THE FALL OF THE DOLLAR EMPIRE

THE FALL OF THE DOLLAR EMPIRE

PROTECTIONISM, DE-DOLLARIZATION,
&
THE RISE OF A NEW FINANCIAL ORDER

RANGA CHAND

For Sylvia, Jason, and Erwin

CONTENTS

PREFACE

Empires rise. Empires fall. Financial ones are no different. The U.S. dollar, long the undisputed ruler of global finance, now stands at a crossroads. The economic order it once upheld is fracturing, as protectionism, geopolitical rifts, and financial realignment accelerate changes that, just a decade ago, would have seemed unthinkable.

For much of the modern era, the dollar wasn't just a currency—it was power itself. Woven into the fabric of global trade, investment, and monetary policy, it dictated the rules of international finance. Oil flowed in dollars, debt was settled in dollars, and economies bent to the will of the dollar. Its dominance was so entrenched that few dared to question it. But cracks are forming. The financial empire built on the greenback is no longer unchallenged.

New economic blocs are emerging. Trade agreements are bypassing the dollar. Global powers are hedging their bets, seeking alternatives. This raises a fundamental question: Is the world witnessing the slow unraveling of the dollar's reign, or is its role simply evolving into something new?

As this shift unfolds, the United States itself enters an era of deep uncertainty. At the time of writing, President Donald J. Trump has returned to office in 2025, bringing with him a renewed wave of economic nationalism. While his full policy agenda remains unclear, early signals point to an escalation of protectionist measures—moves that could further fracture global trade and financial stability.

If Washington doubles down on economic isolationism, it may do more than reshape international markets; it could accelerate the decline of its most powerful financial weapon—the dollar. In a world still anchored to U.S. monetary influence, any drastic shift will have far-reaching consequences, amplifying the forces of fragmentation explored in this book.

Why This Book Matters

The question of the dollar's future is not just a financial curiosity—it is a defining issue for the global economic order. Every modern financial crisis, from the 1997 Asian currency crisis to the 2008 global meltdown, has been shaped by the dollar's dominance. But what happens when that dominance erodes?

Today, new challenges loom large. The weaponization of the dollar in international sanctions, the U.S.-China trade war, the emergence of digital currencies, and the growing influence of regional economic alliances are redrawing the financial map. The world is slowly diversifying away from the dollar, not through a single event, but through a series of strategic shifts that, over time, could fundamentally alter global finance.

This book is for those seeking to understand these seismic shifts—policymakers navigating an increasingly fragmented economic landscape, investors assessing risk in a multi-currency world, economists evaluating the implications of monetary realignment, and everyday citizens who want to grasp how these global forces affect their savings, purchasing power, and economic security.

This is not a book predicting the dollar's collapse, nor is it a defense of American financial hegemony. Rather, it is an exploration of the forces reshaping global finance and what they mean for the future. It examines the shifting dynamics of trade, monetary policy, and geopolitical strategy, offering a clearer understanding of the evolving financial landscape.

How This Book Is Different

The discussion surrounding the dollar's future is often framed in binary terms—either the U.S. currency will reign supreme indefinitely, or it will soon be replaced by a new global standard. The reality is far more complex. While the dollar remains deeply entrenched in global finance, a growing web of economic, political, and technological shifts is relentlessly eroding its unchallenged supremacy, creating a future that is neither absolute dominance nor abrupt displacement, but something in between.

Unlike many works that focus exclusively on monetary policy, this book connects the dots between financial realignment, trade shifts, and geopolitical trends. It examines de-dollarization as it is happening, drawing on real-world case studies, economic data, and historical precedents to provide a nuanced perspective. It does not assume inevitabilities but rather explores the conditions under which certain scenarios may unfold.

The Journey of Writing This Book

This book is the product of extensive research across financial history, macroeconomic trends, and trade policies. It draws from global data sources, including the World Bank, the International Monetary Fund (IMF), and central bank reports, while also incorporating analysis of past financial transitions—such as the decline of the British pound as the world's dominant currency.

One of the greatest challenges in writing this book was distinguishing between short-term volatility and long-term structural change. Is a declining share of U.S. dollar reserves in global foreign exchange holdings a sign of de-dollarization, or merely a cyclical rebalancing? Are alternative payment systems being adopted out of necessity, or are they genuine attempts to dethrone the dollar?

The answers are not always clear-cut, but this book aims to provide a framework to evaluate these questions with clarity.

A Word on Objectivity and Bias

It is important to acknowledge that discussions about the future of the dollar are often politicized. Some believe U.S. financial dominance is immutable, while others see the current shifts as the beginning of an irreversible decline.

This book does not take a side—it presents the evidence, considers multiple perspectives, and lays out plausible scenarios. The goal is not to persuade but to illuminate.

How to Read This Book

The structure of this book allows readers to follow a logical progression—from the rise of U.S. financial dominance to the challenges emerging in the present day, and ultimately, to the potential futures that lie ahead.

Each chapter builds upon the last, but readers can also explore individual sections that align with their specific interests. Whether one is interested in trade wars, monetary realignment, or the geopolitical dimensions of currency power, this book offers a comprehensive yet accessible exploration of these themes.

A Final Thought – The Stakes of This Moment

The fall of a financial empire does not happen overnight, nor does it happen without consequences. The forces reshaping global finance are not a distant concern—they are unfolding now. Whether the world moves toward a fractured financial system, a multipolar order, or a desperate attempt to reinforce U.S. dominance, the choices made in the coming years will shape the course of global power for generations to come.

We are witnessing history unfold.

.

INTRODUCTION

For nearly eight decades, the U.S. dollar has stood as the foundation of global finance, shaping trade, investment, and economic stability. From its enshrinement at Bretton Woods in 1944 to its evolution as the world's unrivaled reserve currency, the dollar has been more than just legal tender—it has been the linchpin of American financial dominance. Its deep liquidity, integration into global markets, and status as the default medium for trade cemented its role as the backbone of the global economy.

Today, however, the dollar's supremacy is no longer assured. A new financial order is taking shape, driven by mounting protectionism, economic realignments, and a growing global revolt against dollar dependency. What once seemed unthinkable—the decline of U.S. financial hegemony—is now a very real possibility. The question is no longer whether the dollar's dominance will be tested, but how rapidly and decisively its empire will erode.

The Dollar's Rise & The Making of an Empire

The dollar's transformation from a national currency to the nerve center of global finance was no accident. It was the result of a carefully crafted economic order, in which the United States positioned itself as the world's ultimate financial safe haven. Under the Bretton Woods system, the dollar was as good as gold, providing stability to a world recovering from war. Even after the Nixon Shock of 1971 severed that gold link, the dollar maintained its supremacy through the petrodollar system, the depth of U.S. capital markets, and Washington's ability to dictate the rules of global finance.

For decades, countries stockpiled dollar reserves as a hedge against crisis, reinforcing the currency's global grip. The strength of U.S. institutions, the transparency of its markets, and the lack of viable alternatives kept the dollar unchallenged—even in times of financial turmoil. But that era of unchallenged financial hegemony may be coming to an end.

Introduction

The Winds of Change: A Global Revolt Against the Dollar

A seismic shift is underway, as economic and geopolitical forces erode the very foundations of the dollar empire. What was once an unchallenged pillar of global finance is now facing mounting resistance from both adversaries and longtime allies. The forces driving this transformation are varied—some rooted in U.S. policy miscalculations, others in deliberate efforts by competing powers to challenge American financial dominance. Taken together, they signal a world that is increasingly moving beyond the dollar.

One of the most defining shifts has been the rise of protectionism and economic nationalism, particularly within the United States. The very country that once championed free markets and globalization is now turning inward, erecting trade barriers, imposing tariffs, and rewriting the rules of global commerce.

What was once considered an outlier approach has now become mainstream economic strategy, fueled by both political ideology and a desire to shield domestic industries from foreign competition. Yet, in attempting to fortify its own economy, Washington has inadvertently alienated key trading partners, pushing them to explore alternative financial arrangements. Frustration with U.S. policies has accelerated efforts to bypass the dollar, as economic powerhouses seek to insulate themselves from the political volatility that increasingly defines American trade policy.

At the heart of this push is de-dollarization, a movement that has gained remarkable traction in recent years. What was once dismissed as a symbolic gesture has now evolved into a coordinated global strategy. China and Russia—both eager to challenge U.S. financial hegemony—have aggressively reduced their reliance on the dollar in trade and investment.

Beijing has expanded its Cross-Border Interbank Payment System (CIPS), providing an alternative to SWIFT (the dominant global financial messaging network that facilitates cross-border transactions), while deepening bilateral currency agreements that allow major trading partners to settle transactions in yuan. Russia, after years of U.S. sanctions, has forged a closer financial alliance with China, moving much of its trade away from dollar settlements. As more nations seek to reduce exposure to U.S. financial controls, the growing integration of CIPS with other non-dollar payment systems signals a broader shift toward a multipolar financial order.

Even some U.S. allies—mindful of Washington's frequent use of economic sanctions as a geopolitical weapon—have begun exploring ways to diversify their reserves and reduce their vulnerability to dollar-based disruptions. The rise of regional trade agreements, central bank digital currencies (CBDCs), and direct currency swaps is chipping away at the dollar's once-unquestioned dominance.

Adding to these pressures is the Federal Reserve's evolving role in this financial realignment. In response to inflationary pressures at home, the Fed has pursued an aggressive tightening cycle, sharply raising interest rates to curb rising prices. While these policies are aimed at stabilizing the domestic economy, their global ramifications have been profound. Higher U.S. interest rates have made dollar-denominated debt significantly more expensive, straining economies that rely on cheap dollar financing. Emerging markets, already grappling with rising costs of imports and weakening local currencies, have been hit particularly hard.

The dollar's recent surge in strength—while a testament to its enduring influence—has also exposed its vulnerabilities. If the global economy continues shifting toward a multipolar financial system, the very factors that once made the dollar indispensable could accelerate its decline.

These shifts do not signal an immediate collapse of dollar dominance, but they do suggest a changing financial order—one in which the dollar is no longer the undisputed king. The coming years will determine whether these trends remain incremental adjustments or the beginning of a fundamental transformation in global finance.

The Key Questions

This book seeks to answer the most pressing questions shaping the future of global finance:

1. Is de-dollarization an inevitable trend, or can the U.S. maintain its financial hegemony?
2. How will protectionism, trade wars, and economic nationalism accelerate the dollar's decline?
3. Could a global shift away from the dollar trigger a financial crisis?

4. What would a post-dollar world look like, and how would the U.S. navigate this transition?
5. Are we witnessing the final chapter of the dollar's dominance, or will it adapt and endure?

These are not abstract or theoretical concerns—they carry real consequences for governments, businesses, and individuals alike.

How This Book is Structured

To understand the forces reshaping the global financial order, this book is divided into five parts:

*   **PART I: THE RISE OF THE DOLLAR EMPIRE** – Traces the dollar's ascent and the key moments that cemented its dominance.
*   **PART II: THE DOLLAR'S SELF-INFLICTED WOUNDS: PROTECTIONISM AND THE SEEDS OF DECLINE** – Examines how trade wars, tariffs, and economic nationalism are accelerating the financial realignment.
*   **PART III: THE GLOBAL REVOLT – HOW DE-DOLLARIZATION IS BREAKING THE DOLLAR'S GRIP** – Explores how other economies are actively challenging dollar supremacy and whether the trend is irreversible.
*   **PART IV: THE U.S. AT A CROSSROADS – THE FRAGILE FUTURE OF DOLLAR HEGEMONY** – Evaluates the long-term economic impact on the U.S. and its ability to maintain financial leadership.
*   **PART V: THE NEXT GLOBAL ORDER: A POST-DOLLAR WORLD?** – Considers possible scenarios: a multipolar system, an alternative reserve currency, or an adaptation of the dollar itself.

Why This Matters

The future of the dollar is about more than currency markets—it is about power, influence, and the ability to shape global affairs. For decades, the U.S. has leveraged the dollar's dominance to impose sanctions, influence monetary policy worldwide, and sustain its own economic deficits without immediate repercussions. If this power erodes, the geopolitical and financial consequences will be profound. This unparalleled advantage has allowed the U.S. to project economic strength far beyond its borders, reinforcing its leadership in global finance and trade.

Introduction

As the dollar empire faces its reckoning, the choices made by policymakers, central banks, and market participants will determine whether the dollar remains dominant, gradually declines, or is replaced by an entirely new financial order. The speed and nature of this transition will not only shape global markets but also redefine the balance of economic power for generations to come.

The next decade will be decisive. Will the dollar adapt and endure, or are we witnessing the final unraveling of its global supremacy? The answer to that question will define the next era of global finance.

The coming years will test the resilience of the dollar system as economic, technological, and geopolitical forces converge to reshape global finance. Emerging powers are accelerating efforts to reduce their reliance on U.S. monetary influence, while innovations such as digital currencies and alternative payment networks threaten to erode the dollar's centrality. At the same time, America's own fiscal and trade policies will determine whether the dollar withstands these pressures or succumbs to the forces of fragmentation. What happens next will not only impact financial markets but also redefine the levers of global economic power.

As this transition unfolds, the world is entering uncharted territory. A fragmented monetary system could grant some nations greater financial autonomy but also increase volatility, as no single currency may fully replace the dollar's role. Whether the shift is orderly or disruptive will depend on Washington's policy responses and global market dynamics. One thing is certain—the era of unquestioned dollar hegemony is ending, and the choices made today will shape global finance for decades to come.

PART I

THE RISE OF THE DOLLAR EMPIRE

"He who controls the wealth of a nation commands its destiny."
— Aristotle

The dollar's rise to global supremacy was no accident. Part I examines the economic and political forces that forged the U.S.-led financial order, from the post-World War II architecture that established the dollar's primacy to the era of globalization that extended its reach across every corner of the world. Through two pivotal chapters, this section reveals how U.S. economic dominance was built and how the dollar became indispensable to global trade, finance, and investment—setting the stage for the challenges and transformations it faces today.

CHAPTER 1

THE BIRTH OF THE DOLLAR EMPIRE

The global financial system we know today did not emerge overnight. Chapter 1 explores the transformation from a fragmented world of competing currencies to one dominated by the U.S. dollar. Beginning with the pre-dollar era, where gold and regional currencies shaped trade, it examines the pivotal Bretton Woods Agreement that cemented U.S. financial hegemony. The Nixon Shock, which ended the gold standard, marked a turning point, unleashing the full force of the dollar's influence. Finally, this chapter delves into how the U.S. leveraged its economic and geopolitical power to become the unrivaled financial superpower. As this chapter concludes, readers will grasp how the dollar's dominance was not merely a product of circumstance but of deliberate strategy, setting the stage for its enduring global influence—and the challenges that now threaten it.

1

THE WORLD BEFORE THE DOLLAR

On September 21, 1931, anxious crowds gathered outside the Bank of England. The weight of an empire's financial supremacy rested on the decisions being made inside, yet those emerging from the building carried an announcement that would reverberate across the global economy: Britain was abandoning the gold standard. After nearly a century as the anchor of international finance, the British pound— once as good as gold—had been devalued. For much of the world, this moment symbolized the unraveling of a monetary order that had held firm for generations. Britain, the undisputed financial hegemon of the 19th century, was conceding that it could no longer maintain the system upon which global trade and investment had been built.

The collapse of the pound's gold backing was not an isolated event but the culmination of economic forces that had been straining the international monetary system for decades. Before the rise of the U.S. dollar, the global financial order had been a fragmented and precarious balance between dominant imperial currencies, regional monetary systems, and a reliance on gold as the ultimate store of value. Britain had emerged as the financial epicenter in the 19th century, its currency underpinning global trade, but its dominance— like the empires before it—was built on foundations that would eventually crack under economic pressures, war, and shifting global power.

The British Pound: The King of Global Trade

By the dawn of the 20th century, the British pound was the undisputed king of international finance. At the height of the British Empire, London stood at the center of global commerce, with sterling accounting for the bulk of the world's foreign exchange reserves. Britain controlled nearly a quarter of global trade, and its financial system was the nerve center of international transactions. The pound's supremacy was reinforced by an extensive network of banks, financial houses, and commercial institutions that facilitated global capital flows.

The Bank of England, with its reputation as the world's most influential central bank, held vast gold reserves that provided the foundation for confidence in the pound. By 1900, Britain's official gold holdings exceeded £120 million, an amount equivalent to approximately £15.5 billion today. British financial institutions, including the powerful banking dynasties of the Rothschilds, Barings, and Lloyds, played a pivotal role in financing global infrastructure projects. Railroads in Argentina, industrial expansions in India, and development projects across Africa and Asia were all underwritten by British capital, strengthening sterling's position as the de facto global currency.

Sterling's influence extended beyond Britain's formal empire. Even nations outside British rule pegged their currencies to the pound, effectively adopting it as a global standard. By 1913, nearly 60% of global trade invoices were denominated in pounds, and more than half of all international bonds were issued in sterling. This dominance meant that the fate of the global economy was tied to Britain's financial stability. But beneath the surface, vulnerabilities were forming. The pound's strength was reliant on Britain maintaining trade surpluses and a steady flow of gold—two conditions that would prove increasingly difficult to sustain in the face of war, economic shifts, and rising industrial competitors.

The Role of Gold in Pre-WWI Finance

Before paper money became the backbone of modern economies, gold reigned supreme. By the late 19th century, nearly every major economy adhered to a gold-backed system, a monetary framework that tied the value of national currencies to fixed amounts of gold. Under this system, governments were required to maintain gold reserves sufficient to back the money they issued, ensuring that paper currency could be converted into gold on demand. This arrangement created a self-regulating mechanism: a nation that imported more than it exported had to settle its trade deficit by shipping gold abroad. As gold reserves dwindled, central banks were forced to respond by raising interest rates, tightening credit, and contracting their economies to restore balance.

While the gold standard provided monetary stability, it also imposed severe constraints. Because governments could not print money freely or engage in aggressive monetary stimulus, economic downturns were often prolonged and painful. A country experiencing financial distress could not simply devalue its currency or inject liquidity into the system; it had to endure economic contraction until the natural flow of gold reversed course. This rigidity made the gold standard a double-edged sword—while it ensured long-term financial discipline, it also made financial crises inevitable and sometimes catastrophic.

The Panic of 1893: A Case Study in Gold Standard Fragility

The inherent weaknesses of the gold standard became evident during economic shocks, none more so than the Panic of 1893. In the years leading up to the crisis, reckless railroad expansion fueled a speculative boom in the United States. Investors and banks poured capital into new railway lines, convinced that demand for rail transport would continue to soar. Many railroad companies borrowed heavily, taking on debts far exceeding their earnings in the expectation of future profitability.

When demand failed to keep pace with projections, overleveraged railroads found themselves unable to meet their debt payments. The collapse of the Philadelphia and Reading Railroad in early 1893 triggered a financial panic. Investors, fearing widespread bankruptcies, rushed to liquidate their holdings, setting off a 40% collapse in the stock market. More than 500 banks failed, many of which had extended credit to struggling railroad companies.

As confidence in the financial system evaporated, foreign creditors and domestic banks sought refuge in gold. This sparked a massive outflow of U.S. gold reserves as investors scrambled to convert their dollars into gold, anticipating that the government might suspend convertibility. The drain on reserves brought the U.S. dangerously close to a monetary crisis, with gold holdings shrinking so rapidly that the Treasury was forced to seek outside intervention. In a dramatic move, J.P. Morgan orchestrated a $65 million gold bailout—equivalent to more than $2 billion today—by assembling a syndicate of international financiers to purchase U.S. bonds in exchange for gold. The bailout averted total collapse, but the crisis had exposed a harsh reality: under the gold standard, financial shocks were amplified, not mitigated, as any downturn could set off a cycle of gold depletion, economic contraction, and rising unemployment.

The Gold Standard's Global Strains: Britain, France, and Beyond

The United States was not alone in facing these pressures. Britain and France, two of the world's most powerful economies, found themselves repeatedly constrained by the rigidities of the gold standard. For Britain, adherence to the system meant that during periods of trade deficits—when the country imported more than it exported—gold reserves flowed out of the country. To prevent further depletion, the Bank of England had to raise interest rates, making borrowing more expensive and slowing economic growth. This policy often deepened recessions, as businesses cut investment and workers lost jobs. Industries such as coal, textiles, and steel— once the backbone of Britain's industrial power—faced severe contractions, leading to double-digit unemployment rates during downturns.

France, despite holding some of the largest gold reserves in Europe, was not immune to financial instability. The French government had a habit of hoarding gold rather than allowing it to circulate, creating periodic monetary tightening that slowed economic growth. At the same time, capital flight—investors pulling their money out of the country due to fears of instability— destabilized France's financial system. Wealthy individuals and institutions moved their assets abroad, often to Britain or the United States, draining liquidity from French banks. This, in turn, led to lending restrictions, business closures, and heightened public anxiety about the stability of the economy.

Similar patterns emerged across other economies tied to gold-backed currency. Countries that borrowed excessively or expanded beyond their gold reserves were eventually forced into contraction, leading to austerity, rising unemployment, and, in many cases, political unrest. Governments had little flexibility to respond to downturns, as printing more money or adjusting interest rates was constrained by the requirement to maintain gold convertibility.

A System under Pressure: The Gold Standard's Breaking Point

While the gold standard imposed financial discipline, it also amplified economic distress. Currency stability came at the cost of deep recessions, banking panics, and prolonged downturns. The longer an economy remained tethered to gold-backed money, the more vulnerable it became to capital flight and deflationary spirals. The inability to respond flexibly to economic shocks meant that recessions lasted longer and inflicted greater hardship.

By the early 20th century, as global trade expanded and financial markets grew more complex, the constraints of the gold standard became increasingly apparent. Yet despite its flaws, the system remained intact—until the devastation of World War I forced a reckoning. Governments abandoned gold-backed currency to finance military expenditures, shattering confidence in the system's permanence. The war set in motion a new global financial order, one in which economic stability would increasingly depend not on gold, but on the flexibility of national policies and, eventually, the dominance of the U.S. dollar.

The Decline of Britain and the Rise of the U.S.

By the dawn of the 20th century, Britain remained the dominant financial power, with London at the center of global banking and the pound sterling anchoring trade. Yet beneath this dominance, economic imbalances were mounting. Britain's supremacy depended on three pillars: maintaining a trade surplus, vast colonial wealth, and commitment to the gold standard. As the global economy evolved, each came under strain.

The first challenge came from rising industrial competitors. The United States and Germany—once secondary players in global manufacturing—were closing the gap. By 1913, the U.S. had overtaken Britain as the world's largest economy, contributing over 19% of global industrial output compared to Britain's 14%. American factories, powered by innovation and mass production, out-produced British counterparts in steel, automobiles, and industrial machinery. Meanwhile, Germany's state-backed industrial policies and close cooperation between banks and manufacturers enabled it to surpass Britain in steel, chemistry, and heavy industry.

At the same time, Britain's adherence to the gold standard, once a pillar of its financial strength, became a liability. By tying the pound to gold, Britain couldn't adjust its currency to changing conditions. When its trade balance weakened, the Bank of England had little choice but to raise interest rates to attract foreign capital, often at the expense of industry and employment. This rigid monetary discipline contrasted with newer industrial economies like the U.S. and Germany, which had more financial flexibility.

Britain's empire, once an advantage, also became a financial strain. Colonies provided raw materials and markets, but maintaining imperial dominance grew costly. Military expenditures to protect trade routes, governance costs, and rising nationalist movements in India, Egypt, and elsewhere placed increasing pressure on Britain's finances.

The final and most devastating blow came with World War I. Britain, financing a prolonged war, borrowed heavily from the U.S. By 1918, it had accumulated over $4 billion in debt to the U.S., marking a historic reversal from its pre-war status as the world's leading creditor. The war also forced Britain to suspend the gold standard, breaking a key pillar of its financial system.

By the end of the war, the global financial hierarchy had shifted. The United States emerged as the world's largest creditor, and Wall Street, once subordinate to London, became the epicenter of global capital markets. While Britain attempted to restore its financial dominance in the 1920s, its grip on global finance was slipping.

The Great Depression & the End of the Pound's Dominance

After World War I, Britain sought to restore the pound's global prestige by rejoining the gold standard in 1925 at its pre-war parity of £4.86 per U.S. dollar, effectively setting the price of gold at £3.17 per ounce. The decision, led by Chancellor of the Exchequer Winston Churchill, was meant to reaffirm Britain's financial dominance, instill confidence in the currency, and stabilize international trade. However, it quickly proved to be a costly miscalculation.

The fundamental problem was that Britain's economy had changed dramatically since 1914. During the war, Britain had abandoned the gold standard and allowed the pound to depreciate naturally. By the early 1920s, market forces had settled on an exchange rate closer to £4.40 per dollar, reflecting the weakened state of British industry and the lingering economic scars of wartime borrowing. By locking itself into an overvalued exchange rate, Britain crushed its export competitiveness. Foreign buyers turned to cheaper alternatives, forcing domestic manufacturers—especially in coal, steel, and textiles—to slash production and lay off workers. High unemployment gripped industrial regions, surpassing 10% throughout the late 1920s.

To defend the overvalued currency, the Bank of England maintained high interest rates, hoping to attract foreign capital and sustain confidence in the pound. But this approach deepened economic stagnation—borrowing became expensive, investment slowed, and deflationary pressures increased the real burden of debt on businesses and households. These contractionary policies made it nearly impossible for Britain to grow its way out of the economic malaise, turning the gold standard into a financial straitjacket rather than a stabilizing force.

Beyond its domestic repercussions, Britain's return to gold at an unsustainable parity also contributed to global economic instability. As the pound struggled, the Bank of England had to rely on foreign loans and short-term capital inflows to maintain its gold reserves, making the economy highly vulnerable to external shocks. When the Great Depression struck in 1929, the rigidity of the gold standard exacerbated deflation and prolonged the downturn.

By 1931, Britain could no longer bear the economic strain and abandoned the gold standard, allowing the pound to depreciate. The move boosted exports, relieved deflationary pressures, and marked a turning point in British monetary policy. In hindsight, Churchill himself recognized the failure, later calling it the "greatest political blunder of my life." The episode serves as a cautionary tale of how misguided monetary policies—particularly currency overvaluation—can crush industrial competitiveness and prolong economic stagnation.

Britain's failed return to gold was not an isolated misstep but part of a broader trend in the interwar period, where economic rigidity and poor policy choices contributed to global instability. The experience reinforced the dangers of tying currency policy to outdated economic realities—a lesson that would resurface again in later financial crises.

Chapter 1: The Birth of the Dollar Empire

World War II and the Final Shift to the Dollar

If the Great Depression had weakened Britain's financial dominance, World War II delivered the final blow. Britain's war effort required massive government spending, pushing the national debt to unprecedented levels. By 1945, Britain's debt had soared to over 200% of GDP, leaving its economy in a precarious state. Wartime production had drained resources, devastated industries, and left Britain reliant on U.S. financial support.

In contrast, the United States emerged from the war as the world's economic superpower. While Europe and Asia lay in ruins, American factories had been operating at full capacity, supplying weapons, machinery, and consumer goods. The war had nearly doubled the size of the U.S. economy, and by the time it ended, the United States controlled over 70% of the world's gold reserves.

Bretton Woods: The Dollar Replaces the Pound

Recognizing Britain's weakened state, the United States moved to reshape the global financial system in its own image. In July 1944, 44 nations gathered at the Bretton Woods Conference in New Hampshire to establish a new international monetary order. The result was a framework in which the U.S. dollar, rather than the pound, became the world's primary reserve currency.

The new system pegged major currencies to the U.S. dollar, which in turn was tied to gold at a fixed rate of $35 per ounce. Unlike the pre-war gold standard, where all currencies were directly linked to gold, Bretton Woods positioned the U.S. dollar as the world's financial anchor. The dollar was convertible to gold at $35 per ounce, while other currencies were pegged to the dollar—effectively making the Federal Reserve the new custodian of global monetary stability.

The agreement marked the official transfer of financial power from London to Washington. The pound, which had anchored the global economy for over a century, had now been relegated to a secondary role. This shift was not merely symbolic; it reflected the changing realities of global trade, finance, and military power in the postwar world. With its vast industrial base untouched by the war and its gold reserves swelling, the United States was uniquely positioned to assume the role of the world's economic leader.

Chapter 1: The Birth of the Dollar Empire

The Pound's Fall and the U.S. Dollar's Global Ascent

Britain, once the world's financial epicenter, had become a debtor nation reliant on American loans. The $3.75 billion loan package provided by the U.S. in 1946 was not just a financial lifeline—it was the final confirmation that the pound was no longer the world's dominant currency. The U.S. dollar, backed by America's industrial strength and vast gold reserves, had officially replaced sterling as the cornerstone of the global economy.

By the end of World War II, the transformation was complete. The pound had fallen, the United States had emerged as the world's economic hegemon, and the U.S. dollar had replaced sterling as the foundation of international trade and investment. Britain, though still a major economic power, would never again wield the financial dominance it once enjoyed. The world had entered the age of the dollar, a new era of American financial supremacy that would define the global economy for decades to come.

2

THE BRETTON WOODS SYSTEM

By the time World War II drew to a close in 1945, the global economy stood in shambles. The devastation that had swept across Europe and Asia had left once-mighty economies in ruins. Cities lay in rubble, industries had been hollowed out, and financial systems were on the brink of collapse. Britain, the empire that had dominated global finance for more than a century, was no longer in a position to dictate monetary order. London, once the heart of the world's financial system, had become a debtor, burdened by war loans owed primarily to the United States. France, Germany, and much of Western Europe faced an even bleaker outlook, with governments struggling to feed their populations, let alone revive economic activity.

In stark contrast, the United States had emerged from the war not just victorious but economically unrivaled. While European cities smoldered, American factories thrived. The war had transformed the U.S. into the world's largest creditor, lender, and industrial producer. By 1945, it held over 20,000 metric tons of gold—nearly 70% of the world's total reserves, an accumulation that made the U.S. dollar the most trusted currency in circulation. The war had accelerated a shift that had already been underway for decades: the dollar was no longer just an American currency—it was the de facto monetary foundation of the modern world.

But dominance alone was not enough. The global economy needed stability, and without a new financial framework, there was a real danger that the postwar world would descend into the same economic fragmentation and currency wars that had defined the interwar years. In the absence of a functioning monetary system, the world risked repeating the catastrophic mistakes of the 1930s, when competitive devaluations and trade protectionism had deepened the Great Depression and fueled geopolitical tensions. The solution had to be comprehensive—one that would prevent the type of financial chaos that had preceded the war while securing the United States' newfound economic supremacy.

With this in mind, world leaders convened a historic summit in July 1944 in a small resort town in New Hampshire. Over 700 delegates from 44 nations gathered at the Mount Washington Hotel in Bretton Woods, where they would negotiate the terms of a new global financial order. The stakes could not have been higher. The outcome of the conference would determine not just the rules of international finance but also the structure of global power for decades to come.

The Birth of Dollar Supremacy

The conference at Bretton Woods was not simply about designing a stable financial system—it was a struggle for monetary dominance. Two competing visions emerged, each reflecting the ambitions of the world's leading economic powers. On one side stood John Maynard Keynes, representing Britain, who proposed the creation of a new international reserve currency called the bancor. Keynes argued that the world needed a neutral, supranational currency—one managed by a global clearinghouse rather than controlled by any single nation. Such a system, he believed, would prevent the kind of trade imbalances that had plagued the global economy before the war.

On the other side was Harry Dexter White, the chief negotiator for the United States, who had no interest in Keynes's proposal. The U.S. was now the world's financial superpower, and White was determined to secure American economic dominance. Instead of a neutral global currency, White proposed a system where the U.S. dollar—rather than the bancor—would become the world's primary reserve currency. Under this arrangement, all major currencies would be pegged to the dollar at fixed exchange rates, and the dollar alone would be convertible into gold at a fixed rate of $35 per ounce. This effectively made the U.S. the anchor of the global financial system, ensuring that every central bank in the world had to hold dollars as part of their reserves.

The outcome was never truly in doubt. Keynes, despite his intellectual brilliance, was negotiating from a position of weakness. Britain was financially dependent on U.S. loans for its postwar reconstruction and had little choice but to accept American terms. The agreement finalized at Bretton Woods enshrined the dollar as the linchpin of the new international system, marking the official transfer of financial power from London to Washington.

But the agreement went beyond just currency pegs. To support this new system, two major financial institutions were created: the International Monetary Fund (IMF) and the World Bank. The IMF was established with an initial lending capacity of $8.8 billion to provide short-term loans to countries facing balance-of-payments crises, preventing economic shocks from spiraling into full-blown depressions.

Meanwhile, the World Bank, with an initial capital of $10 billion, was designed to finance long-term reconstruction and development projects, particularly in war-ravaged Europe and underdeveloped regions. These institutions, though ostensibly created for global economic stability, were structurally dominated by the United States, ensuring that Washington maintained significant control over international finance.

How the Bretton Woods System Worked

The mechanics of the Bretton Woods system were straightforward: the U.S. dollar was pegged to gold at $35 per ounce, while all other major currencies were fixed to the dollar. If a country's currency deviated too far from its fixed rate, its central bank was required to intervene—either by buying or selling its currency in the market or by adjusting domestic economic policies to maintain stability. This ensured that exchange rates remained stable, encouraging trade and investment by reducing the uncertainty caused by currency fluctuations. This framework created a predictable monetary environment, fostering postwar economic growth and reinforcing the dollar's role as the anchor of the global financial system.

The U.S. played a unique role in this system. Because the dollar was tied to gold, other nations viewed it as a reliable store of value. Countries running trade surpluses with the U.S. accumulated dollars rather than gold, reinforcing the dollar's role as the world's primary reserve currency. This arrangement provided economic security, as nations could always exchange their surplus dollars for gold if needed. In practice, however, few did—most countries preferred to hold onto their dollar reserves, using them for trade and investment rather than converting them into gold.

Chapter 1: The Birth of the Dollar Empire

Trade Dynamics and the Recycling of Dollars

At first, the Bretton Woods system functioned as intended. The United States, enjoying a massive trade surplus, provided the world with dollars through exports and foreign aid. Postwar Europe and Japan, still rebuilding their industries, eagerly absorbed American goods and capital. The Marshall Plan, launched in 1948, injected $13 billion into Western Europe to finance reconstruction, further reinforcing the dollar's dominance.

But as the 1950s gave way to the 1960s, the global trade balance began to shift. As West Germany and Japan rebuilt their economies, they transitioned from importers of U.S. goods to export powerhouses. For the first time, the United States was running consistent trade deficits—buying more from the world than it was selling. This shift led to a growing accumulation of U.S. dollars abroad, particularly in the central banks of Germany, Japan, and later, France.

Rather than redeeming these excess dollars for gold—which would have drained U.S. reserves—foreign central banks reinvested their surplus dollars into U.S. financial markets, primarily through purchases of U.S. Treasury bonds. This process, known as dollar recycling, ensured a continuous demand for the dollar, even as the U.S. trade deficit widened. Foreign nations found it easier and more profitable to hold their reserves in U.S. assets rather than gold, further entrenching the dollar's role as the global reserve currency.

The Seeds of Instability

At first, this system worked in America's favor. The United States could finance its deficits without suffering the usual consequences of devaluation because the rest of the world needed dollars. But by the late 1960s, cracks in the system had begun to emerge. As Europe and Japan accumulated larger and larger reserves of dollars, confidence in America's ability to uphold the $35 per ounce gold peg began to erode. Foreign governments, particularly France, started demanding gold for their excess dollars, raising fears that the U.S. did not have enough gold to back the growing money supply.

The U.S. faced a dilemma: maintaining the gold standard required strict monetary discipline, but the demands of the Vietnam War and Great Society programs led to rising government spending and deficits. Rather than curbing expenditures or raising taxes, policymakers relied on printing more dollars, further fueling inflationary pressures. Meanwhile, speculative attacks on the dollar intensified as investors and central banks grew wary of America's ability to sustain gold convertibility. The prospect of a run on U.S. gold reserves loomed larger, forcing Washington into an increasingly untenable position.

The system was approaching a breaking point. Would the U.S. be able to maintain its gold commitments, or was a monetary crisis inevitable? The answer would come in 1971, when President Richard Nixon made a decision that would fundamentally alter the global financial order.

3

THE NIXON SHOCK: THE END OF GOLD

By the late 1960s, the global financial system was facing an existential crisis. The very foundations of the Bretton Woods Agreement, which had anchored the world economy for more than two decades, were beginning to crack under the weight of mounting U.S. deficits and shifting trade dynamics. When the system was first established in 1944, the United States stood as the undisputed economic powerhouse, its factories supplying the world, its currency commanding international trust, and its gold reserves forming the bedrock of global financial stability. But over time, the assumptions that had sustained this arrangement began to unravel.

The Pressures That Led to the Crisis

For years after World War II, the United States enjoyed a comfortable trade surplus, exporting industrial goods to Europe and Japan while maintaining a vast hoard of gold. The dollar was scarce outside U.S. borders, reinforcing its value and credibility. However, as Western Europe and Japan rapidly recovered, their economies transformed from war-torn dependents into formidable industrial competitors. By the 1960s, nations such as West Germany and Japan had built world-class manufacturing sectors, chipping away at America's longstanding dominance in global trade. Once a net exporter, the United States now faced a growing trade deficit, as American consumers increasingly purchased foreign goods while U.S. exports struggled to compete in price and quality.

The erosion of U.S. trade supremacy coincided with a dramatic expansion of federal spending. The Vietnam War, which escalated in the 1960s, placed enormous pressure on the national budget. Military expenditures soared, reaching nearly $30 billion annually by 1969, and as the war dragged on, so did the costs. Simultaneously, President Lyndon B. Johnson's Great Society programs, designed to combat poverty and expand social welfare, injected vast sums into domestic spending. While these programs provided crucial social support, they also flooded the global economy with U.S. dollars, a reality that was becoming impossible to ignore.

With more dollars in circulation abroad than could be redeemed in gold, the fundamental contradiction at the heart of Bretton Woods became glaringly apparent. The United States had promised to maintain the dollar's convertibility into gold at $35 per ounce, yet by 1971, foreign central banks collectively held far more dollars than the U.S. had gold to cover. The world had, in effect, become oversaturated with dollars, and confidence in the system was beginning to erode.

The French Challenge and the Global Run on Gold

Nowhere was this loss of confidence more evident than in the actions of French President Charles de Gaulle. A fierce critic of the dollar's privileged status, de Gaulle viewed the postwar monetary system as an arrangement that unfairly favored the United States at the expense of the rest of the world. Under the existing structure, the U.S. could print dollars freely while other nations had to earn them through trade. To de Gaulle, this amounted to a monetary empire, one that allowed the U.S. to finance its deficits simply by issuing more currency rather than maintaining discipline like other countries.

France, unlike many of its allies, decided to take a stand. In the late 1960s, de Gaulle's government began redeeming its dollar reserves for gold, a move that sent ripples through the global financial system. To emphasize his point, he dispatched a French naval vessel to New York, instructing it to retrieve France's gold reserves from the U.S. Federal Reserve. The message was clear: France was unwilling to hold a currency that it believed to be overextended and increasingly untrustworthy.

This action triggered a chain reaction. Other countries, witnessing France's assertiveness, began following suit. Between 1958 and 1971, U.S. gold reserves fell from 20,000 metric tons to just 8,133 metric tons, as European and Asian central banks scrambled to convert their dollar holdings before it was too late. By the summer of 1971, gold was flowing out of the United States at an alarming rate—nearly 100 metric tons per day—as nations rushed to secure their share of a rapidly dwindling reserve.

The situation was spiraling out of control. If the run on U.S. gold continued, the United States would soon exhaust its reserves and be unable to meet its obligations under Bretton Woods. The system, already on life support, was nearing its breaking point.

The Nixon Shock: Ending the Gold Standard

The crisis left President Richard Nixon with a stark choice. One option was to dramatically devalue the dollar, acknowledging that the U.S. had issued more dollars than it could back with gold. Such a move would have been an admission of weakness, signaling to the world that the dollar was no longer as strong as it claimed to be. The other, more radical option was to sever the dollar's link to gold entirely, dismantling the monetary system that had defined global finance for decades.

On August 15, 1971, Nixon made his decision. In a nationally televised address, he announced that the United States would "suspend temporarily the convertibility of the dollar into gold." The decision, framed as a short-term measure to stabilize the economy, was in reality a permanent rupture with the past. Overnight, the gold standard was gone.

The Consequences: A New Financial Order

The immediate impact of Nixon's decision was financial turmoil. Without a gold anchor, the value of the dollar plunged against other major currencies, leading to a period of instability in global markets. The price of gold, which had been fixed at $35 per ounce, skyrocketed to over $200 per ounce by the late 1970s, reflecting the market's belief that the dollar had been artificially overvalued for years.

At the same time, the loss of monetary discipline ushered in a new era of inflation. Without the constraints of gold convertibility, governments—especially the United States—could expand the money supply without direct consequences, leading to a prolonged period of stagflation, where inflation soared while economic growth stagnated.

To restore confidence in the dollar, the U.S. sought a new foundation for its global dominance. In 1974, Washington brokered a critical deal with Saudi Arabia and OPEC: in exchange for U.S. military protection and economic cooperation, Saudi Arabia agreed to price all of its oil exports in U.S. dollars. This arrangement, which soon extended to the entire OPEC bloc, ensured that global demand for dollars remained high. The petrodollar system was born, and with it, a new era of American financial hegemony.

The Rise of Wall Street and a Fiat-Based Financial System

Beyond energy markets, the severing of gold convertibility also accelerated the rise of Wall Street as the epicenter of global finance. With currency values now dictated by investor sentiment rather than gold reserves, financial speculation became a dominant force in global markets. The U.S. Treasury market, already a cornerstone of international finance, grew even more central as foreign governments parked their surplus dollars in American debt rather than demanding gold.

Freed from the constraints of gold-backed money, financial institutions embraced a new era of innovation—one that emphasized leverage, derivatives, and complex financial instruments. The 1980s and 1990s witnessed the explosive growth of global capital markets, fueled by deregulation and technological advancements. Wall Street's powerhouses—investment banks, hedge funds, and private equity firms—flourished as capital flowed across borders with unprecedented speed. This shift reinforced the dollar's dominance, as most international transactions, from sovereign debt issuance to corporate mergers, were denominated in dollars, further entrenching its role as the world's reserve currency.

At the same time, the shift to a fiat-based system allowed the U.S. government greater fiscal and monetary flexibility. No longer bound by the discipline of gold reserves, the Federal Reserve and the Treasury could expand the money supply to stimulate growth, respond to economic crises, and finance government spending without the immediate fear of depleting gold reserves. This newfound flexibility proved instrumental in managing economic downturns, including the inflationary shocks of the 1970s and the financial crises that followed in later decades. However, it also introduced new risks—most notably, the temptation to rely on deficit spending and monetary expansion as permanent economic tools rather than short-term solutions.

Rather than weakening the dollar, Nixon's decision had reshaped its dominance. The world, no longer bound to a fixed monetary system, had no choice but to accept a fiat-based regime where the dollar's value rested not on physical gold, but on the sheer size and influence of the U.S. economy, military, and capital markets.

The Shift to a New Monetary Era

The Nixon Shock marked a decisive turning point in global finance. The constraints of the gold standard had been removed, giving the United States unprecedented monetary flexibility—but also exposing the global economy to new risks. Without gold backing, inflationary pressures would become a recurring challenge, financial crises would grow more frequent, and economic stability would increasingly depend on the actions of central banks rather than the discipline of gold reserves.

Yet, far from signaling the decline of American financial power, the Nixon Shock reinforced the dollar's centrality. In the years that followed, the petrodollar system, financial deregulation, and the expansion of Wall Street would solidify the U.S. currency's role as the world's unrivaled financial anchor. The next section will explore how this transition unfolded—how trade liberalization, financial engineering, and global investment flows ensured that, even in a world without gold-backed money, the dollar remained the foundation of the global economy.

4

HOW THE DOLLAR BECAME KING

By the time World War II came to an end, the United States had emerged as the undisputed economic leader of the world. The war had left Europe in ruins, its cities shattered, its economies crippled, and its financial institutions weakened beyond recognition. The British Empire, once the backbone of global trade and finance, was now drowning in debt, forced to borrow heavily from the United States to sustain itself. In contrast, America had grown stronger. Its industrial base had expanded, its financial markets were intact, and most crucially, it controlled more than 70% of the world's gold reserves—a staggering reversal of the prewar balance of power.

As the dust settled, the global financial order took on a new shape, one that was no longer centered around the British pound but around the U.S. dollar. The Bretton Woods Agreement, signed in 1944, had already set the stage for this transition, officially establishing the dollar as the world's primary reserve currency. But while the agreement provided the legal and institutional framework for American financial dominance, the real consolidation of U.S. hegemony came in the years that followed. Through a combination of strategic policies, military alliances, and financial engineering, the United States ensured that the world would not only rely on the dollar but would become increasingly dependent on it.

The Petrodollar: Securing Global Dollar Demand

The collapse of the Bretton Woods system in 1971, when President Richard Nixon severed the dollar's convertibility to gold, could have jeopardized America's financial supremacy. In theory, removing the gold standard should have weakened confidence in the dollar. Without a hard asset backing it, why would the world continue to trust U.S. currency? But Instead of undermining the dollar, the Nixon administration quickly found another way to cement its status: oil.

In the early 1970s, the United States struck a landmark agreement with Saudi Arabia, the world's largest oil exporter, to ensure that all oil transactions would be priced exclusively in dollars. In return, the U.S. provided military protection, economic aid, and access to American financial markets. The deal soon expanded to include other members of OPEC (Organization of the Petroleum Exporting Countries), effectively creating the petrodollar system. Under this arrangement, any country that wanted to purchase oil on global markets first had to acquire U.S. dollars, creating a built-in demand for the currency.

The implications of this system were profound. Since every country required oil, and oil could only be bought in dollars, central banks around the world needed to hold significant reserves of U.S. currency. This guaranteed demand for dollars even in countries that had no direct trade with the United States. As a result, the dollar remained the world's dominant currency even after the end of the gold standard, backed not by precious metals but by the essential commodity that powered modern economies.

Beyond securing the dollar's role in global trade, the petrodollar system also provided the U.S. government with an extraordinary financial advantage. Because oil-exporting nations accumulated vast amounts of dollars, they needed a place to invest them. The most attractive and secure option? U.S. Treasury bonds. This created a cycle in which petrodollars flowed back into American financial markets, helping to finance the U.S. government's spending at low borrowing costs.

For Washington, it was a perfect arrangement. The U.S. could print dollars at will, and because the world needed them to buy oil, it faced no immediate consequences for running large deficits. While most nations had to be mindful of overspending to avoid currency depreciation, the U.S. could simply export inflation, as excess dollars were absorbed by foreign economies. The petrodollar system thus became the invisible engine that fueled American financial dominance for decades to come. This unique privilege allowed the U.S. to finance wars, stimulus programs, and economic expansions with minimal constraint, reinforcing its global influence while other nations remained tethered to fiscal discipline.

Chapter 1: The Birth of the Dollar Empire

Wall Street and the Financialization of the Global Economy

While the petrodollar system ensured global reliance on the dollar, another major force was reshaping America's role in the world economy—the rise of Wall Street as the epicenter of global finance.

Following the collapse of Bretton Woods, international capital markets underwent a dramatic transformation. With currencies no longer fixed to gold, exchange rates fluctuated based on supply and demand, giving rise to a new era of financial speculation. Wall Street, already a major player in global finance, seized this opportunity. The deregulation of banking in the 1980s and the explosion of financial innovations—including derivatives, mortgage-backed securities, and hedge funds—turned the U.S. into the nerve center of global capital flows.

American investment banks and hedge funds began expanding aggressively overseas, setting up operations in Europe, Asia, and Latin America. The New York Stock Exchange (NYSE) and NASDAQ became the largest and most liquid equity markets in the world, attracting capital from every corner of the globe. Foreign governments, multinational corporations, and individual investors alike poured money into U.S. markets, seeking the stability and high returns that Wall Street offered.

At the same time, the Eurodollar market—offshore dollars held outside the U.S.—expanded rapidly, further embedding the dollar into global finance. Because most international lending was conducted in dollars, foreign banks and corporations had no choice but to transact in the currency, reinforcing its dominance. This process of financialization ensured that even as U.S. manufacturing declined, its financial institutions remained at the center of the global economic order.

The U.S. Treasury Bond Market: The World's Safe Haven

If global trade and Wall Street cemented the dollar's dominance, the U.S. Treasury bond market ensured its long-term endurance.

As foreign nations accumulated dollar reserves—whether from oil sales, trade surpluses, or financial investments—they needed a place to store them. The safest and most liquid asset available was U.S. government debt. Treasury bonds, backed by the full faith and credit of the U.S. government, became the preferred investment vehicle for central banks worldwide. Nations such as China, Japan, Germany, and the oil-rich Gulf states became some of the largest holders of U.S. debt, collectively holding trillions in Treasury securities.

This demand for Treasuries granted the U.S. an extraordinary advantage: the ability to finance its deficits at exceptionally low interest rates. Unlike emerging economies, which often struggled to attract foreign capital, the U.S. faced no such issue. In times of financial crises—whether during the 1997 Asian Financial Crisis, the 2008 Global Financial Crisis, or the COVID-19 pandemic—global investors rushed into U.S. bonds as the ultimate safe-haven asset.

Even countries that had tense political relations with Washington—such as China and Russia—continued to hold Treasuries simply because there was no viable alternative. No other financial market was as deep, liquid, or trusted as the U.S. bond market.

Why No Other Currency Could Challenge the Dollar

Despite periodic discussions about de-dollarization, no currency has come close to replacing the U.S. dollar as the world's reserve currency. The euro, despite its importance, suffers from political fragmentation within the European Union. The Chinese yuan, despite Beijing's ambitions, remains hindered by strict capital controls and government intervention. Cryptocurrencies, while promising in theory, lack the stability and institutional backing required for large-scale adoption.

But beyond economic considerations, the dollar's dominance is also reinforced by U.S. military and geopolitical power. The United States maintains over 750 military bases in more than 80 countries, ensuring its economic and strategic interests remain protected. This military presence provides an added layer of security that no other currency issuer can offer. Nations conducting trade in dollars know that the U.S. has both the economic strength and military reach to enforce financial stability when necessary.

5

THE DOLLAR'S DOMINION: UNRIVALED, FOR NOW

By the late 20th century, the U.S. had achieved something unprecedented: total financial hegemony without direct colonial rule. The dollar was not just a currency; it was the foundation of the global financial system. The petrodollar ensured steady demand, Wall Street attracted the world's capital, and U.S. Treasuries provided the safest store of value.

This dominance was built on more than economic strength—it was underpinned by trust in U.S. institutions, the rule of law, and an unrivaled ability to project military and political power globally. The U.S. dollar became the default currency for international trade, foreign reserves, and cross-border investments, creating a self-reinforcing cycle that entrenched American financial supremacy. The influence of institutions like the Federal Reserve and the International Monetary Fund, both heavily shaped by U.S. policies, further bolstered this dominance, giving Washington an unparalleled ability to shape global economic outcomes.

Yet, no hegemony is without its vulnerabilities. As the 21st century unfolds, new forces—including rising global debt, financial fragmentation, and emerging economic powers—are beginning to test the resilience of the dollar-based system. The rapid ascent of China as an economic superpower, growing calls for de-dollarization, and technological innovations such as digital currencies are challenging the status quo. At the same time, the U.S. faces internal pressures, from political polarization to mounting fiscal deficits, raising questions about its long-term financial stability.

Whether these shifts will erode or merely reshape U.S. financial supremacy remains the defining question of the modern era. The dollar's dominance, though deeply entrenched, is no longer unassailable. The coming decades will reveal whether the U.S. can adapt to new realities or whether the world will witness the gradual decline of its financial empire—an empire built not on territory, but on trust, trade, and the power of a single currency.

One of the greatest strengths of the dollar system has been its network effect—its dominance reinforced by the sheer volume of global transactions conducted in dollars, the deep liquidity of U.S. financial markets, and the lack of viable alternatives. Even as challengers emerge, inertia favors the status quo. Most global trade contracts are still priced in dollars, multinational corporations conduct business in greenbacks, and central banks hold the majority of their reserves in U.S. assets. This entrenched position makes a sudden shift away from the dollar unlikely. However, history suggests that financial systems do not remain static. The same network effect that once propelled the dollar to supremacy could, under the right conditions, work in reverse, accelerating a pivot toward a more multipolar financial order.

At the heart of this transition is the question of confidence. The dollar's global role has always depended not just on economic fundamentals but on trust—trust in U.S. fiscal responsibility, trust in the stability of its institutions, and trust in the rule of law governing its financial system. If this confidence erodes—whether due to reckless monetary policy, escalating political dysfunction, or aggressive financial sanctions that push nations toward alternatives—the world may find itself in a self-reinforcing cycle of de-dollarization. While no single currency is poised to immediately replace the dollar, the growing adoption of alternative financial systems, from China's yuan-based trade agreements to the rise of digital currencies, suggests that the foundation of American financial dominance is not as unshakable as it once seemed.

CHAPTER 2

GLOBALIZATION AND THE DOLLAR'S REACH

The era of globalization propelled the U.S. dollar from a position of strength to one of unrivaled dominance. Chapter 2 examines how trade liberalization expanded the dollar's influence as the primary currency for global transactions, while U.S. financial markets provided stability and liquidity that the world came to rely on. This chapter explores why central banks and corporations accumulate U.S. dollars, from trust in U.S. economic leadership to the liquidity offered by dollar-denominated assets. Yet, even as the dollar remains central to global finance, the first signs of strain are emerging. With rising geopolitical tensions, economic fragmentation, and growing calls for financial independence from U.S. influence, early de-dollarization efforts signal potential cracks in the system. This chapter concludes by highlighting the paradox of the dollar's continued dominance amidst growing vulnerabilities, setting the stage for deeper discussions on the future of global finance.

1

GLOBALIZATION AND THE DOLLAR'S TAKEOVER

When the United States severed the dollar's link to gold in 1971, the world entered a period of profound financial uncertainty. For nearly three decades, the Bretton Woods system had provided stability through fixed exchange rates, allowing governments to conduct trade with minimal fluctuations in currency values. But by the early 1970s, the system that had underpinned the postwar global economy was no longer sustainable. The United States, no longer able to maintain the gold convertibility of the dollar, had set the world on a new course — one where currency values would be determined not by central bank gold reserves, but by the open market.

This transition to *floating exchange rates* fundamentally altered global trade. Under the old system, exchange rates had remained stable, giving businesses confidence that international transactions would not be disrupted by sudden currency swings. But in the years following the Nixon Shock, currency markets became increasingly volatile, forcing nations to adapt to a financial order in which governments could no longer guarantee the stability of their money.

For the United States, the collapse of Bretton Woods initially seemed like a moment of vulnerability. Without the gold standard, the dollar's credibility now depended entirely on the strength of the U.S. economy and the willingness of other nations to continue using it as a medium of exchange. Yet, rather than diminishing the dollar's dominance, the shift to floating rates ultimately reinforced it.

Unlike other currencies, which suffered from bouts of speculative pressure and instability, the dollar remained the most trusted and liquid asset in global markets. Its unrivaled status was further cemented by a powerful new reality: the rise of trade liberalization and financial deregulation, both of which expanded the role of the dollar far beyond what had been possible under the fixed-exchange system of Bretton Woods.

Dollar Expansion through Trade Agreements

The 1970s and 1980s marked a pivotal era in which nations increasingly embraced free trade as a path to economic growth. As global economies recovered from the oil shocks of the 1970s and the inflationary turmoil of the early 1980s, policymakers around the world pushed for deeper integration of markets, dismantling trade barriers and promoting cross-border investment.

At the forefront of this movement was the United States, which sought to leverage its financial and industrial strength to solidify its economic influence. The Reagan administration championed trade liberalization, advocating for reduced tariffs, fewer restrictions on foreign investment, and a more open financial system. These efforts culminated in a series of trade agreements that would bind much of the global economy even more tightly to the dollar.

Nowhere was this shift more evident than in North America. In 1994, the United States, Canada, and Mexico signed the North American Free Trade Agreement (NAFTA), eliminating most trade barriers between the three countries and dramatically increasing the volume of cross-border transactions. The impact was immediate. Supply chains became more interconnected, with companies operating seamlessly across national borders. American multinational corporations expanded aggressively, setting up manufacturing and distribution hubs throughout Mexico and Canada, all while conducting transactions in U.S. dollars.

Beyond North America, a wave of trade agreements swept through Europe and Asia. The formation of the European Union's single market in the early 1990s and the rapid expansion of free trade zones in East Asia signaled a shift toward global economic integration. But despite the growing role of regional trade blocs, one factor remained constant—the dominance of the dollar in global trade settlements. Even as countries strengthened economic ties with their neighbors, they continued to invoice their exports and imports in dollars, reinforcing the currency's role as the world's primary medium of exchange.

For developing economies, the appeal of dollar-based trade was undeniable. Nations that sought to integrate into global markets recognized that pricing goods in dollars provided stability and reduced transaction costs. Given the dollar's liquidity and its presence in every major financial hub, businesses across the world found it far easier to settle transactions in dollars than in their own national currencies. This was particularly true for commodities—whether oil, steel, or agricultural products—where dollar pricing had long been the standard. The dollar was not just the world's reserve currency; it was the language of international trade.

China's WTO Entry and the Dollar's Global Rise

By the late 20th century, globalization had become a defining force in the world economy. No country exemplified this transformation more than China. For much of the Cold War era, China had remained largely closed off from global trade, operating under a state-controlled economy that prioritized self-sufficiency over international commerce. But in the 1980s and 1990s, a dramatic shift was underway.

Under the leadership of Deng Xiaoping, China embarked on a series of economic reforms that opened its markets to foreign investment and trade. Special economic zones were established along the country's coastline, attracting multinational corporations eager to tap into China's vast pool of low-cost labor. Factories sprung up at an astonishing rate, producing goods not just for domestic consumption, but for export to markets around the world.

This process reached a defining moment in 2001, when China was admitted to the World Trade Organization (WTO). The agreement marked China's full entry into the global trading system, removing many of the trade barriers that had previously restricted its exports and giving it unprecedented access to Western markets. Almost overnight, China became the world's factory, producing everything from textiles to electronics on a scale never before seen.

But while China's manufacturing dominance was rapidly growing, its financial system remained deeply tied to the dollar. Chinese firms, eager to expand their presence in global markets, conducted the overwhelming majority of their trade in dollars, just as their counterparts in Europe, Japan, and other export-driven economies had done before them. Even as China's economic output surged, it relied on dollar-based transactions to conduct business with the rest of the world.

This dynamic created a paradox. While China was emerging as the world's second-largest economy, it was also becoming the largest holder of U.S. dollars. As Chinese exports flooded global markets, a massive accumulation of dollars flowed back into China's financial system. Rather than converting these reserves into yuan, the Chinese government chose to reinvest them into U.S. Treasury bonds and other dollar-denominated assets, further entrenching the dollar's global dominance. By the mid-2000s, China held more than $1 trillion in U.S. Treasuries, making it one of the largest financiers of American government debt.

For the United States, this arrangement proved beneficial. China's dollar holdings ensured a steady demand for U.S. debt, allowing Washington to finance its deficits at historically low interest rates. At the same time, American consumers benefited from a flood of cheap Chinese goods, keeping inflation in check and fueling an era of economic expansion.

Yet, beneath this mutually beneficial relationship, tensions were brewing. As China's economic power grew, so too did its desire to reduce its dependence on the U.S. financial system. While Beijing remained committed to global trade, it began exploring alternatives to dollar reliance, setting the stage for future conflicts over currency dominance.

The Dollar's Deepening Grip on Global Trade

The post-Bretton Woods era saw the dollar's dominance expand far beyond what even its architects had envisioned. The collapse of fixed exchange rates did not weaken the dollar; instead, it allowed American financial markets, multinational corporations, and global trade networks to reinforce its role as the world's undisputed currency.

Trade liberalization ensured that businesses around the world continued to rely on dollar-based transactions, while China's rise further cemented the dollar's global grip. By the early 21st century, more than 80% of global trade was invoiced in dollars, even in transactions that did not directly involve the United States. The dollar had transcended national borders, becoming the foundation of the global economic order.

Yet, as the next section will explore, financial markets—not just trade—played an equally critical role in maintaining this dominance. The integration of global capital markets, the rise of U.S. Treasury bonds as the world's safest asset, and the deepening influence of Wall Street all contributed to the dollar's unrivaled position. But could this financial strength also be a source of vulnerability? As financial markets expanded, so too did the risks of overreliance on the U.S. system—a reality that would become increasingly clear in the decades ahead.

2

THE ROLE OF U.S. FINANCIAL MARKETS IN GLOBAL STABILITY

Few nations in history have been able to sustain global economic dominance as the United States has. At the heart of this dominance lies a financial system so deeply embedded in global trade and investment that it remains the bedrock of international finance even as geopolitical shifts and technological changes reshape the world economy. The ability of U.S. financial markets to absorb capital, provide stability in times of crisis, and finance government deficits at low cost has given the United States an unparalleled advantage—a privilege that has long shielded it from many of the economic constraints faced by other nations. But this privilege is not immune to pressure. While the U.S. remains the epicenter of global finance, cracks are beginning to show in the very system that has upheld its dominance for decades.

The U.S. Treasury Market: The Backbone of Global Finance

The foundation of America's financial supremacy lies in the U.S. Treasury market. For decades, U.S. government bonds have been the world's most trusted financial instrument, serving as both a store of value and a benchmark for global interest rates. Unlike other countries, where government bonds can fluctuate wildly based on domestic instability or market skepticism, U.S. Treasuries are viewed as risk-free assets.

Foreign governments, central banks, and institutional investors hold trillions of dollars in U.S. debt, not out of charity or political allegiance, but because of the unrivaled depth, liquidity, and security that the Treasury market offers. The scale of this market is staggering. As of 2024, foreign central banks hold over $7.6 trillion in U.S. Treasury securities, accounting for nearly a third of all outstanding U.S. government debt. At its peak, China alone held over $1.3 trillion in Treasuries, though its holdings have since declined as Beijing gradually diversifies its reserves. Japan, another major player, remains one of the largest foreign holders, reinforcing the global reliance on the U.S. bond market.

This demand for Treasuries gives Washington an enormous strategic advantage. It allows the U.S. to borrow on exceptionally favorable terms, running persistent deficits without suffering the currency crises or interest rate spikes that plague emerging economies. No other country enjoys this kind of financial flexibility. While developing nations must carefully balance their borrowing with investor confidence, the United States can issue new debt almost at will, knowing that global demand will absorb it. This is what makes the U.S. Treasury market the backbone of global finance — its size, its stability, and, crucially, its ability to function as the world's primary safe asset.

Why Foreign Governments Accumulate U.S. Debt

For many nations, holding U.S. debt is not simply a financial decision but an economic necessity. The structure of global trade ensures that dollars accumulate in foreign reserves, and those dollars must be reinvested somewhere. With limited alternatives, U.S. Treasuries remain the preferred choice.

Countries that run trade surpluses with the United States, such as China, Japan, and Germany, end up accumulating vast reserves of U.S. dollars. Instead of holding idle cash, central banks reinvest these reserves in Treasuries, ensuring a stable return while keeping their foreign exchange markets liquid. This creates a reinforcing cycle: nations that trade heavily with the U.S. accumulate dollars and recycle them back into the American financial system.

Beyond trade dynamics, holding Treasuries provides foreign governments with financial insurance. In times of uncertainty, access to liquid dollar assets can stabilize a nation's currency and financial system. This was evident during the 2008 global financial crisis, when even countries skeptical of U.S. economic policy rushed to increase their dollar reserves, recognizing Treasuries as the safest place to store capital during market turmoil. The same pattern emerged during the COVID-19 pandemic, when a flight to safety saw demand for U.S. debt surge, driving bond yields to historic lows.

The Global Safe Haven: U.S. Treasuries in Times of Crisis

When financial panic sets in, capital flees to safety. Again and again, history has shown that no asset is perceived as safer than U.S. government bonds. This status as the global safe haven has allowed the U.S. to maintain investor confidence even in periods of deep economic distress.

During the 1997 Asian Financial Crisis, when Thailand, Indonesia, and South Korea saw their currencies collapse under the weight of speculative attacks, investors rushed to U.S. Treasuries, driving down yields while leaving emerging markets struggling to attract capital. A similar flight to safety occurred during the Eurozone debt crisis of the early 2010s, when fears of sovereign defaults in Greece, Italy, and Spain sent European investors scrambling to park their money in dollars. Even in moments of domestic instability, the U.S. bond market has remained the global anchor.

Perhaps the most telling example of this paradox came in 2008, when the global financial crisis originated in the United States itself. Despite the meltdown of major American financial institutions and a housing collapse that triggered global recession, investors still flooded into U.S. Treasuries. In a rational market, one might have expected capital to flee the very country responsible for the crisis, but the reality was different — no other financial system offered the same level of liquidity, legal protection, and perceived security.

This ability to attract capital even in times of domestic turmoil is a testament to the entrenched power of U.S. financial markets. It is also a privilege that no other country has been able to replicate.

Wall Street's Influence on Global Capital Flows

Beyond government bonds, the dominance of U.S. financial markets extends to equities, corporate debt, and capital investment. The New York Stock Exchange (NYSE) and NASDAQ remain the largest and most liquid stock markets in the world, drawing investors from every continent. American multinational corporations, from Apple and Microsoft to Boeing and ExxonMobil, issue bonds and raise capital in U.S. dollars, reinforcing the greenback's role as the de facto currency of global business.

Wall Street investment banks and asset managers exert enormous influence over global capital flows. Firms like BlackRock, JPMorgan, and Goldman Sachs not only allocate trillions in investment capital but also shape international financial policy through their advisory roles in sovereign wealth funds, pension systems, and corporate finance. This gives the United States financial leverage that extends far beyond Washington's direct policy tools.

The Eurodollar market—offshore dollar deposits held outside the United States—further illustrates the scale of Wall Street's reach. Even when transactions take place entirely outside of U.S. borders, they are often conducted in dollars, reinforcing American financial influence over global banking.

The Exorbitant Privilege: Why the U.S. Can Borrow Without Limits

French President Valéry Giscard d'Estaing once described the U.S. dollar's unique role as an *exorbitant privilege*—a reference to America's ability to borrow cheaply in its own currency while forcing the rest of the world to earn dollars through trade or investment. Unlike emerging markets that must manage their dollar reserves carefully, the United States faces no such constraint. It can issue debt freely, knowing that global demand for Treasuries remains robust.

While most nations must worry about external debt denominated in a foreign currency, the U.S. can print the very money it borrows. This advantage has allowed the U.S. government to run persistent deficits without triggering financial crises, a luxury that no other economy enjoys.

Emerging Challenges: Financial Sanctions and Rising U.S. Debt

Yet, despite its dominance, the U.S. financial system is not without vulnerabilities. One of the most significant risks to dollar hegemony comes from the overuse of financial sanctions. When the U.S. froze over $300 billion in Russian foreign reserves in response to the 2022 invasion of Ukraine, it sent shockwaves through central banks worldwide. Many nations, including China, Saudi Arabia, and India, saw this as a warning—if the dollar could be used as a geopolitical weapon, should they continue to rely on it so heavily?

At the same time, the rising U.S. national debt, now surpassing $34 trillion, has raised concerns about long-term sustainability. While demand for Treasuries remains strong, the growing fiscal burden has led some investors to question whether the U.S. can continue borrowing at current levels indefinitely.

For now, the U.S. financial system remains unmatched in depth, liquidity, and global influence. But the forces that sustain its dominance are beginning to shift. The coming years will test whether America can adapt to an evolving financial landscape—or whether its *exorbitant privilege* is slowly slipping away.

3

WHY THE WORLD ACCUMULATES U.S. DOLLARS

For much of the modern era, the U.S. dollar has been the bedrock of the global financial system. Nations, corporations, and financial institutions have accumulated vast reserves of dollars—not always by choice, but often out of necessity. Whether for trade, investment, or financial stability, the dollar's role as the primary global currency has shaped international markets in ways that no other currency has been able to replicate.

Yet beneath this dominance, there are growing questions about whether the world's reliance on the dollar is sustainable. The sheer scale of dollar holdings across central banks, private institutions, and corporate balance sheets has created both stability and vulnerability. The financial system remains deeply entrenched in a dollar-based framework, but a slow and deliberate shift is underway as nations seek to diversify their reserves and hedge against future disruptions.

The Dollar as the World's Reserve Currency

The foundation of the dollar's global supremacy was laid in 1944 at Bretton Woods, where the United States cemented its position as the anchor of the international monetary system. Even after President Nixon severed the link between the dollar and gold in 1971, the currency maintained its status as the world's primary reserve asset. For much of the postwar period, global markets accepted the dollar as the safest, most liquid, and most reliable currency available.

At its peak in the late 1990s, the dollar accounted for more than 70% of global foreign exchange reserves—a level of dominance no other currency in modern history had achieved. Today, that figure has declined to around 58%, according to the International Monetary Fund (IMF). While this signals a gradual diversification away from the dollar, no alternative has yet emerged to fully challenge its position. The euro, despite its importance, suffers from political fragmentation. The Chinese yuan, despite Beijing's ambitions, remains tightly controlled by the Chinese government and is still used in less than 3% of global transactions.

For central banks, the decision to hold dollars is not merely a reflection of trust in the U.S. economy—it is a matter of necessity. The dollar remains the most widely used currency in international trade, serving as the default for commodities, manufacturing goods, and financial settlements. Even countries that trade little with the United States still conduct much of their business in dollars, reinforcing the currency's dominance.

Financial crises have only strengthened this pattern. During times of uncertainty, investors and central banks flock to U.S. Treasuries, viewing them as the ultimate safe-haven asset. This was evident during the 2008 financial crisis, when paradoxically, capital rushed into the U.S. dollar even though the crisis had originated in the United States. The same dynamic played out in 2020, when the COVID-19 pandemic sent shockwaves through the global economy, prompting a scramble for dollar liquidity.

Even China, which has sought to reduce its exposure to the dollar, remains one of the largest holders of U.S. Treasury bonds. As of 2023, China held over $800 billion in U.S. government debt, reflecting a careful balancing act—diversifying into alternative assets while still relying on the dollar as a critical financial instrument. This paradox extends to many other nations that recognize the risks of overreliance on the U.S. financial system but find themselves too deeply embedded in it to break away entirely.

The Weight of Dollar-Denominated Debt

If central banks accumulate dollars as reserves, private borrowers do so out of necessity. The sheer scale of dollar-denominated debt across the world is staggering. As of 2023, over $13 trillion in global debt was denominated in U.S. dollars, according to the Bank for International Settlements (BIS). This debt is not just held by U.S. institutions but by corporations, governments, and financial entities across emerging and developed economies alike.

For many countries, borrowing in dollars offers significant advantages. U.S. financial markets provide unmatched liquidity, lower interest rates, and access to a vast pool of global investors.

Borrowers, particularly in emerging markets, often find it easier to issue debt in dollars rather than their own local currencies, which may be more volatile and less trusted by international investors.

Yet, this reliance comes at a cost—particularly when the Federal Reserve tightens monetary policy. The cycle is a familiar one: when the Fed raises interest rates, the value of the dollar rises, making it more expensive for foreign borrowers to service their debt. For economies heavily reliant on external financing, this can trigger severe financial stress.

Sri Lanka's 2022 default serves as a stark example of this dynamic. As the Fed embarked on one of the most aggressive rate-hiking cycles in modern history to combat inflation, the dollar strengthened dramatically. Sri Lanka, already burdened by excessive external debt, found itself unable to meet its repayment obligations. The country's dwindling foreign exchange reserves, rising import costs, and higher debt servicing requirements pushed it into an economic crisis, ultimately forcing a default on its sovereign debt for the first time in history.

This scenario has played out repeatedly across emerging markets. From Turkey to Argentina to Pakistan, economies that rely on dollar financing find themselves vulnerable to sudden shifts in U.S. monetary policy. When the dollar strengthens, these nations must devote more of their economic resources to repaying debt rather than investing in growth. This has led to an ongoing debate about whether developing economies should seek alternatives to dollar-denominated borrowing, yet no viable substitute has emerged.

The Petrodollar System: The Foundation of Dollar Demand

While trade and debt have played crucial roles in the dollar's global standing, no factor has been more important than the petrodollar system in ensuring continuous demand for U.S. currency. The origins of this system trace back to the 1970s, following the collapse of the Bretton Woods framework.

After abandoning the gold standard, the U.S. faced a critical challenge: how to sustain the dollar's dominance without the backing of a tangible asset. The answer came through a strategic agreement with Saudi Arabia and OPEC, in which oil would be priced exclusively in dollars. In return, the U.S. would provide military protection and economic support to the Saudi regime. Over time, this arrangement was extended to all major oil-exporting nations, effectively binding the global energy market to the dollar.

The implications of this system were profound. Any country that wished to purchase oil needed to hold dollars, creating a self-reinforcing global demand. Oil-exporting nations, in turn, accumulated vast reserves of U.S. dollars, which they often recycled into U.S. assets—particularly Treasury bonds. This cycle ensured that the dollar remained at the center of global finance, even in the absence of gold backing.

Yet, the petrodollar system is no longer as unshakable as it once was. In recent years, China, Russia, and other major economies have begun experimenting with oil transactions in alternative currencies. In 2023, Beijing secured agreements with Saudi Arabia and Russia to settle some oil trade in yuan, marking a significant shift. While the dollar remains dominant in global energy markets, these developments highlight a growing willingness to explore alternatives—an early sign of potential fragmentation in the system.

The Paradox of Dollar Dependence

Despite growing concerns over U.S. financial dominance, the reality remains that the global economy is deeply entrenched in a dollar-based system. For decades, the dollar's role as the primary reserve currency has been cemented by historical precedent, economic inertia, and structural advantages that few alternatives can match. Even as countries take steps to diversify, a full-scale shift away from the dollar is far from imminent.

The dominance of the dollar extends beyond trade—it permeates global finance, from central bank reserves to corporate debt issuance. More than half of global trade invoices are denominated in dollars, even in transactions that do not involve the United States. The global demand for dollars ensures that the Federal Reserve's monetary policy has far-reaching consequences, influencing everything from emerging-market debt to commodity prices.

For many nations, the costs of abandoning the dollar far outweigh the benefits. The depth of U.S. financial markets, the liquidity of dollar-denominated assets, and the entrenched nature of the petrodollar system all ensure that the dollar remains indispensable—for now. The world may be slowly diversifying, but there is no immediate alternative that offers the same level of trust, stability, and ease of use.

Yet, history suggests that no currency retains dominance forever. While no immediate rival exists, the cracks in the system are becoming more visible. The weaponization of the dollar through financial sanctions has accelerated efforts by some nations to explore alternatives. The U.S. government's ability to freeze foreign assets and restrict access to SWIFT (the global financial messaging system) has raised concerns among even its allies. In response, regional trade blocs are experimenting with bilateral trade settlements in local currencies, and digital payment systems are being developed to bypass dollar reliance altogether.

The rise of alternative payment networks, the increased use of yuan in trade settlements, and the continued accumulation of gold by central banks all signal an evolving financial landscape. While the dollar is unlikely to be dethroned in the near future, the long-term trajectory suggests that the world is inching toward a more multipolar monetary order—one where reliance on a single currency becomes increasingly impractical.

4

DE-DOLLARIZATION: THE FIRST CRACKS

For decades, the U.S. dollar has reigned as the unquestioned anchor of the global financial system. It has been the primary medium for international trade, the dominant reserve currency for central banks, and the ultimate safe-haven asset in times of crisis. But history has shown that no currency maintains supremacy forever. Beneath the surface of dollar dominance, signs of change are beginning to emerge. A slow but persistent shift is underway, driven by financial crises, geopolitical tensions, and the emergence of alternative financial networks.

While no single event has been powerful enough to dethrone the dollar outright, each shock to the system has chipped away at its foundation. The first major warning came with the 2008 financial crisis, which exposed the risks of excessive dependence on the U.S. banking system. More recently, the weaponization of the dollar through sanctions, particularly against Russia, has raised alarm among nations that once viewed dollar reserves as a neutral store of value. Meanwhile, the rise of China and Russia as financial counterweights, the declining reliance on U.S. Treasuries, and the slow but significant push toward non-dollar trade settlements have all signaled that the era of unquestioned dollar hegemony may be entering a new phase.

The 2008 Financial Crisis: The First Warning Sign

The first serious cracks in the dollar-based system appeared in 2008 when the global financial crisis, triggered by the collapse of the U.S. subprime mortgage market, sent shockwaves through economies worldwide. For a system built on the promise of stability, the sudden unraveling of major American financial institutions—including the bankruptcy of Lehman Brothers—was a stark reminder that even the world's most powerful economy was not immune to systemic failures.

For decades, central banks and foreign investors had parked their reserves in U.S. Treasury bonds and dollar-denominated assets, viewing them as the safest investments available. But the 2008 crisis forced a painful reassessment. The reckless expansion of U.S. credit markets, the failure of regulatory oversight, and the near-collapse of the global banking system exposed vulnerabilities that had long been overlooked. Nations that had built their financial models around dollar stability suddenly found themselves at the mercy of the U.S. Federal Reserve's emergency measures.

As Washington scrambled to contain the crisis, the Federal Reserve slashed interest rates to near zero and launched quantitative easing (QE)—a policy that flooded markets with newly created dollars in an attempt to stabilize financial institutions. While this approach helped to prevent a full-scale depression in the U.S., it had unintended consequences abroad. Emerging economies that had relied on dollar financing saw their currencies fluctuate wildly, and their foreign exchange reserves—much of which were tied to U.S. debt—were now caught in a system that seemed increasingly unpredictable.

In the aftermath of the crisis, China, Russia, and other major economies began quietly reassessing their exposure to the dollar-based system. The People's Bank of China (PBOC) gradually diversified its reserves, increasing holdings of gold, euros, and alternative assets, while Russia steadily reduced its dependence on U.S. Treasuries. The crisis had revealed an uncomfortable truth: the global financial system was not as stable as many had believed, and its foundation—the U.S. dollar—was not immune to shocks originating from within the United States itself.

Dollar Offensive: U.S. Sanctions on Russia

If 2008 was a wake-up call, the events of 2022 marked a turning point. When the United States and its allies froze over $300 billion of Russian foreign reserves in response to the Ukraine invasion, it sent an unmistakable message to the rest of the world: the global financial system, long thought to be a neutral framework for trade and investment, could be weaponized at any moment.

For decades, the U.S. dollar's dominance had been built on trust—on the idea that central banks and sovereign wealth funds could hold their reserves in dollars without fear of political interference. That assumption was shattered when Washington effectively cut off Russia from the global financial system, barring it from using its own reserves. While these sanctions were intended to cripple Russia's economy, they also raised uncomfortable questions for other countries. If a G20 economy like Russia could have its dollar reserves frozen overnight, what would stop the U.S. from doing the same to other nations in the future?

This realization accelerated efforts to build alternative financial networks that bypass the dollar. China and Russia quickly expanded the use of their own national currencies for trade, while the BRICS nations (Brazil, Russia, India, China, and South Africa) began discussing the possibility of creating a new reserve currency independent of the U.S.-led financial order. At the same time, Moscow and Beijing ramped up transactions through China's Cross-Border Interbank Payment System (CIPS)—a potential competitor to SWIFT—allowing Russian banks to process payments outside of the dollar-based system.

China & Russia: Challenging the Financial Order

China's strategy for reducing its dollar dependence has been unfolding for years, but recent events have pushed Beijing to accelerate these efforts. The Belt and Road Initiative (BRI), China's massive infrastructure investment program, has played a key role in this transition. Instead of relying on the dollar for international financing, China has increasingly encouraged the use of renminbi-denominated loans for infrastructure projects across Asia, Africa, and Latin America.

At the same time, Russia has made a dramatic shift in its financial strategy, particularly after being cut off from much of the Western banking system. By 2023, over 70% of Russia-China bilateral trade was conducted in non-dollar currencies, primarily in yuan and rubles—a sharp contrast to previous years when the majority of trade was settled in dollars. This trend extends beyond China. India, Saudi Arabia, and Brazil have all explored similar arrangements, gradually reducing their reliance on the dollar in key trade relationships.

While these moves have not yet fundamentally altered the global financial order, they represent the first meaningful steps toward a multi-currency world, where the dollar is no longer the default medium of exchange for every major transaction.

CBDCs and the Push for De-Dollarization

Another challenge to dollar dominance comes from the rise of central bank digital currencies (CBDCs)—government-backed digital money designed to facilitate transactions outside of traditional banking networks. China has been the most aggressive in this space, launching the digital yuan as a tool to settle trade transactions without relying on Western payment systems.

Unlike traditional reserve assets, which must be physically held in banks, CBDCs offer an alternative form of liquidity that can be transferred instantly across borders. If widely adopted, they could provide an entirely new way for countries to bypass dollar-based clearing systems altogether. This potential shift has led many in Washington to worry that digital currencies could erode U.S. influence in global finance, particularly if major trading blocs begin settling transactions in digital yuan, rupees, or rubles instead of dollars.

The Global Retreat from U.S. Treasuries

A more immediate concern for U.S. policymakers is the slow but steady decline in foreign holdings of U.S. Treasury bonds. Once seen as the safest and most liquid asset in the world, Treasuries have long been the foundation of the global financial system. But in recent years, major economies—including China, Japan, and Saudi Arabia— have gradually reduced their purchases, opting instead to diversify their reserves into gold and other assets.

China, which at its peak held over $1.3 trillion in U.S. debt, has cut its holdings to below $800 billion as of 2023. Japan, once the largest foreign holder of Treasuries, has steadily reduced its holdings from $1.15 trillion in early 2024 to $1.128 trillion by mid-year, reflecting a measured but ongoing shift. Meanwhile, Saudi Arabia has lowered its U.S. debt holdings from over $180 billion in 2020 to around $110 billion in 2023, redirecting its reserves toward alternative assets, including gold and other foreign investments. While these moves have been incremental, they signal a broader trend of reserve diversification, suggesting that the world is becoming less willing to finance America's ever-growing debt burden.

Petrodollar Under Threat: Is the Shift Underway?

Perhaps the greatest challenge to dollar dominance would come from a shift in the global oil trade, which has historically been conducted in U.S. dollars. Since the 1970s, the petrodollar system has forced nations to accumulate dollars to purchase crude oil, ensuring perpetual demand for the currency. But this system is no longer unchallenged.

Saudi Arabia, once the bedrock of the petrodollar agreement, has signaled openness to accepting payments in yuan, particularly for Chinese oil sales. Meanwhile, Russia and Iran have already begun trading oil in euros, yuan, and even gold, bypassing the dollar entirely.

For now, the dollar remains the dominant global currency, but the cracks in the system are undeniable. Whether these shifts amount to a gradual erosion of U.S. financial power or the beginning of a larger realignment remains to be seen.

5

THE DOLLAR'S FRAGILE THRONE

For much of the postwar era, the U.S. dollar has functioned as the backbone of the global financial system, a role cemented by deep capital markets, the petrodollar system, and the sheer inertia of international trade networks. Even as global economic power has begun shifting toward emerging markets, the world's reliance on the dollar has remained largely intact.

Yet beneath the surface, signs of change are becoming increasingly difficult to ignore. While the dollar still accounts for the majority of global trade transactions and foreign exchange reserves, its dominance has been gradually eroding. In 2000, over 70% of global reserves were held in dollars. By 2023, that figure had fallen to around 58%, according to the International Monetary Fund. The decline has been slow, but it reflects a growing willingness among central banks and financial institutions to diversify their holdings.

The shift is most visible in trade settlements. China has aggressively pushed for yuan-based transactions, particularly with oil-exporting nations. Russia, following Western sanctions in response to its invasion of Ukraine, has expanded non-dollar trade arrangements with China, India, and Iran. Even longtime U.S. partners such as Saudi Arabia have signaled a greater openness to accepting alternative currencies, a move that would have been unthinkable just a decade ago.

Despite these developments, no single challenger has emerged to replace the dollar. The euro, which was once seen as a serious competitor, remains constrained by the European Union's fragmented fiscal system. The Chinese yuan, though gaining traction, remains hindered by strict capital controls and limited convertibility. Even as calls for a multipolar currency system grow louder, the world has yet to establish a credible alternative to the dollar's unique combination of liquidity, stability, and global acceptance.

The Dollar's Future in a Fractured Economy

While no immediate replacement for the dollar exists, the structure of global finance is becoming more fragmented. The post-World War II financial order, in which the dollar was the undisputed linchpin of international trade, is gradually giving way to a system where multiple currencies play a role.

This fragmentation is already apparent in the proliferation of bilateral trade agreements that bypass the dollar. India and the UAE settled their first oil trade in rupees in 2023. China and Brazil have moved to conduct portions of their trade in yuan, while Russia has shifted the majority of its energy exports away from dollar pricing. The growth of Central Bank Digital Currencies (CBDCs) further complicates the picture, as nations explore alternative financial architectures that could reduce their exposure to U.S. monetary policy.

At the same time, the dollar's role in financial markets remains deeply entrenched. During times of crisis, global investors still flock to U.S. Treasuries, reinforcing the perception that the dollar remains the world's safest asset. This dynamic was evident during the 2008 financial crisis, the COVID-19 pandemic, and the 2022 Russian invasion of Ukraine, when dollar-denominated assets surged in demand despite economic turmoil. The paradox is clear—while the world increasingly seeks alternatives to the dollar, it continues to depend on it when financial uncertainty strikes.

The United States, however, cannot afford complacency. The mechanisms that have long supported dollar supremacy—deep capital markets, trade dominance, and global confidence in U.S. financial institutions—are facing challenges unlike any seen in previous decades. If financial fragmentation continues, and alternative trading blocs successfully reduce their reliance on the dollar, Washington may find itself navigating an economic order where the dollar remains central but no longer unchallenged.

Will Protectionism Doom the Dollar?

The greatest risk to the dollar may not come from external challengers, but from within the United States itself. Rising protectionism, economic nationalism, and an increasing reliance on financial sanctions have created unintended consequences that could weaken the very system that has sustained American dominance.

Trade has long been a pillar of the dollar's global role. The postwar expansion of free trade agreements ensured that businesses and governments had a vested interest in conducting transactions in dollars, reinforcing its status as the default global currency. However, the rise of protectionist measures, including tariffs and trade restrictions, has begun to undermine these foundations.

The U.S.-China trade war, initiated in 2018, disrupted global supply chains and encouraged Beijing to accelerate its efforts to reduce dollar dependency. Sanctions on Russia, while isolating Moscow from Western financial markets, also prompted it to expand non-dollar trade partnerships. Even U.S. allies have quietly begun exploring alternatives, wary of Washington's increasing willingness to weaponize the global financial system for political objectives.

History has shown that financial dominance is rarely lost overnight, but it can be eroded over time through a combination of external competition and self-inflicted policy missteps. The risk for the United States is that by pushing too aggressively toward economic nationalism, it may accelerate the shift toward a multi-currency world rather than preventing it. If trading partners find it more convenient—or politically necessary—to transact outside the dollar system, the erosion of dollar dominance could occur faster than anticipated.

For now, the dollar remains the world's undisputed reserve currency, but the structural forces shaping the global economy suggest that change is already underway. Whether that change leads to a slow realignment of financial power or a more disruptive shift remains an open question—one that the U.S. cannot afford to ignore.

PART II

THE DOLLAR'S SELF-INFLICTED WOUNDS
Protectionism and the Seeds of Decline

"An empire that shuts its gates to the world invites decay within."
— Marcus Aurelius

As globalization's golden era wanes, protectionism is making a resurgent and contentious return. Part II explores how the reintroduction of tariffs—once considered relics of a bygone era—has reshaped global trade. From the escalating U.S.-China trade war to broader nationalist economic policies, this section delves into the motivations behind protectionist measures and the ripple effects they create. Across two chapters, it reveals how tariffs disrupt supply chains, strain diplomatic ties, and threaten economic stability, raising a critical question: Are these short-term gains worth the long-term costs to global prosperity and U.S. economic leadership?

CHAPTER 3

THE RETURN OF TARIFFS: A DANGEROUS GAME

Tariffs have long been wielded as economic weapons, often justified as shields for domestic industries. Yet history shows they frequently backfire, triggering trade wars, economic slowdowns, and unintended consequences. This chapter explores the cyclical nature of protectionism, from historical failures to President Trump's first-term trade war with China, analyzing its motivations, execution, and fallout. With Trump's return to office in 2025, trade policy appears to be shifting back toward protectionism, echoing his first-term tariffs on China, Europe, and other trading partners. While the scope of new measures is still emerging, the risk of greater economic fragmentation looms, reinforcing the themes explored in this chapter. As history shows, tariffs rarely deliver on their promises. Instead, they raise consumer costs, disrupt supply chains, and strain international alliances, leaving one question: Are tariffs a safeguard against unfair trade—or a high-stakes gamble that could destabilize the global economy?

1

HISTORICAL LESSONS:
WHEN PROTECTIONISM BACKFIRES

For centuries, nations have sought to shield their industries from foreign competition, believing that high tariffs and trade barriers would insulate domestic markets from external shocks. The logic is simple: restrict imports, stimulate local production, and create jobs at home. Yet history tells a different story. More often than not, protectionist policies have set off economic retaliation, strangled trade, and inadvertently harmed the very industries they were meant to protect. From the Great Depression to modern trade wars, the lesson is clear—tariffs may be politically expedient, but they rarely deliver the economic results their proponents expect.

The Smoot-Hawley Tariff Act: A Self-Inflicted Wound

Perhaps the most infamous case of protectionism gone wrong is the Smoot-Hawley Tariff Act of 1930. Passed in the throes of the Great Depression, it was meant to be a lifeline for struggling American farmers and manufacturers by raising duties on over 20,000 imported goods. The bill's sponsors, Senator Reed Smoot and Representative Willis Hawley, insisted that higher tariffs would force Americans to buy domestic goods, sparking an economic revival. But they underestimated one critical factor—the rest of the world would not stand idly by.

Retaliation was swift. In response, Canada, Britain, Germany, and France imposed their own tariffs on U.S. exports, slashing demand for American goods overseas. International trade collapsed by 65%, and instead of creating jobs, the act exacerbated factory closures. U.S. exports plummeted by over 60% between 1929 and 1933, deepening the economic crisis. Farmers, the very group Smoot-Hawley was designed to protect, found themselves cut off from global markets, with surplus crops rotting in fields as prices crashed.

Meanwhile, industrial production fell, unemployment soared to 25%, and the nation sank deeper into economic despair.

By the time Franklin D. Roosevelt took office in 1933, it was clear that Smoot-Hawley had done more harm than good. His administration worked quickly to reverse course, signing reciprocal trade agreements to lower tariffs and restore global commerce. But the damage had been done. The Great Depression dragged on, and economists would later cite Smoot-Hawley as a textbook example of how protectionism can turn a crisis into catastrophe.

The U.S.-Japan Trade War: When Tariffs Hurt Their Own

Fast forward to the 1980s, and the United States was once again facing a perceived threat—this time, from Japan's booming manufacturing sector. Japanese automakers, electronics firms, and steel producers were rapidly gaining global market share, often outcompeting American firms on price and quality. Fearing economic displacement, the U.S. launched a series of protectionist measures, imposing tariffs on Japanese steel, semiconductors, and cars. The goal was simple: protect U.S. manufacturers by making Japanese imports more expensive.

But instead of reviving American industry, these tariffs had unintended consequences. In the auto sector, rather than cutting back production, Japanese automakers outmaneuvered the tariffs by setting up manufacturing plants in the United States. Toyota, Honda, and Nissan built factories in states like Kentucky, Ohio, and Tennessee, hiring thousands of American workers while still dominating the market. Meanwhile, U.S. car prices rose, as domestic automakers, now shielded from competition, failed to innovate and simply passed costs on to consumers.

In the electronics sector, U.S. semiconductor firms—ironically the ones tariffs were meant to protect—faced higher costs for imported Japanese components, making them less competitive. Many companies simply rerouted their supply chains, sourcing parts from South Korea and Taiwan to bypass restrictions. Rather than stifling Japan's dominance, the tariffs accelerated the globalization of production, reinforcing the reality that supply chains adapt faster than trade policy.

The U.S.-Japan trade war is often remembered not for its success, but for its failure to protect American industries in the long run. By the late 1990s, Japan remained a global manufacturing powerhouse, while U.S. automakers continued to struggle with efficiency and cost competitiveness. The experience reinforced a crucial lesson—tariffs may provide short-term relief, but they rarely address the root causes of industrial decline.

Europe's Tariffs on Chinese Steel: A Modern Parallel

More recently, the European Union attempted its own version of protectionism, this time aimed at China's steel industry. Throughout the 2010s, China flooded global markets with cheap steel, undercutting European producers. In response, the EU imposed anti-dumping tariffs as high as 35%, hoping to curb imports and protect domestic jobs.

At first glance, the tariffs seemed to work—Chinese steel exports to Europe declined. But the ripple effects soon became apparent. European industries that relied on cheap steel—such as construction, automotive manufacturing, and heavy machinery—faced rising costs, making their final products more expensive. Rather than curbing China's dominance, the tariffs forced European manufacturers to look for alternative suppliers, increasing their dependence on non-EU markets.

Meanwhile, China simply redirected its steel exports to Southeast Asia and Africa, strengthening its economic influence in those regions. The policy had, in effect, pushed China to expand its global trade footprint rather than diminish it. As with Smoot-Hawley and the U.S.-Japan trade war, the lesson remained the same—tariffs rarely work in a world where supply chains and markets can shift rapidly.

Why Protectionism Fails: The Global Economic Reality

Across history, one thing is clear—tariffs rarely deliver on their promises. Time and again, protectionist policies have been sold as a means to revive domestic industries, yet they often do more harm than good. Rather than safeguarding jobs and strengthening economies, they tend to inflict collateral damage, raising costs for consumers, straining international relations, and triggering retaliatory measures that shrink global trade.

Protectionism has an inherent flaw: *it invites countermeasures*. No country operates in isolation, and when one nation imposes tariffs, others respond in kind. The Smoot-Hawley Tariff Act didn't just restrict imports into the United States—it provoked a chain reaction that decimated global commerce. Likewise, U.S. tariffs on Japan in the 1980s didn't restore American industrial supremacy; they merely encouraged Japanese automakers to outmaneuver the restrictions by setting up production inside the U.S. More recently, when the European Union imposed tariffs on Chinese steel, it didn't weaken China's grip on the market. Instead, China simply redirected its exports elsewhere, tightening its economic foothold in other regions.

The reality is that industries adapt far more quickly than trade policy. Policymakers assume that tariffs will force companies to rely on domestic suppliers, but businesses are rarely so easily cornered. When one market closes, another opens. When Japanese car manufacturers faced U.S. restrictions, they didn't retreat—they expanded by building factories in America. When the EU raised tariffs on Chinese steel, European manufacturers turned to alternative suppliers, sometimes at higher costs, while China shifted its focus to Asia and Africa. Protectionism does not stop globalization; it simply forces it to evolve in unexpected ways.

And while tariffs may shield certain industries, they almost always raise costs elsewhere. Steel tariffs, for example, may help domestic steel mills, but they simultaneously increase prices for industries that depend on steel—automakers, construction firms, and manufacturers. These businesses, in turn, pass the added expenses onto consumers, driving up prices for everything from cars to home appliances. The same holds true for agricultural tariffs. While they may be intended to protect farmers, they can cut off export markets, leaving surplus goods to pile up, forcing governments to step in with subsidies—an ironic twist where taxpayers end up footing the bill for a crisis tariffs were supposed to prevent.

At its core, protectionism is built on the illusion of economic self-sufficiency. Tariff advocates argue that restricting imports will force domestic industries to grow stronger, but history suggests otherwise. A nation cannot tariff its way to innovation. Real industrial competitiveness does not come from shielding companies from competition; it comes from investment in technology, efficiency, and adaptability. Without addressing these deeper structural issues, protectionism serves as little more than a temporary bandage over long-term economic weaknesses.

Yet despite these repeated failures, protectionism is once again gaining traction. Across the world, leaders are dusting off old arguments, promising that tariffs will restore national greatness and correct trade imbalances. The United States, in particular, has taken a hard turn toward economic nationalism, reviving trade wars under the banner of fairness and self-reliance.

But have policymakers learned from past mistakes, or are they simply repeating history? In the next section, we turn to the Trump administration's trade war with China—one of the most aggressive tariff battles in modern history—and examine whether it reinforced American economic strength or simply set the stage for another costly lesson in the dangers of protectionism.

2

TRUMP'S TRADE WAR:
THE EROSION OF U.S. FINANCIAL POWER

For decades, the United States maintained a delicate balance in global trade, advocating for open markets while wrestling with the complexities of economic competition. By the time Donald Trump entered office in 2017, however, the political mood had shifted. The U.S. trade deficit had become a rallying cry for economic nationalists, and nowhere was the imbalance more pronounced than in America's relationship with China. Trump's campaign had drawn heavily on the promise of restoring American manufacturing, bringing back jobs, and punishing trade partners for what he called "unfair" practices. Once in power, he pursued that vision with the most aggressive tariff regime in modern U.S. history.

The numbers alone tell the scale of this experiment. Between 2018 and 2019, the U.S. imposed new tariffs on over $550 billion worth of imports, primarily targeting China, but also Canada, Mexico, and the European Union (EU). What began as an effort to correct trade imbalances quickly escalated into a global trade war, as affected nations retaliated in kind. The consequences rippled across industries, disrupting supply chains, driving up costs, and forcing businesses and consumers alike to bear the burden of Washington's newfound protectionism.

The U.S.-China Trade War: From Policy to Fallout

At the center of Trump's trade war was China, the world's second-largest economy and America's most formidable trading partner. U.S. officials accused Beijing of widespread economic misconduct — currency manipulation, forced technology transfers, and the theft of intellectual property — and tariffs, they argued, were the necessary corrective force to rebalance the playing field.

The first tariffs landed in July 2018, when the U.S. imposed a 25% duty on $34 billion worth of Chinese goods, targeting industrial machinery, auto parts, and electronics. China responded almost immediately, slapping retaliatory tariffs on $34 billion of American exports, including soybeans, pork, and automobiles. Yet this was only the beginning. Over the next eighteen months, the U.S. expanded its tariff list three more times, adding a 10% tariff on another $200 billion in imports by September 2018, later increasing it to 25% in 2019. By December 2019, Trump had raised total tariffs to $550 billion, covering nearly two-thirds of all imports from China.

If the goal was to force Beijing into submission, the results were mixed at best. China, unwilling to be strong-armed, retaliated with increasing severity. It imposed tariffs on $185 billion worth of American goods, with a strategy carefully designed to inflict economic pain on Trump's political base—farmers and manufacturers in the Midwest. The hardest hit were soybean farmers, who watched as China, previously their largest buyer, cut purchases by 75% in 2018, turning instead to Brazil for supply. The damage was so severe that the U.S. government had to step in with $28 billion in bailout funds, effectively forcing American taxpayers to subsidize a trade war they had never signed up for.

The Cost to American Consumers and Businesses

One of the great illusions of tariff policy is the belief that foreign exporters bear the cost. In reality, tariffs function as a tax on the importing country, with the cost passed down the supply chain until it ultimately reaches consumers and businesses. This became painfully evident as the trade war escalated.

By 2019, American manufacturers dependent on Chinese components were struggling to absorb rising costs. Companies that relied on imported steel and aluminum—such as automakers, appliance manufacturers, and construction firms—found themselves paying significantly more for raw materials. Ford and General Motors each reported a $1 billion increase in production costs, forcing them to either raise vehicle prices or absorb the losses. Harley-Davidson, the iconic American motorcycle manufacturer, decided to shift some of its production to Thailand, avoiding the retaliatory tariffs imposed by the EU.

For retailers, the effects were just as severe. The National Retail Federation warned that tariffs were increasing prices on everyday goods, from electronics to clothing. Walmart, America's largest retailer, confirmed that the cost of some consumer products had risen significantly due to the tariffs, disproportionately affecting lower-income households. A study by the Federal Reserve and the National Bureau of Economic Research (NBER) estimated that the 2018-2019 tariffs cost the average U.S. household $1,277 per year, erasing the gains from Trump's tax cuts for many families.

Even Apple, a company that had carefully balanced its supply chain across multiple countries, found itself in a difficult position. The tariffs affected components used in iPhones, forcing Apple to increase some prices or absorb the cost. In a rare public move, CEO Tim Cook personally lobbied the Trump administration for tariff exemptions, underscoring the economic strain that protectionism had placed on U.S. businesses.

Retaliation from U.S. Trade Partners

Trump's tariffs were not confined to China. Other trade partners — many of them long-time U.S. allies—soon found themselves in the crosshairs.

In June 2018, the U.S. imposed 25% tariffs on Canadian and Mexican steel and 10% on aluminum, citing "national security" concerns. The move stunned U.S. neighbors, especially since Canada was America's largest steel supplier. Canadian officials reacted swiftly, imposing $12.6 billion in retaliatory tariffs on U.S. goods, strategically targeting products such as whiskey, dairy, and steel. Mexico, too, responded with countermeasures, hitting U.S. pork, cheese, and bourbon—directly impacting American farmers and food producers. The trade standoff was only resolved in May 2019, but not before it had damaged long-standing economic relationships.

Europe was next. The Trump administration imposed tariffs on European cars and aircraft, escalating a long-standing dispute over subsidies to Airbus. The European Union hit back with tariffs on $7.5 billion worth of American exports, carefully selecting products with symbolic and economic importance—Harley-Davidson motorcycles, bourbon whiskey, and Florida orange juice.

For the first time in decades, a fundamental shift was occurring in global trade dynamics. Nations that had previously depended on the U.S. for economic leadership were now looking elsewhere. In response to the tariffs, European and Asian economies deepened trade ties with each other, accelerating efforts to reduce their dependence on the U.S. market.

The Trade War's Economic Legacy: Did It Work?

The fundamental question remains: Did the trade war accomplish what it set out to do?

If the objective was to reduce the U.S. trade deficit, it failed. Despite the tariffs, the U.S. trade deficit with China remained over $300 billion in 2019, as companies and suppliers found ways to work around the restrictions. Many Chinese goods were simply rerouted through third countries like Vietnam and Taiwan, allowing them to bypass duties while still reaching U.S. consumers. The trade imbalance that tariffs were supposed to correct remained largely unchanged, demonstrating how deeply entrenched global supply chains had become.

If the goal was to revive U.S. manufacturing, the results were mixed. Some companies, such as Caterpillar and Whirlpool, re-shored production to avoid tariffs, but others adapted in ways that circumvented the intended impact. Instead of bringing jobs back to American workers, businesses pursued alternative strategies to maintain profitability. Apple shifted part of its supply chain to India, while Nike and Adidas expanded production in Vietnam. Mexico, too, emerged as a key beneficiary, attracting manufacturers seeking proximity to the U.S. without the added cost of tariffs.

Rather than forcing a domestic manufacturing revival, the tariffs had the unintended effect of reshuffling global trade relationships. The real winners weren't necessarily American workers, but rather economies that could offer lower labor costs and fewer trade restrictions. Vietnam's exports to the U.S. surged by over 40% between 2018 and 2019, as companies sought a tariff-free alternative to China. India, once on the periphery of global manufacturing, saw a wave of new investment from firms eager to diversify away from U.S.-China tensions. Even European suppliers capitalized on trade disruptions, positioning themselves as alternative sourcing hubs.

For many American companies, the logic was simple—if production couldn't be moved back to the U.S. without significantly raising costs, it was more practical to relocate to other competitive markets. The result was not a victory for domestic manufacturing, but rather a strategic reallocation of global supply chains. Tariffs had not strengthened American industry as intended; they had merely reshaped trade flows in favor of countries that could adapt more efficiently.

If the aim was to punish China for unfair trade practices, the strategy had only limited success. While tariffs inflicted short-term economic pain, China found new trading partners and accelerated efforts to reduce reliance on the U.S. — a move that could permanently alter global trade patterns. Instead of capitulating under pressure, China deepened its trade relationships with Europe, Southeast Asia, and Africa, reinforcing its long-term strategy of diversification.

Perhaps the most ironic outcome of the trade war was its impact on American farmers, the very group tariffs were supposed to protect. Retaliatory tariffs from China cut off key agricultural exports, particularly soybeans, forcing farmers to rely on billions of dollars in government subsidies to stay afloat. Instead of revitalizing rural America, tariffs shifted the economic burden from private industry to taxpayers, raising the question of whether the trade war's costs outweighed its supposed benefits.

What began as an attempt to restore American economic power ended up accelerating shifts in global trade that may leave the U.S. more isolated in the long run. And as nations increasingly seek alternatives to both American goods and the U.S. financial system, an even more profound consequence looms on the horizon — the rise of de-dollarization. Could the very tariffs intended to strengthen the U.S. economy ultimately weaken the dollar's dominance in global trade? That is the question we turn to next.

A Self-Inflicted Wound: The Cost of Misguided Policy

Trump's tariffs, though politically popular, became a case study in the unintended consequences of protectionism. Rather than forcing adversaries into submission, they invited retaliation, drove up prices, and disrupted industries that had long relied on stable trade relationships. The trade war did not bring manufacturing back to the United States in any meaningful way, nor did it significantly reduce the trade deficit. Instead, it pushed businesses to seek alternative markets, rewarded other low-cost manufacturing hubs, and strained relations with key allies and trading partners.

More critically, the tariffs accelerated a trend that Washington had long feared—China's push toward economic self-sufficiency and the global shift away from U.S. economic leadership. Rather than making China more dependent on the American market, tariffs reinforced Beijing's resolve to diversify its supply chains, deepen trade ties with emerging economies, and develop technological independence.

But the consequences of protectionism extend beyond trade alone. Tariffs do more than disrupt commerce—they distort global currency flows, fuel inflation, and trigger a feedback loop that can destabilize entire economies. The U.S. may have sought to strengthen its position through aggressive trade policies, but in doing so, it may have inadvertently accelerated the emergence of a multi-polar economic order—one in which the dollar's dominance, once unquestioned, is increasingly being challenged.

Trump's Second-Term Agenda: A Renewed Protectionist Push?

With Trump's return to office in 2025, his administration's stance on trade and tariffs is once again at the center of global economic debates. While it is still early in his second term, initial indications suggest that protectionist policies may remain a defining feature of U.S. economic strategy. The question now is whether his second presidency will escalate the trade tensions of his first term—or whether evolving geopolitical and financial conditions will force a recalibration of U.S. policy.

Early signs suggest that Trump's administration is doubling down on trade barriers, particularly against China, with renewed emphasis on reshoring manufacturing and reducing supply chain dependence on foreign competitors. However, the economic landscape has shifted significantly since 2017. Many of the trade partners targeted by U.S. tariffs during his first term have since deepened regional trade alliances, developed alternative financial systems, and taken steps to reduce reliance on the dollar. This means that a new round of aggressive tariffs may not have the same leverage as before.

Another key question is whether Trump's second-term trade policies will collide with financial realities. The U.S. fiscal deficit has ballooned past $34 trillion, and rising interest rates have strained both corporate and government finances. If protectionist measures trigger further inflationary pressures or supply chain disruptions, the long-term costs of tariffs may be harder to justify. Moreover, major economies—including China, the EU, and India—have already begun restructuring trade flows in response to past U.S. tariffs, suggesting that America may face a more fragmented and less cooperative global trading environment.

The consequences of protectionism extend beyond trade alone. Tariffs distort currency flows, amplify inflationary pressures, and accelerate the global search for alternatives to the dollar-based system. If Trump's second term follows a similar trajectory to his first, the risk is that rather than reinforcing U.S. economic leadership, trade policy could further weaken Washington's influence in the global financial order.

3

THE POLITICAL APPEAL OF PROTECTIONISM

Tariffs have always been more than just an economic tool—they are a political weapon, wielded to stir national pride, mobilize voters, and project strength. Unlike monetary policy or complex fiscal decisions, tariffs are easy to explain, easy to defend, and easy to sell to the public. They create a clear villain, usually a foreign competitor accused of undercutting domestic industries, and promise a simple solution—shutting out the competition and bringing jobs back home.

From Herbert Hoover to Ronald Reagan to Donald Trump, American leaders have repeatedly turned to tariffs as a way to win elections and consolidate political power. Yet, while tariffs may produce short-term political victories, their long-term economic consequences often tell a different story. History has shown that tariffs frequently fail to deliver the prosperity they promise, instead triggering trade retaliation, higher consumer prices, and economic stagnation.

The Power of the "Us vs. Them" Narrative

Trade is complicated. Supply chains are deeply interconnected, spanning multiple continents and involving countless unseen transactions. Most voters don't have the time—or the interest—to untangle the complexities of global trade flows. But a tariff? A tariff is simple. It can be framed as a patriotic measure, a necessary defense against foreign economic aggression. The message is clear: "We are protecting our industries. We are standing up for our workers. We are stopping unfair trade practices."

This is why tariffs remain wildly popular, even when they fail to achieve their intended economic goals. Politicians understand this, and they have long used protectionist rhetoric to tap into economic anxieties. During times of recession or industrial decline, tariffs are presented as a lifeline for struggling workers, a way to reverse job losses and revive domestic manufacturing. The reality, however, is often far less straightforward.

Take the Smoot-Hawley Tariff Act of 1930, a piece of legislation that was sold as a way to protect American farmers and manufacturers from foreign competition during the Great Depression. Supporters claimed that by raising tariffs on over 20,000 imported goods, the United States could insulate itself from global economic turmoil. But instead of ushering in a new era of prosperity, Smoot-Hawley triggered a global trade war, as other countries retaliated with their own tariffs. Within just a few years, global trade collapsed by nearly 65%, worsening the very economic downturn the tariffs were supposed to alleviate.

Similar logic was used during the U.S.-Japan trade tensions of the 1980s, when Washington imposed quotas and tariffs on Japanese cars and electronics, fearing that Japan's rapid industrial rise would hollow out American manufacturing. While these measures temporarily slowed Japanese exports, they also drove up prices for American consumers and pushed production elsewhere, particularly to South Korea and Taiwan. In the end, the tariffs did little to restore U.S. industrial dominance but did succeed in reshaping global supply chains in unexpected ways.

This cycle repeats because the political benefits of protectionism are immediate, while the economic costs take time to materialize. A factory closure due to foreign competition is a visible and painful event, often making headlines and fueling public resentment. But the inflationary effects of tariffs, the hidden costs passed on to consumers, and the broader economic distortions they create? Those unfold more gradually, making them easier to ignore.

How Tariffs Became a Campaign Strategy

Few modern politicians have understood the political power of tariffs as well as Donald Trump. His 2016 campaign was built on the idea that unfair trade deals had devastated American manufacturing, and tariffs were his weapon of choice to reverse that trend. He accused China of "ripping off the United States", promised to punish Mexico for job losses, and declared that globalization had left American workers behind.

Once in office, he followed through on his rhetoric, launching a full-scale trade war with China, imposing 25% tariffs on $550 billion worth of Chinese imports, and targeting steel and aluminum from Canada, Mexico, and the European Union. The economic results were mixed. While some domestic industries benefited, others faced higher input costs, retaliatory tariffs, and lost export markets. Farmers, particularly soybean producers, were hit hard when China redirected its agricultural purchases to Brazil, forcing the U.S. government to step in with $28 billion in subsidies to offset the damage.

Yet, despite the disruptions and contradictions, Trump's tariffs remained popular with his base. They were framed as a bold, decisive move, proof that he was taking action while previous leaders had done nothing. This underscores a key reality: *tariffs are not just an economic tool—they are a political symbol*. They provide visible proof that a leader is "fighting" for domestic workers, regardless of whether the policy actually improves their economic well-being.

This political appeal extends far beyond the United States. Around the world, governments have turned to tariffs as a means of asserting economic sovereignty. In Europe, the European Union has used anti-dumping tariffs on Chinese steel to shield its domestic producers. In India, high tariffs on electronics and automobiles have been justified as a way to promote local industry. These measures are often popular with domestic voters, even when they raise consumer prices and limit competition.

The Illusion of Economic Protection

One of the strongest arguments made in favor of tariffs is the "infant industry" argument—the idea that new industries need temporary protection before they can compete on the global stage. South Korea's industrial rise in the 1960s and 1970s is often cited as an example of how government intervention, including trade restrictions, helped nurture domestic champions like Samsung and Hyundai.

But there's an important distinction. In South Korea's case, protectionist policies were temporary and targeted, designed to boost exports rather than limit imports. Once South Korean firms became competitive, trade barriers were gradually removed, allowing them to expand globally. The problem with modern tariff policies is that they often fail to follow this model. Instead of serving as short-term support for emerging industries, they become permanent fixtures, shielding inefficient businesses and distorting markets.

In many cases, tariffs end up hurting the very industries they are supposed to protect. When the U.S. imposed steel tariffs in 2018, domestic steelmakers initially benefited, but American manufacturers that relied on steel faced higher costs, making them less competitive internationally. Similarly, when India imposed high tariffs on imported smartphones, it encouraged local assembly but failed to develop a globally competitive electronics sector.

The fundamental problem with tariffs is that they create more losers than winners. They might protect one industry, but they raise costs for others. They shield domestic producers, but they invite retaliation from trade partners. They might create short-term jobs, but they reduce long-term competitiveness.

The Future of Tariff Politics

Despite these risks, protectionism is not going away. In the United States, both Republicans and Democrats have embraced selective tariffs, signaling that economic nationalism is now a bipartisan issue. China, once the target of U.S. tariffs, is building its own protectionist measures, strengthening domestic supply chains and encouraging yuan-based trade. Around the world, regional trade blocs are emerging, with nations prioritizing economic security over globalization.

The question now is: Can the world balance economic security with open trade? Or will rising protectionism fracture the global economy into competing, tariff-protected blocs? As we will explore in the next section, tariffs do more than restrict trade—they disrupt global financial flows, weaken international currencies, and accelerate the economic fragmentation already underway.

4

UNINTENDED CONSEQUENCES OF TARIFFS

Tariffs are often sold to the public as a patriotic tool to defend domestic industries and protect American jobs. In reality, however, they function as a hidden tax on consumers and businesses, driving up costs, disrupting supply chains, and provoking retaliatory measures that weaken the very industries they are meant to support. While they may provide the illusion of economic strength, the long-term consequences can be far more damaging than the problems they claim to solve.

Tariffs as a Hidden Tax on Consumers

Despite the political rhetoric that portrays tariffs as a way to force foreign nations to "pay their fair share," it is ultimately domestic consumers who bear the financial burden. When the U.S. imposes tariffs on imported goods, the cost is rarely absorbed by foreign exporters. Instead, it is passed down through the supply chain, pushing prices higher for American businesses and consumers alike.

The impact of tariffs became particularly evident during the Trump administration's trade war with China. A study by the Federal Reserve Bank of New York found that the full cost of these tariffs was transferred to American consumers and businesses, raising prices on affected goods by an average of 25%. This was felt most acutely in everyday consumer products, from smartphones and laptops to washing machines and automobiles. As manufacturers struggled to adjust, companies such as Ford and General Motors saw their material costs rise by nearly $1 billion, forcing them to pass these expenses onto consumers through higher car prices.

The price hikes were not limited to direct importers of Chinese goods. Many American businesses that did not source products from China still felt the pinch because they relied on components or raw materials that originated there. A study by the National Bureau of Economic Research (NBER) estimated that by 2020, U.S. companies had paid an additional $46 billion in tariff-related costs, much of which was passed on to consumers in the form of higher retail prices.

For ordinary Americans, the effects of tariffs were most noticeable at the checkout counter. The higher cost of essential goods effectively eroded any wage gains workers had received in the same period, chipping away at their purchasing power. While protectionist policies were intended to shield American consumers and workers from foreign competition, they instead contributed to inflationary pressures, leading to a decline in overall living standards.

Supply Chain Disruptions and the Shift to New Markets

Tariffs do not merely affect pricing—they also trigger long-lasting disruptions in global supply chains, often in ways that policymakers fail to anticipate.

During the U.S.-China trade war, Washington imposed tariffs on $550 billion worth of Chinese goods, expecting that higher import costs would incentivize American businesses to bring manufacturing back home. Instead, companies took a different approach: they shifted production to alternative low-cost economies, ensuring that their supply chains remained intact while bypassing U.S. tariffs.

Vietnam quickly emerged as a major beneficiary of this shift. Between 2018 and 2020, Vietnamese exports to the U.S. surged by 35%, as manufacturers sought new production hubs outside China. Mexico, too, saw a sharp rise in exports, becoming the largest U.S. trading partner in 2019, overtaking China for the first time in decades. Apple, Samsung, and other multinational firms redirected key components of their production to Vietnam, India, and Taiwan, ensuring that they could continue operating at competitive costs without being subject to U.S. tariffs.

This shift was not just a temporary response—it represented a fundamental restructuring of global supply chains. Once companies relocate production, they invest billions in new factories, supplier contracts, and logistical infrastructure. As a result, even when tariffs are lifted, businesses are unlikely to revert to their original suppliers. Instead of bringing manufacturing back to the U.S., tariffs had the unintended effect of reinforcing globalization, merely redistributing production to new markets rather than eliminating dependence on foreign suppliers.

The ripple effects of these shifts became even more pronounced during the COVID-19 pandemic, when supply chain fragility became evident. The semiconductor shortage that crippled U.S. car production in 2021 was exacerbated by previous disruptions caused by tariffs, as key suppliers had already been forced to relocate and adjust to new trade barriers. By attempting to force production back to the U.S. through tariffs, policymakers had inadvertently destabilized supply chains, leading to higher costs and greater uncertainty for businesses struggling to meet consumer demand.

The Global Ripple: Retaliation and Market Distortions

One of the most dangerous aspects of tariffs is that they rarely go unanswered. History has shown that when one country imposes tariffs, its trading partners respond in kind, setting off a chain reaction that compounds economic damage.

The trade war launched by the Trump administration provoked swift retaliation from key trading partners. China, Canada, the EU, and Mexico all imposed countermeasures targeting politically sensitive American industries. Beijing placed tariffs on U.S. soybeans, pork, and seafood, effectively shutting American farmers out of a crucial export market. Canada and the EU retaliated with tariffs on U.S. steel, bourbon, and motorcycles, striking at major manufacturing hubs. Mexico, another vital trading partner, responded by slapping tariffs on American dairy and meat exports, undercutting U.S. agricultural sales in Latin America.

The economic consequences were immediate and severe. U.S. soybean exports to China, which had once totaled 32.9 million metric tons in 2017, collapsed by 75% in 2018, forcing American farmers to seek alternative markets. In an attempt to offset their losses, the U.S. government had to provide $28 billion in bailout payments to struggling farmers—an ironic turn of events, considering that tariffs were meant to strengthen domestic industries.

Beyond immediate financial losses, the damage to trade relationships proved long-lasting. China, once heavily reliant on U.S. agricultural products, began to diversify its suppliers, increasing imports from Brazil and Argentina. By the time trade tensions eased, China had already built stronger partnerships with South American producers, permanently reducing its dependence on American exports.

The same pattern repeated in manufacturing. Major U.S. companies, including Harley-Davidson, shifted production overseas to avoid the rising costs of retaliatory tariffs. Instead of protecting American jobs, tariffs had inadvertently incentivized businesses to move more of their operations abroad.

The Paradox of Protectionism: Who Really Wins?

Tariffs are often presented as a straightforward solution to complex economic problems. With the stroke of a pen, policymakers promise to revive domestic industries, bring back lost jobs, and restore economic sovereignty. The logic seems airtight—by making foreign goods more expensive, tariffs should encourage Americans to buy domestic, spurring production and strengthening the national economy. But history suggests otherwise. Rather than shielding workers and industries from foreign competition, tariffs often inflict the greatest harm on those they are designed to protect.

For the average consumer, the impact is immediate and tangible. Prices rise as the cost of imported goods climbs, forcing households to stretch their budgets further for everyday essentials. American manufacturers, many of whom rely on foreign raw materials, are caught in the crossfire. Higher input costs squeeze profit margins, forcing businesses to either pass the expense onto consumers or scale back operations. Supply chains, which have been fine-tuned for decades to optimize efficiency, are suddenly thrown into disarray. Companies scramble to adapt, but instead of bringing production back to U.S. soil, many find it more practical to shift their operations elsewhere—Vietnam, Mexico, or Southeast Asia—where they can sidestep tariffs altogether.

Meanwhile, exporters suffer an entirely different set of consequences. For every tariff the United States imposes, trading partners retaliate, erecting their own barriers against American goods. Markets that once eagerly absorbed U.S. agricultural products, industrial machinery, and electronics begin turning elsewhere. A Chinese manufacturer that once sourced American-made components now looks to Europe. A Canadian buyer that once imported U.S. steel considers a supplier in Brazil. What began as a measure to strengthen domestic industry ends up eroding its global competitiveness.

Rather than revitalizing American manufacturing, tariffs often produce a cycle of short-term disruption, long-term price inflation, and strained international relations. Countries that once relied on American goods diversify their suppliers, reducing their dependence on the U.S. market. Firms that once operated comfortably in the United States rethink their strategy, seeking out more cost-effective production bases abroad. And all the while, the supposed beneficiaries—the workers and industries tariffs were meant to protect—find themselves dealing with job insecurity, rising costs, and uncertain futures.

Tariffs promise economic sovereignty, but they rarely deliver it. Instead, they accelerate inflation, fragment global supply chains, and provoke retaliatory measures that leave domestic industries more vulnerable, not less. They may shift economic activity, but they do not create new growth—only new inefficiencies.

And yet, the consequences of protectionism extend far beyond rising prices and disrupted trade flows. There is a deeper, more profound shift underway, one that could have long-term ramifications for the global financial system. As the U.S. imposes tariffs and alienates key trading partners, many countries are looking for ways to reduce their reliance on the American economy altogether. In the next chapter, we explore an unintended but perhaps inevitable consequence of these trade wars—the de-dollarization trend. Could tariffs, intended to reinforce American dominance, actually accelerate the decline of the dollar's supremacy in global trade?

CHAPTER 4

HOW TARIFFS DISRUPT THE GLOBAL ECONOMY

Tariffs may seem like straightforward policy tools, but their ripple effects are anything but simple. Chapter 4 analyses how protectionist measures disrupt the global economy, starting with the restriction of dollar flows that lubricate international trade and investment. It explores how tariffs often trigger currency devaluation and inflation, creating a feedback loop that affects not just the countries directly involved, but the broader global market. This chapter also highlights the looming threat of retaliation, as trade wars escalate and nations impose countermeasures, leading to fractured supply chains, price volatility, and strained diplomatic relations. As economic borders tighten, the costs are borne not just by corporations and governments, but by everyday consumers and workers, both at home and abroad. This chapter offers a sobering analysis of how tariffs can destabilize the very systems they aim to protect, posing critical risks to global economic stability.

1

CHOKING THE DOLLAR FLOW
TO GLOBAL MARKETS

For decades, the United States has acted as the engine of the global economy, fueling trade, investment, and financial stability with its seemingly limitless supply of dollars. Every time an American consumer buys a German car, a Chinese smartphone, or a Brazilian coffee, dollars leave the U.S. and flow into the pockets of foreign businesses and governments. These dollars do more than just pay for goods—they circulate through the world's financial system, serving as reserves in central banks, collateral for global debt, and the lifeblood of international trade.

But tariffs disrupt this system at its core. The moment the U.S. government slaps a 10%, 20%, or even 50% tariff on imports, the flow of dollars slows dramatically. American businesses begin sourcing goods domestically, or they simply import less. Consumers, facing higher prices, cut back on spending. And as the demand for foreign goods declines, so too does the outward movement of dollars. The result is an economic shock wave that extends far beyond American borders, particularly in economies that depend on exports to the U.S.

The Dollar's Role: The Lifeblood of Global Trade

For many nations, U.S. dollar inflows are not just a convenience—they are a necessity. The dollar is the foundation of global commerce, woven into nearly every major economic transaction. Over 88% of all foreign exchange transactions involve the dollar. More than half of the world's foreign exchange reserves are held in dollars. Oil, wheat, industrial metals—virtually every major commodity is priced in dollars, making access to the currency a matter of survival for economies reliant on imports. When Washington decides to restrict the outflow of dollars through tariffs, it doesn't just alter trade balances. It starves global markets of the very currency they rely on to function.

The impact is particularly devastating for countries that lack strong domestic financial markets or deep currency reserves. Without a steady stream of dollars from exports, these nations must find a way to acquire the currency elsewhere. Some attempt to boost their own exports to alternative markets, but if tariffs extend beyond just the U.S. — if other nations retaliate with trade restrictions of their own — options begin to dwindle.

In desperation, central banks are often forced to intervene, spending their foreign reserves to prop up their national currencies. The cycle quickly spirals: as reserves deplete, confidence in the local currency weakens. Investors pull their money, fearful of instability. The currency falls further. Inflation takes hold, driving up the price of imports, squeezing consumers, and destabilizing entire economies.

The Mexican Peso Crisis (1994-95): A Cautionary Tale

This is not an abstract theory. The world has seen this cycle before. In December 1994, Mexico's financial system imploded almost overnight. For years, the country had thrived on the strength of its exports to the United States, accumulating billions of dollars in trade revenue and foreign investment. But when confidence in the Mexican economy wavered and capital began flowing out instead of in, the peso collapsed. In a matter of weeks, its value was cut in half. Inflation soared. The Mexican government was left scrambling for an emergency bailout, ultimately requiring a $50 billion rescue package from the United States and the IMF just to stabilize its economy.

What triggered the crisis was simple: a sudden shortage of U.S. dollars. Mexico needed dollars to service its foreign debt, to pay for imported goods, and to maintain confidence in its currency. But as dollar flows contracted, investors lost faith, dumping the peso in favor of safer assets. It was a brutal lesson in economic fragility — one that is still playing out across the world today.

Tariff Shockwaves: China and Emerging Markets

A similar dynamic emerged during the U.S.-China trade war in 2018 and 2019. As tariffs took effect, Chinese exports to the U.S. plummeted. Factories that had long relied on American demand faced declining revenues. China's foreign exchange reserves, largely held in U.S. dollars, began to shrink as capital outflows surged. The yuan weakened under pressure, and the Chinese government was forced to step in, spending vast sums to stabilize its currency.

Yet the pain did not stop at China's borders. Across Asia and Latin America, nations that relied on Chinese trade found themselves caught in the storm. With fewer dollars circulating in global markets, currencies in India, Brazil, and Indonesia weakened. Inflation surged in nations that depended on dollar-priced imports, particularly in commodities like oil and food. What had begun as a tariff dispute between two superpowers had rapidly transformed into a global financial disruption.

A Chain Reaction of Dollar Shortages and Economic Pain

The consequences of restricting the flow of U.S. dollars extend far beyond trade figures and corporate earnings reports. When America cuts off a major source of dollar supply, it creates ripple effects that extend into currency markets, debt markets, and even the price of basic consumer goods. A shortage of dollars forces governments to take drastic measures—selling off reserves, devaluing their currencies, and, in some cases, imposing their own restrictions on capital flows to stem the damage. But these measures only reinforce the cycle. A weakening currency makes it more expensive to buy imported goods, fueling inflation. Inflation erodes consumer purchasing power, leading to economic slowdowns. In the worst cases, these conditions spark investor panic, leading to capital flight and full-blown financial crises.

The warning signs are already flashing. In 2022, the euro fell below parity with the dollar for the first time in two decades, largely due to capital outflows seeking the safety of U.S. assets. The Japanese yen plunged to its weakest level in more than 30 years as investors, uncertain about global trade conditions, fled to the dollar. The Brazilian real and Australian dollar both came under pressure, reflecting broader instability in global currency markets.

Today, the risk of another widespread currency crisis is higher than ever. Tariff policies—if implemented aggressively—could accelerate dollar shortages, leading to financial instability across multiple continents. If the U.S. further restricts trade with tariffs, these trends will intensify, making it harder for emerging economies to sustain their financial stability. The cracks in the system are already visible, and history suggests that prolonged disruptions in dollar circulation often precede deeper financial crises.

Weaponizing Tariffs, Starving the World of Dollars

When politicians talk about tariffs, they frame them as domestic policy tools—a way to bring back jobs, protect industries, or reduce dependency on foreign goods. But the reality is far larger and more dangerous. By restricting trade, the U.S. is not just reshaping the flow of goods—it's cutting off the very currency that keeps the global economy running.

The next great financial crisis may not originate from a Wall Street banking collapse or a housing bubble. Instead, it could be triggered by something far less obvious yet just as devastating—a trade war that chokes the global economy by starving it of U.S. dollars. The world's financial system runs on liquidity, and that liquidity depends on the seamless circulation of dollars through trade, investment, and capital flows.

By weaponizing tariffs and restricting trade, the U.S. risks not only disrupting supply chains but also severing the financial arteries that sustain global markets. As dollar shortages deepen, emerging economies could face currency crises, multinational corporations could struggle to settle cross-border transactions, and central banks might be forced into drastic measures to stabilize their reserves. In an interconnected world, economic dominance cannot be maintained in isolation. The real danger is not just trade retaliation—it's the potential unraveling of the very system that has upheld U.S. financial supremacy for decades.

2

THE DEVALUATION-INFLATION SPIRAL

Tariffs are often framed as a tool to protect domestic industries, but their impact stretches far beyond national borders. When the United States imposes tariffs on foreign imports, it does more than just reduce trade flows—it disrupts the delicate balance of global finance, setting off a cascade of currency devaluations and inflationary pressures that can spiral into full-blown economic crises. This is the unseen ripple effect, a feedback loop that begins with trade barriers but ultimately destabilizes entire economies.

How Currency Devaluation Triggers Inflation

Tariffs are rarely considered outside the realm of trade policy, yet their impact reaches far beyond simple price adjustments. By restricting imports, they set off a series of financial disruptions that ripple through global markets, often with unintended consequences. At the heart of this disruption is the U.S. dollar, the currency that underpins global trade and finance. When the United States imposes tariffs, it reduces the outflow of dollars to trading partners, tightening the supply of the world's most widely used reserve currency. For many economies, this creates an immediate problem—one that forces them into a dangerous cycle of currency devaluation, inflation, and financial instability.

The mechanism is straightforward but devastating. When fewer dollars flow into an economy, its local currency begins to weaken against the dollar in foreign exchange markets. This depreciation is often swift and severe. Take, for example, the Turkish lira. In 2018, after the U.S. imposed tariffs on Turkish steel and aluminum, the lira plunged from 4.75 per dollar to 7.20 per dollar in just three months— a staggering 52% decline. Overnight, imported goods became dramatically more expensive for Turkish consumers, fueling an inflationary spiral that pushed prices up by 25% year-over-year. The cost of basic essentials, from fuel to food, surged, eroding household incomes and triggering a nationwide economic crisis.

A similar pattern unfolds whenever a country's access to dollars is restricted. As the local currency weakens, the cost of imports—especially critical commodities such as oil, wheat, and industrial materials—rises. Japan, for example, saw its yen depreciate from 115 per U.S. dollar in early 2022 to over 150 by October of the same year, a drop of nearly 30%. This devaluation sent shockwaves through the Japanese economy, as the country relies on imported energy priced in dollars. As a direct result, Japan's import costs rose by 42% over the same period, intensifying inflationary pressures that had been largely absent from the country for decades.

For emerging economies, the stakes are even higher. Many of these nations carry significant amounts of dollar-denominated debt, meaning that a weaker local currency makes repaying loans much more expensive. In Argentina, where the peso has been in near-constant decline, the exchange rate deteriorated from 60 pesos per dollar in 2019 to over 350 by late 2023, a depreciation of more than 80%. The immediate consequence was skyrocketing inflation, which surpassed 120% annually, forcing the central bank to impose capital controls and raise interest rates in a desperate bid to stabilize the currency.

Once this cycle begins, escaping it becomes nearly impossible. As inflation rises, investors and businesses lose confidence in the local economy, prompting further capital flight. This exodus of money further weakens the currency, necessitating yet another round of interventions—higher interest rates, currency market interventions, and, in many cases, negotiations with international lenders such as the International Monetary Fund. The story is eerily familiar in countries from Sri Lanka to Nigeria, where a dependence on dollar inflows has left them vulnerable to external shocks, particularly when U.S. trade policy tightens global dollar liquidity.

The tariff-driven dollar squeeze is a global doom loop—a cycle where currency devaluation leads to inflation, eroding economic stability and forcing governments into desperate measures to prevent collapse. The long-term effects are devastating. Nations trapped in this cycle face rising living costs, social unrest, and struggle to attract foreign investment as capital flees to safer markets. Once confidence in a currency is lost, the downward spiral becomes self-reinforcing.

This feedback loop explains why, when the U.S. raises tariffs, the effects extend beyond trade. What starts as a domestic policy quickly triggers global economic shocks, setting off chain reactions in currency and debt markets. These crises may seem disconnected from U.S. tariffs, but the link is undeniable. By disrupting dollar flows, tariffs weaken currencies, fuel inflation, and push vulnerable economies into distress—a pattern seen time and again, from the Turkish lira crisis to the Argentine peso collapse.

3

WHEN CURRENCIES COLLAPSE

Lessons From 1997–2022

Throughout modern history, currency collapses have rarely occurred in isolation. Instead, they are often the result of a complex interplay between domestic vulnerabilities and external shocks—many of which stem from policy decisions beyond national borders. From speculative attacks to trade restrictions and shifting investor sentiment, the forces that drive financial crises share striking similarities across different economies and eras. The following case studies, spanning 1997 to 2022, illustrate how abrupt shifts in capital flows, rising debt burdens, and external pressures—such as tariffs and monetary tightening—can trigger devastating currency spirals, reshaping entire economies in their wake.

The 1997 Asian Financial Crisis

The collapse of currencies in the 1997 Asian Financial Crisis serves as a stark reminder of what happens when nations experience a sudden shortfall of U.S. dollars. Though this crisis was not triggered by tariffs, the underlying mechanism—a rapid decline in dollar inflows leading to currency depreciation, inflation, and financial turmoil—mirrors what many economies face when protectionist trade policies restrict their access to dollars. The lessons from this crisis are particularly relevant today as tariffs once again disrupt global dollar flows, putting many nations in similar positions of vulnerability.

Capital Inflows and the Fragile Dollar Peg

In the years leading up to 1997, several fast-growing Asian economies—including Thailand, Indonesia, Malaysia, and South Korea—had pegged their currencies to the U.S. dollar. This system worked well when capital was flowing in, as it allowed these nations to borrow cheaply in dollars while keeping their exchange rates stable. Foreign investors poured money into these economies, drawn by high growth rates and promising returns. Governments and corporations took advantage of this confidence, accumulating billions in U.S. dollar-denominated debt under the assumption that strong exports and continued capital inflows would allow them to service their obligations easily.

However, trouble began when the U.S. Federal Reserve raised interest rates in 1994-1995, making dollar-denominated assets more attractive and pulling capital back to the United States. At the same time, global demand for Asian exports weakened, reducing the inflow of dollars into these economies. This double shock—higher borrowing costs and fewer dollars coming in from trade—placed severe strain on the region's currency pegs. Investors began questioning whether these nations had enough reserves to defend their fixed exchange rates, and once uncertainty set in, panic took hold.

The Domino Effect: From Thailand to the Region

The first domino to fall was Thailand. In early 1997, Thailand's baht was pegged at approximately 25 baht per U.S. dollar, but as capital outflows accelerated and the country's dollar reserves dwindled, the peg became unsustainable. In July 1997, Thailand abandoned its dollar peg, and the baht immediately plummeted past 50 per dollar—a 100% devaluation in just months. This triggered a contagion effect across the region.

Indonesia's rupiah, which had traded at 2,400 per dollar, collapsed to 16,000 per dollar by early 1998, an astonishing 85% depreciation. South Korea's won followed, falling from 800 per dollar to over 1,700 in a matter of months. Malaysia and the Philippines suffered similar fates, with their currencies declining by 50% or more. These devaluations unleashed a wave of economic devastation, as the cost of imports—particularly energy, food, and essential goods—skyrocketed overnight. Inflation surged into double digits, eroding household purchasing power and forcing businesses to cut back on production, lay off workers, or shut down entirely.

For companies and governments that had borrowed in U.S. dollars, the crisis was catastrophic. A loan that once required 100 million baht to repay now demanded 200 million baht, simply due to currency depreciation. Unable to meet their obligations, companies defaulted in droves, triggering banking collapses and requiring emergency bailouts from the International Monetary Fund (IMF). In South Korea alone, seven of the country's top 30 conglomerates went bankrupt, and the IMF had to step in with a $58 billion rescue package to stabilize the economy. Indonesia fared even worse, as inflation surged to over 80%, unemployment skyrocketed, and the government was ultimately overthrown amid mass protests.

The Asian Financial Crisis proved how fragile an economy becomes when it depends on steady dollar inflows to sustain growth, only to collapse when those flows are disrupted. This is precisely the risk that modern tariffs and protectionist policies pose today. When the U.S. reduces imports through tariffs, it doesn't just impact trade volumes—it reduces the amount of dollars circulating through global markets, putting pressure on nations with high dollar-denominated debt and vulnerable exchange rates. The domino effect seen in 1997 could easily be repeated in today's global economy, especially in emerging markets that are already battling inflation and currency weakness.

While the 1997 crisis was triggered by capital flight and speculative attacks, a similar dynamic unfolds when tariffs restrict global access to U.S. dollars. Countries that cannot secure enough dollars to meet their trade and debt obligations are at risk of the same self-reinforcing cycle of currency depreciation, inflation, capital flight, and financial collapse. The question is no longer whether these risks exist—it is whether history is on the verge of repeating itself.

Modern Parallels: U.S. Tariffs and the Currency Collapse of 2022

The lessons of the 1997 Asian Financial Crisis remain more relevant than ever, as global markets witnessed a similar unraveling in 2022. While the trigger this time was not an explicit financial panic, the fundamental mechanism remained the same: a sudden shortage of U.S. dollars, a sharp depreciation in foreign currencies, and inflationary shocks rippling through economies worldwide. Unlike in 1997, where investor panic led to capital flight, this crisis was driven by a combination of U.S. protectionist trade policies, Federal Reserve interest rate hikes, and global disruptions caused by supply chain shocks and sanctions.

At the center of the 2022 crisis was a dramatic strengthening of the U.S. dollar, which sent shockwaves through global markets. The dollar's surge was fueled by aggressive Federal Reserve interest rate hikes, as the U.S. central bank moved swiftly to combat inflation. Between March and December 2022, the Fed raised rates from 0.25% to 4.5%, marking one of the fastest tightening cycles in history. This had the immediate effect of making U.S. assets more attractive, drawing capital out of emerging markets and back into the dollar. In just a few months, the dollar index (DXY)—which measures the dollar's strength against a basket of major currencies—rose from 95 to over 114, a 20-year high.

For many countries, this surge in dollar strength was devastating. The Japanese yen collapsed from 115 per U.S. dollar in early 2022 to over 150 by October, a 30% depreciation. Japan, an energy-dependent nation that imports almost all of its oil, suddenly faced a 42% increase in energy costs, putting immense strain on consumers and businesses. The country's central bank was forced to intervene in currency markets for the first time in decades, spending $68 billion in a single month in an attempt to stabilize the yen.

Europe faced its own struggles as the euro fell below parity with the dollar for the first time in 20 years, reaching a low of 0.96 in September 2022. This depreciation was particularly damaging in the wake of the Russia-Ukraine war, which had already sent energy prices soaring. European countries found themselves paying significantly more for dollar-priced commodities like natural gas and crude oil, exacerbating an inflation crisis that saw annual price increases surpass 10% in multiple Eurozone economies.

Emerging Markets in Currency Freefall

Emerging markets bore the brunt of the storm. The Indian rupee hit an all-time low of 83 per dollar, the South African rand plunged to 18 per dollar, and Brazil's real weakened by 15% in just a few months. However, the most severe impacts were felt in countries with high levels of dollar-denominated debt, as their repayment burdens skyrocketed. In Sri Lanka, where external debt had already exceeded 100% of GDP, the government was left with no option but to default on its foreign obligations for the first time in history. The Sri Lankan rupee lost over 75% of its value, causing fuel shortages, political turmoil, and the collapse of the ruling government.

A similar fate unfolded in Argentina, where the peso tumbled from 200 per U.S. dollar to over 350 within a year, forcing the central bank to impose severe capital controls to prevent further financial hemorrhaging. Inflation soared past 120% annually, making Argentina one of the most unstable economies in the world. The situation was so dire that the country was forced to negotiate a $44 billion bailout with the International Monetary Fund, yet the crisis remained far from over.

Protectionism and the Global Dollar Shortage

This currency collapse in 2022 was not merely a function of monetary policy—it was exacerbated by the economic strain caused by protectionist U.S. trade policies. The tariff wars initiated in previous years had already put pressure on export-dependent economies, reducing their ability to earn U.S. dollars. Countries that had once relied on dollar inflows from trade found themselves in a double bind: fewer exports due to tariffs and higher costs due to currency depreciation.

The crisis of 2022 illustrated how the U.S. dollar, though seen as a pillar of global stability, can quickly become a weapon of financial destruction when its strength rises too rapidly. By tightening its grip on global markets—whether through higher interest rates or trade barriers—the U.S. creates an environment where weaker economies are forced into financial distress. When dollar access is restricted, either by capital flight or by trade disruptions, nations with heavy dollar liabilities scramble to secure scarce dollars, further weakening their local currencies in a vicious cycle.

This is the modern doom loop, one in which nations that are heavily integrated into the dollar-based global trade system find themselves caught between inflation, currency depreciation, and an ever-rising burden of external debt. The events of 2022 serve as a warning that any large-scale restriction of dollar flows—whether from tariffs, capital flight, or monetary tightening—can create a domino effect of financial crises across multiple regions.

As history has shown, when the dollar tightens its grip, economies that depend on its availability suffer the most. The world saw it in

1997, again in 2022, and the conditions are in place for another round of currency turmoil in the years ahead. The real question is whether global markets have learned the lessons of the past, or whether another financial storm is already brewing beneath the surface.

4

THE INFLATION SHOCK AND THE DOLLAR

A currency in freefall is not just a financial abstraction; it has direct and devastating consequences on everyday life. When the value of a nation's currency declines sharply against the U.S. dollar, the cost of essential imports—oil, food, medicine, and industrial raw materials—rises almost instantly. For countries that rely heavily on imports, this can unleash a powerful wave of inflation, eroding the purchasing power of households, slashing business profit margins, and creating a deep sense of economic insecurity. The stronger the dollar, the higher the cost for economies dependent on global trade, and when those costs surge, inflation becomes a relentless force that policymakers struggle to contain.

Currency Depreciation and Inflation: Global Case Studies

Few places exemplify this dynamic better than Turkey, a country that has been caught in the grip of a severe currency depreciation and inflation crisis for years. The Turkish lira, which traded at 4 per U.S. dollar in early 2018, collapsed to 18 per dollar by the end of 2022, marking a 77% depreciation. The immediate consequence was an import-driven inflationary shock, particularly in energy prices. Turkey, which imports almost all of its oil and gas, saw its energy costs spiral, leading to inflation surpassing 80% in 2022, one of the highest rates in the world. For ordinary citizens, this translated into basic necessities becoming unaffordable. The price of cooking oil doubled in a year, electricity bills soared, and bread prices skyrocketed, pushing millions of middle-class families to the brink.

Argentina's experience was even more severe. With a long history of currency instability, the country faced yet another inflationary catastrophe in 2023. The Argentine peso, which stood at 60 per U.S. dollar in 2019, crumbled to over 350 per dollar just four years later, a decline of nearly 85%. Inflation surged past 120% annually, with wages failing to keep pace, wiping out savings and forcing businesses to continuously raise prices just to survive. Grocery stores in Buenos Aires began implementing daily price changes, as the cost of flour, meat, and household goods surged uncontrollably. Faced with a collapsing peso, Argentines rushed to convert their earnings into dollars, worsening the crisis as demand for the greenback soared.

While Argentina's currency woes are often attributed to mismanagement, the inflationary shock of a weaker currency is a pattern repeated across multiple economies. Sri Lanka's economic collapse in 2022 was a textbook case of what happens when a country loses access to dollars. The Sri Lankan rupee, which had been relatively stable at 180 per U.S. dollar, plummeted past 360 per dollar in just a few months—a 100% devaluation. This currency collapse sent fuel prices soaring by 150%, leading to nationwide shortages, mass protests, and eventually the downfall of the government. Inflation spiked to 73%, with food prices rising so high that many households were forced to skip meals or rely on government rations. Without enough foreign exchange reserves to pay for essential imports, Sri Lanka experienced rolling blackouts, empty gas stations, and a full-fledged economic meltdown.

A similar pattern emerged in Egypt, where the Egyptian pound lost nearly 50% of its value in 2022, pushing inflation above 35%. Imported wheat, critical for the country's bread supply, became prohibitively expensive, triggering government intervention to maintain food security. In Nigeria, a sharp currency devaluation in 2023 saw inflation spike beyond 30%, fueling public discontent and social unrest. Across Africa, Asia, and Latin America, the combination of a strong U.S. dollar and weakening local currencies created a financial squeeze that central banks struggled to manage.

The Ripple Effect: Economic Strain and Social Unrest

The relationship between currency depreciation and inflation is straightforward: when a country imports a large portion of its goods, a weaker currency means those imports cost more in local terms. This is especially dangerous for economies that rely on dollar-priced commodities such as oil and food staples. A country like Japan, which imports nearly 90% of its energy, felt this acutely in 2022 when the yen weakened from 115 per U.S. dollar to 150, driving up fuel costs by over 40%.

What makes the inflationary impact even more damaging is that it disproportionately hurts low-income households, who spend a higher percentage of their earnings on food, transportation, and utilities. When prices surge due to currency depreciation, wage growth rarely keeps pace, leading to declining living standards and increasing economic hardship. This was evident in Pakistan in 2023, where a sharp 40% depreciation of the rupee against the dollar led to inflation surpassing 38%, with food prices rising even faster. For many families, basic necessities such as wheat flour and cooking oil became unaffordable, forcing the government to introduce emergency subsidies.

Even countries with relatively strong financial systems are not immune. In the United Kingdom, the British pound fell to a historic low of $1.03 against the U.S. dollar in late 2022, the weakest level in decades. This triggered an immediate spike in imported energy prices, worsening an already severe cost-of-living crisis. The government was forced to step in with emergency measures to cap electricity and heating costs for millions of households.

Meanwhile, in the Eurozone, surging inflation and an energy crisis following Russia's invasion of Ukraine placed immense strain on major economies like Germany and France. By mid-2022, the euro had fallen to parity with the U.S. dollar for the first time in two decades, reflecting investor concerns over economic stability. The weaker currency intensified the cost burden of dollar-denominated imports, including natural gas and oil, forcing European policymakers to implement extensive subsidies and fiscal support measures to shield households and businesses from mounting financial stress.

The broader lesson from these crises is that when access to dollars becomes restricted—whether due to tariffs, monetary policy, or capital flight—currencies suffer, and inflation follows. The pattern has played out in multiple regions, across different economic systems, and in varying degrees of severity. Once a country enters the cycle of currency depreciation, import-driven inflation, and rising external debt burdens, escaping it becomes a long and painful process.

For policymakers, the challenge is immense. Raising interest rates to stabilize the currency can slow inflation but often comes at the cost of recession and job losses. Letting the currency fall too quickly risks a hyperinflationary spiral, where confidence collapses and local savings become worthless. The longer a currency remains weak, the harder it becomes to restore stability, as inflationary expectations become embedded in the economy.

The inflationary shock from weaker currencies is not just an emerging market problem. It is a global phenomenon, and as long as the U.S. dollar remains the dominant reserve currency, fluctuations in its value will continue to dictate economic conditions worldwide. The events of 2022 and 2023 proved that when the U.S. dollar surges, no economy is truly safe from its inflationary impact.

5

IS THE DOLLAR THE NEXT CASUALTY?

The strength of the U.S. dollar has long been viewed as a symbol of America's economic dominance. For decades, global trade, finance, and commodity pricing have revolved around the dollar, giving the United States an unparalleled advantage in shaping global economic policy. But history has shown that no currency remains dominant forever. The same forces that drive the dollar's strength today—protectionist trade policies, aggressive monetary tightening, and a worldwide scramble for dollars—could ultimately undermine its position as the world's reserve currency.

A strong dollar, while seemingly a sign of economic power, is not without its risks. When the dollar appreciates too rapidly, it places enormous strain on global financial markets. Emerging economies, many of which owe significant amounts of dollar-denominated debt, struggle to make payments as their local currencies weaken. At the same time, multinational corporations that rely on overseas revenue see their earnings shrink when converted back into dollars, making U.S. businesses less competitive globally. This was evident in 2022, when major American firms, from Apple to Microsoft to Procter & Gamble, warned that the strong dollar had erased billions in revenue, forcing them to revise their earnings forecasts downward.

Yet, the real risk to the dollar's dominance lies not in short-term fluctuations but in long-term structural shifts in global trade and finance. As more nations experience currency instability due to U.S. trade policies and monetary decisions, they are increasingly looking for alternatives to the dollar. This de-dollarization trend is no longer a fringe movement—it is gaining traction among some of the world's largest economies. If this momentum continues, the gradual erosion of dollar reliance could accelerate into a systemic realignment, fundamentally reshaping the global financial order.

De-Dollarization: A Growing Threat to U.S. Financial Supremacy

Consider China's push for the internationalization of the yuan. Over the past decade, China has systematically reduced its dependence on the dollar by encouraging trade settlements in yuan. In 2023, more than 25% of China's trade was settled in yuan, a sharp increase from less than 2% a decade earlier. The Belt and Road Initiative, which has extended hundreds of billions in infrastructure loans across Asia, Africa, and Latin America, has also been used as a vehicle for increasing yuan-denominated lending, further reducing reliance on the dollar.

At the same time, the BRICS bloc—comprising Brazil, Russia, India, China, and South Africa—is actively working to create an alternative financial system. In 2023, BRICS nations announced plans to develop a new reserve currency, potentially backed by a basket of commodities including gold, oil, and rare earth metals. While such a system remains in its infancy, its very existence reflects a growing desire among major economies to reduce their exposure to the U.S. dollar.

Russia's experience following Western sanctions in 2022 accelerated this shift. After the United States and its allies froze $300 billion in Russian foreign exchange reserves, the Kremlin moved swiftly to de-dollarize its economy, conducting trade with China and India in yuan and rupees instead of dollars. By 2023, more than 80% of Russia-China trade was settled in yuan, a dramatic shift that would have been unthinkable just a few years earlier. The lesson was clear: the dollar's weaponization through financial sanctions had pushed nations to seek alternatives, a trend that could gain momentum as geopolitical tensions persist.

Even U.S. allies are reconsidering their reliance on the dollar. Saudi Arabia, long a cornerstone of the petrodollar system, has begun pricing oil in yuan for Chinese buyers. While the vast majority of global oil sales are still conducted in dollars, any erosion of the petrodollar system would deal a serious blow to the dollar's global standing. Meanwhile, France executed its first yuan-denominated liquefied natural gas (LNG) trade in 2023, signaling that even Western economies are open to diversifying their currency exposures. The declining role of the U.S. dollar in global central bank reserves is another warning sign. In 2000, the dollar accounted for roughly 70%

of global foreign exchange reserves. By 2023, that number had fallen to less than 59%, the lowest in decades. While the dollar remains the dominant reserve currency, its gradual erosion signals a growing willingness among central banks to diversify their holdings. Nations such as China, India, and even Germany have been increasing their gold reserves, a move that historically signals a lack of confidence in fiat currencies.

Some of this shift is structural—China, the world's second-largest economy, is simply too big to be ignored in global trade—but much of it is a direct result of U.S. policies. Protectionist trade measures, aggressive sanctions, and weaponization of the financial system have created a strong incentive for other nations to hedge against their reliance on the dollar. The unintended consequence of these policies is that they accelerate the search for alternatives, weakening the very system that has underpinned U.S. financial supremacy for decades.

The Dollar's Dilemma: Power Today, Peril Tomorrow

For now, the dollar remains unchallenged as the world's primary reserve currency, but its dominance is no longer absolute. As the U.S. continues to restrict global access to dollars—whether through tariffs, sanctions, or monetary policy—more countries will look for ways to reduce their exposure. The world may not abandon the dollar overnight, but the cracks in its foundation are beginning to show.

The irony is that the very policies designed to protect the U.S. economy—trade barriers, financial sanctions, and monetary tightening—are the same policies that could ultimately weaken the dollar's role in the global system. If the dollar loses its "exorbitant privilege," the consequences for the United States would be profound: higher borrowing costs, reduced economic influence, and a diminished ability to dictate global financial conditions.

The erosion of the dollar's dominance is not just an abstract geopolitical concern; it has tangible implications for everyday Americans. A diminished global role for the dollar would likely lead to higher inflation at home, as imported goods become more expensive and the U.S. loses its ability to finance deficits cheaply. For decades, the dollar's privileged position allowed the United States to borrow at lower interest rates than other nations, fund expansive fiscal policies, and maintain high living standards without immediate economic repercussions. If the dollar's status wanes, the ripple effects would be felt across the economy—from rising mortgage rates to higher credit card interest rates—and could exacerbate economic inequality as lower-income households bear the brunt of these changes. This potential shift is not just a theoretical concern for policymakers; it is a looming reality that could reshape the financial landscape for millions.

Moreover, the global response to a declining dollar could further accelerate its fall. As more countries diversify their reserves and conduct trade in alternative currencies, a feedback loop may emerge, where diminishing demand for the dollar leads to further devaluation. This scenario, while gradual, would alter the balance of global financial power, giving rise to a more fragmented system where regional currencies play a larger role. The question is not whether the dollar will face challenges, but how swiftly and decisively the United States can adapt to this new reality. History is replete with examples of dominant currencies losing their luster, and the U.S. now stands at a critical juncture: continue policies that alienate global partners or recalibrate its economic strategy to preserve its financial hegemony. The path chosen will determine whether the dollar's legacy endures or becomes a relic of the past.

No currency holds its status forever. The British pound once ruled global trade, only to be overtaken by the dollar in the early 20th century. If current trends continue, the dollar may not disappear, but it could face a multipolar world where it is no longer the undisputed king of global finance. Whether this shift happens in a decade or over several generations remains to be seen, but one thing is clear: if the U.S. continues down the path of economic nationalism, it may find itself the architect of its own currency's decline.

6

TARIFFS: A CATALYST FOR CURRENCY CHAOS

The global economy is an intricate web of interconnected financial flows, supply chains, and currency markets, all of which rely on the steady circulation of U.S. dollars. Tariffs, often framed as a simple tool to protect domestic industries, disrupt this delicate balance in profound and unintended ways. By restricting trade, tariffs reduce the outflow of dollars into global markets, setting off a chain reaction of currency depreciation, inflationary shocks, and financial distress. These effects, initially concentrated in the countries that depend most on U.S. trade, quickly spill over into the broader global economy, creating the conditions for economic instability on a much larger scale.

Tariffs, Currency Turmoil, and Inflation: A Volatile Mix

The relationship between tariffs, currency markets, and inflation is not theoretical—it has been demonstrated time and again. The 1997 Asian Financial Crisis showed how a sudden shortage of dollars can trigger widespread currency collapses and inflationary spirals. The 2022 currency crisis reinforced this lesson, as the U.S. dollar's sharp appreciation—fueled by Federal Reserve rate hikes and protectionist trade policies—crushed multiple currencies, driving inflation and economic hardship across Europe, Japan, and emerging markets. The recent struggles of Turkey, Argentina, Sri Lanka, and Nigeria highlight how vulnerable economies can be devastated by a stronger dollar, particularly when access to foreign exchange reserves becomes restricted.

The irony of tariffs is that while they are designed to protect American industries, they frequently backfire in unexpected ways. In the short term, a tariff-induced drop in imports may seem like a win for domestic manufacturers, but the long-term effects often prove destructive. As foreign economies weaken under the pressure of currency depreciation and dollar shortages, they become less capable of buying American goods and services, reducing demand for U.S. exports. Meanwhile, as other countries struggle to secure dollars, global investors seek safety in U.S. assets, further strengthening the dollar and making American exports even less competitive.

From Trade Wars to Dollar Wars: The Road to De-dollarization

The broader consequence of prolonged tariff policies is the acceleration of de-dollarization efforts. The U.S. dollar has dominated global finance for nearly a century, but every financial shock tied to dollar shortages provides more incentive for foreign economies to seek alternatives. China's aggressive push to settle trade in yuan, Russia's shift to non-dollar trade agreements, and BRICS' exploration of a reserve currency outside the U.S. financial system are all direct responses to the vulnerabilities created by dollar dependence. When tariffs and trade wars make access to dollars unreliable, more countries will take steps to reduce their reliance on the U.S. financial system—a trend that could gradually weaken the dollar's role as the global reserve currency.

If history is any guide, economic nationalism often carries hidden costs. The Smoot-Hawley Tariff Act of 1930, enacted with the goal of protecting American jobs, instead exacerbated the Great Depression by triggering retaliatory tariffs that strangled global trade. The protectionist policies of the 1980s led to soaring deficits and trade imbalances that forced the U.S. into negotiated currency realignments with its trading partners. And in more recent years, tariffs on Chinese goods have failed to bring back American manufacturing in any meaningful way, while simultaneously contributing to higher consumer prices and supply chain disruptions.

The lesson is clear: tariffs are not just about trade. They have far-reaching implications for currency markets, inflation, and financial stability worldwide. When the U.S. restricts dollar flows by imposing trade barriers, it weakens foreign currencies, fuels inflation in vulnerable economies, and accelerates the search for alternatives to the dollar. The unintended consequence is that while tariffs may seem like a tool to strengthen America's economic position, they ultimately weaken the very system that has sustained U.S. financial dominance for decades.

The global economic order is shifting. If the United States continues down the path of protectionism and aggressive monetary tightening, it risks creating the conditions for a fragmented financial system, where competing currencies and trade blocs emerge in response. The real question is whether the U.S. is prepared for a world where the dollar is no longer the undisputed foundation of global commerce. If tariffs continue to fuel financial distress, inflationary shocks, and geopolitical realignments, the United States may discover that its most significant casualty is not foreign competitors—but the dollar itself.

7

TRADE WARS AND THEIR CONSEQUENCES

The assumption that tariffs create a one-sided advantage for the United States overlooks a critical reality: trade is a two-way street. When the U.S. raises tariffs on imports, other nations inevitably respond with their own countermeasures, triggering a cycle of retaliatory tariffs, supply chain disruptions, and economic losses that affect both sides. What starts as an attempt to protect domestic industries quickly escalates into a trade war, imposing higher costs on consumers and businesses alike, distorting global markets, and weakening economic relationships.

History offers numerous lessons on how trade wars, once started, rarely produce clear winners. Instead, they tend to exacerbate economic slowdowns, raise inflation, and fuel uncertainty. The unintended consequences of these conflicts often extend far beyond trade itself, affecting currency markets, investment flows, geopolitical alliances, and long-term economic stability.

The Tariff Trap: How Retaliation Hurts U.S. Businesses

At first glance, tariffs may seem like a logical way to protect domestic industries from foreign competition. By making imports more expensive, they encourage consumers and businesses to buy American-made products instead. However, this logic ignores a fundamental problem: many U.S. industries depend on imports, either as raw materials, intermediate goods, or final products. When tariffs raise the cost of these imports, American businesses face higher production costs, reduced competitiveness, and lower profit margins.

Consider the case of Trump's steel and aluminum tariffs in 2018. Designed to protect American steel manufacturers, these tariffs imposed a 25% duty on imported steel and a 10% duty on imported aluminum. While the U.S. steel industry saw a temporary boost, the unintended victims were manufacturers that rely on steel and aluminum as inputs, including the automotive, aerospace, and construction sectors.

The auto industry, in particular, suffered. U.S. carmakers faced higher input costs, making American-made vehicles more expensive. In response, automakers like Ford and General Motors warned that these tariffs would cost them billions of dollars, forcing them to cut jobs and delay investment projects. By 2019, Ford estimated that the tariffs had cost the company $1 billion, while General Motors projected a hit of nearly $700 million.

Similar consequences played out in agriculture, where retaliatory tariffs from China, Canada, and the European Union targeted U.S. farm exports. In response to U.S. tariffs on Chinese goods, China imposed a 25% tariff on American soybeans, one of the largest U.S. agricultural exports. Almost overnight, U.S. soybean exports to China collapsed by 75%, as Chinese buyers turned to Brazil for their supply. The impact was devastating for U.S. farmers, who faced plummeting prices and unsold inventory. By 2019, the U.S. government was forced to bail out farmers with a $28 billion relief package, effectively offsetting the damage caused by its own trade policies.

The Global Trade War: Retaliation and Escalation

Trade wars rarely remain confined to one or two rounds of tariffs. Instead, they escalate as countries retaliate, expanding the conflict into multiple sectors and regions. The U.S.-China trade war (2018-2019) was a textbook example of this escalation, as each round of tariffs triggered countermeasures that spread uncertainty across global markets.

The first wave of U.S. tariffs targeted $50 billion worth of Chinese imports, focused on industrial goods, semiconductors, and machinery. China responded with tariffs of its own, targeting U.S. agriculture, automobiles, and aircraft. When the U.S. escalated by imposing tariffs on an additional $200 billion in Chinese goods, China retaliated with duties on American soybeans, pork, and liquefied natural gas (LNG). The result was a trade war that disrupted global supply chains, slowed economic growth, and increased costs for businesses and consumers on both sides.

The broader fallout was significant. The International Monetary Fund (IMF) estimated that the U.S.-China trade war reduced global GDP by 0.8% in 2019, wiping out $700 billion in economic output. American consumers bore much of the burden, as businesses passed higher costs onto households, raising prices on everyday goods from electronics to clothing. Meanwhile, manufacturers suffered as supply chains were thrown into chaos, forcing many to shift production out of China—often at higher costs.

Other nations were caught in the crossfire. As China and the U.S. raised tariffs on each other's goods, third-party countries like Germany, Japan, and South Korea saw trade volumes decline. The uncertainty created by the trade war slowed global investment, with foreign direct investment (FDI) into China dropping by 23% in 2019.

Beyond the economic damage, trade wars also erode diplomatic relationships. Canada, Mexico, and the European Union, all long-time U.S. allies, were targeted by tariffs on steel and aluminum under the justification of national security concerns. In response, these countries imposed counter-tariffs on U.S. exports, hitting industries ranging from whiskey to motorcycles to agricultural products. The result was growing frustration with U.S. economic policy, pushing some nations to pursue alternative trade partnerships.

Tariffs and the Rise of Regional Trade

When major economies engage in prolonged trade wars, the incentive for other nations to bypass traditional trade routes and form new alliances grows stronger. Over time, this weakens the role of the United States in global trade and finance.

In response to growing U.S.-China tensions, Asian economies deepened their integration through the Regional Comprehensive Economic Partnership (RCEP), a free trade agreement covering 15 countries, including China, Japan, South Korea, and Australia. RCEP became the largest trade bloc in the world, covering nearly 30% of global GDP, and reducing reliance on the U.S. market.

Similarly, the European Union accelerated trade negotiations with Canada, Japan, and Latin America, signing agreements that reduced their exposure to U.S.-dominated supply chains. Meanwhile, China's Belt and Road Initiative (BRI) continued expanding its economic influence, financing infrastructure projects that shifted global trade routes further away from U.S. dominance.

The long-term consequence of these shifts is clear: the more the U.S. pursues protectionist policies, the more it encourages other nations to develop alternative trade networks. This process does not happen overnight, but the cracks in the existing system are already forming.

The Inflationary Cost of Trade Wars

One of the biggest misconceptions about tariffs is that they primarily hurt foreign exporters. In reality, the costs are often passed on to domestic consumers. When tariffs increase the price of imported goods, businesses typically respond by raising prices, reducing wages, or cutting jobs to offset higher costs. The result is often higher inflation, declining purchasing power, and economic drag.

A 2019 study by the Federal Reserve Bank of New York estimated that the Trump administration's tariffs cost the average U.S. household $1,277 per year through higher prices on consumer goods, raw materials, and manufacturing inputs. Over time, this kind of inflationary pressure reduces economic growth, particularly when combined with rising interest rates and tighter financial conditions.

The economic evidence overwhelmingly suggests that trade wars are costly, inefficient, and damaging to long-term economic growth. Rather than strengthening domestic industries, they often leave them more vulnerable to foreign retaliation and shifting trade alliances.

The High Price of Trade Wars

History has shown that no country truly wins a trade war. Tariffs invite retaliation, disrupt global supply chains, weaken economic alliances, and create inflationary pressures that hurt consumers and businesses alike. In the short term, they may provide temporary relief for certain industries, but over time, the costs far outweigh the benefits.

The ripple effects of these economic conflicts extend beyond spreadsheets and policy papers—they affect everyday lives. From the Midwest farmer grappling with unsold soybeans to the small business owner facing higher input costs, trade wars hit hardest where resilience is already stretched thin. Each tariff imposed and countermeasure enacted not only raises prices but also erodes trust in the global economic system, fostering uncertainty that stifles innovation and investment.

The real danger of prolonged trade conflicts is that they push the global economy toward fragmentation, creating competing trade blocs that reduce the role of the U.S. in global commerce. As nations increasingly seek alternatives, the United States risks isolating itself from the very networks that have long underpinned its economic strength. The irony is sharp: policies meant to shield the American economy may ultimately weaken it, leaving future generations to navigate a world where U.S. economic influence is no longer taken for granted.

As tariffs continue to shape economic policy, the unintended consequences could be far greater than expected—not just for global trade, but for the long-term stability of the U.S. economy itself

.

PART III

THE GLOBAL REVOLT

How De-Dollarization is Breaking
The Dollar's Grip

"Nothing endures but change."
— Heraclitus

As the dollar's supremacy faces mounting pressure, Part III examines the global response to U.S. economic policies. Across three chapters, this section explores the accelerating trend of de-dollarization, driven by sanctions, protectionism, and geopolitical shifts. From emerging economies seeking alternatives to the dollar to the destabilizing effects of currency depreciation, it examines the economic turmoil that follows. Finally, it analyzes the rise of regional economic blocs like BRICS, whose growing influence threatens to reshape global trade and finance, posing a pivotal question: Can the U.S. dollar maintain its dominance in an increasingly multipolar world?

CHAPTER 5

DE-DOLLARIZATION: A GROWING TREND

The U.S. dollar has long been the bedrock of global finance, but this chapter examines how rising geopolitical tensions and economic nationalism are driving a growing trend of de-dollarization. It explores how nations—motivated by the risks of dollar dependence and the weaponization of U.S. financial power—are actively seeking alternatives. From China's yuan-based trade settlements to Russia's response to Western sanctions, de-dollarization is reshaping global financial alliances. This chapter also delves into the economic and political consequences of this shift, highlighting its impact on global markets, currency stability, and U.S. economic influence. As more countries hedge against the dollar, the chapter raises a pressing question: Is the world witnessing the gradual erosion of the dollar's supremacy, and what might the future hold for a global economy no longer anchored by a single dominant currency?

1

IS THE DOLLAR'S REIGN ENDING?

For much of the modern era, the U.S. dollar has been the bedrock of the global economy. No currency has enjoyed such an extensive reach, dictating international trade, investment, and financial stability. It has served as the world's primary reserve currency, the preferred medium for cross-border transactions, and the ultimate safe-haven asset in times of crisis. The dominance of the dollar has granted the United States an unparalleled advantage, allowing it to finance deficits at low cost, impose economic sanctions with impunity, and dictate global liquidity flows with Federal Reserve policy decisions that impact every corner of the world.

Cracks in the Dollar's Dominance

Yet beneath this financial supremacy, cracks are beginning to emerge. The world is changing in ways that challenge the dollar's continued dominance, and while its immediate collapse is unlikely, a gradual erosion is already underway. Nations across the world, particularly emerging powers such as China, Russia, and the broader BRICS alliance, are actively seeking alternatives to the dollar-led system. Their motivation is not simply economic—it is deeply rooted in geopolitical shifts, the strategic weaponization of the dollar by the United States, and a growing desire among nations to regain financial autonomy from Washington's influence.

The events of recent years have accelerated this process. The U.S. decision to freeze Russia's foreign reserves in 2022, in response to its invasion of Ukraine, sent shockwaves through the international financial system. For the first time, a major global power saw a significant portion of its foreign-held assets rendered unusable overnight.

Moscow, once deeply entrenched in the dollar system, found itself scrambling for alternatives, turning to China's yuan and strengthening ties with India to keep its trade flows intact. This moment served as a wake-up call for other nations, particularly those that have long harbored concerns about the U.S. dollar's role as both a financial tool and a political weapon. If Washington could freeze one country's assets, it could do the same to others. The lesson was clear: reliance on the dollar carried a built-in vulnerability that needed to be addressed.

The push for de-dollarization, however, is not merely a response to U.S. sanctions. Structural shifts in the global economy have been reshaping financial relationships for years. As the world's largest economy for most of the 20th and early 21st centuries, the United States naturally commanded influence over global trade and finance. But the rapid economic rise of China, the resurgence of commodity-rich nations like Russia, and the emergence of alternative financial institutions have created an environment where the dollar is no longer the unquestioned default for global transactions.

The Global Shift Away from the Dollar

The share of global reserves held in U.S. dollars has been steadily declining. In the early 2000s, nearly 73% of global foreign exchange reserves were held in dollars, but today that figure has fallen to less than 59%, according to the International Monetary Fund (IMF). While still dominant, the downward trajectory signals that governments are increasingly hedging their bets against a world in which the dollar is no longer the singular reserve currency.

Trade patterns are also shifting in ways that could accelerate de-dollarization. China, now the world's largest trading nation, has been using its economic clout to encourage trading partners to conduct business in yuan instead of dollars. Bilateral currency agreements between China and countries in Africa, Latin America, and the Middle East have allowed for trade settlement in local currencies, bypassing the dollar entirely. Russia and India, once major dollar users, have experimented with ruble-rupee transactions for energy and other commodities. Even Saudi Arabia, long seen as a pillar of the petrodollar system, has expressed willingness to price oil sales in Chinese yuan, a move that would have been unthinkable just a decade ago.

To put these shifts into historical perspective, the decline of a dominant global currency is not unprecedented. The British pound once held a position similar to the dollar's, acting as the world's primary reserve currency throughout the 19th and early 20th centuries. Its dominance, however, was eroded by the economic devastation of two world wars, the financial strain of maintaining the British Empire, and the gradual emergence of the United States as the world's largest economy. The pound was gradually replaced, not through a sudden collapse, but through a decades-long shift in global economic power. A similar transition is now underway, with the dollar facing competition from multiple fronts rather than a single rival currency.

None of this means that the dollar will disappear overnight. The United States. financial system remains the most liquid and trusted in the world, and U.S. Treasuries continue to be the safe-haven asset of choice during economic crises. In moments of global uncertainty, capital still flows into U.S. markets rather than away from them. However, the long-term trajectory tells a different story. If current trends continue, the dollar's absolute dominance will wane, not through an immediate collapse, but through the gradual construction of a more multipolar financial system in which trade, reserves, and investment flows are increasingly diversified.

The question is not whether de-dollarization is happening—it is. The real question is how far it will go and whether the United States will adapt to this shifting landscape or attempt to resist it to its own detriment. History has shown that financial hegemony is never permanent, and those who fail to recognize the changing tides often find themselves left behind. The erosion of dollar dominance may not lead to an immediate collapse, but the longer Washington clings to outdated assumptions, the more it risks accelerating the very shift it seeks to prevent.

.

2

DEEPENING THE CASE FOR DE-DOLLARIZATION

The movement away from the U.S. dollar is not a sudden, isolated phenomenon, but rather the result of years of economic and geopolitical shifts. At its core, de-dollarization reflects a growing realization that dependence on the dollar carries both financial and strategic risks. Several key forces have accelerated this trend, from the United States' increasing use of the dollar as a geopolitical weapon to trade disruptions caused by protectionist policies and the underlying vulnerabilities of the American financial system itself.

The Weaponization of the Dollar: Catalyst for De-Dollarization

For much of the post-World War II era, the global reliance on the U.S. dollar was widely accepted as a stabilizing force. However, over the past two decades, Washington has increasingly used its financial dominance as a tool of coercion, imposing sanctions, freezing foreign assets, and cutting nations off from dollar-based financial networks. This strategy has had profound consequences, making it clear to many governments that their economic stability depends on the goodwill of the United States—a position that few countries are comfortable accepting indefinitely.

One of the most dramatic examples of financial weaponization occurred in 2022, when the United States and its allies imposed unprecedented sanctions on Russia following its invasion of Ukraine. These measures went beyond conventional trade restrictions; Russian banks were expelled from the SWIFT system, and over $300 billion in Russian foreign reserves were effectively frozen. The message to the world was unmistakable: even a country with significant economic power could see its assets rendered useless at the stroke of a pen.

This event was a wake-up call, not just for Russia, but for other nations that had long assumed their dollar reserves were secure. China, already wary of its growing rivalry with the United States, began accelerating efforts to reduce its reliance on the dollar, fearing that it could be the next target of financial warfare. Countries such as India, Iran, and Turkey took notice as well, quietly increasing their use of alternative currencies in trade agreements.

The use of financial sanctions as a tool of foreign policy is not new, but the scale and intensity of recent measures have led many to question the long-term safety of holding dollar reserves. Nations that once viewed the dollar as a neutral global medium of exchange now see it as an instrument of political leverage. This shift in perception has created a strong incentive for countries to explore alternatives, ensuring that their economic sovereignty is not at the mercy of U.S. policy decisions.

Early indications from Trump's second term suggest that economic and financial sanctions will remain a central policy tool. If this trend continues, it may further incentivize nations like China and Russia to reduce their reliance on the dollar, adding momentum to de-dollarization efforts already underway. The fear of financial isolation, particularly for nations that find themselves at odds with U.S. strategic interests, has pushed even traditional allies to reconsider their exposure to dollar-dominated reserves.

The shift away from the dollar is not merely a reaction to U.S. sanctions but also a result of deeper structural forces in the global economy. As emerging markets grow in economic and political influence, their willingness to challenge the existing financial order increases. The world is entering an era where alternatives to the dollar are not just desired — they are actively being constructed.

Trade Wars and Protectionism: Paving the Way for Alternatives

Beyond the use of sanctions, the rising tide of protectionism in the United States has further fueled de-dollarization. For much of the post-Cold War period, the global economy was defined by increasing trade liberalization, with the U.S. at the center of an expanding network of economic partnerships. That began to change in the 2010s, as trade disputes and tariff wars became more frequent, signaling a shift toward a more insular approach.

The U.S.-China trade war, which began under the first Trump administration and has continued in various forms, marked a turning point in global economic relations. Tariffs imposed on hundreds of billions of dollars' worth of Chinese goods disrupted supply chains and created uncertainty in global markets. In response, China intensified its efforts to shift trade away from dollar settlements, expanding the use of the yuan in cross-border transactions. Chinese companies, facing the prospect of higher trade barriers, sought to build stronger economic ties with countries in Africa, the Middle East, and Southeast Asia, many of which were willing to explore non-dollar trade arrangements.

Protectionist policies have not only encouraged de-dollarization among America's rivals but have also led some long-standing allies to reconsider their dependence on U.S. economic policies. The European Union, for example, has explored ways to strengthen the euro's role in international trade, while countries in Latin America have increasingly looked to regional agreements that bypass the dollar. The more the United States imposes tariffs, trade restrictions, and unilateral economic measures, the greater the incentive for other nations to seek alternatives that reduce their exposure to American economic fluctuations.

A historical comparison provides insight into where this trend could lead. In the 1980s, Japan was the target of U.S. trade restrictions designed to limit its growing economic influence. At the time, Japan was the world's second-largest economy, with a trade surplus that threatened American industries. Washington responded with a series of tariffs and trade agreements that forced Japan to appreciate its currency, leading to long-term economic stagnation. While Japan ultimately remained within the U.S.-led financial system, the episode contributed to a shift in global economic power toward China and other emerging markets.

Today, China presents a far greater challenge to the U.S., and protectionist policies may hasten global financial fragmentation. With its economic scale and strategic alliances, China offers real alternatives to the dollar system. If the U.S. weaponizes its financial influence, it risks not just weakening rivals but also alienating allies, undermining dollar supremacy.

3

LESSONS FROM JAPAN:
A WARNING FOR THE U.S. DOLLAR

By the early 1980s, Japan had transformed itself into an economic powerhouse. Its post-war reconstruction, driven by an export-led growth strategy, propelled it to become the world's second-largest economy behind the United States. With a manufacturing sector that emphasized efficiency, quality, and technological innovation, Japan rapidly gained dominance in industries that had long been considered American strongholds—automobiles, consumer electronics, and semiconductors.

The numbers tell the story of an economic surge that became impossible for the U.S. to ignore. In 1965, Japan's trade surplus with the U.S. was negligible, as it was still in the early stages of rebuilding its economy. By 1980, however, that surplus had grown to $10 billion, and within just five years, it had ballooned to over $50 billion. By the late 1980s, Japan accounted for more than 60% of the U.S. trade deficit, making it Washington's primary economic concern.

The automobile industry was at the center of this growing tension. Throughout the 1970s, Japanese automakers—including Toyota, Honda, and Nissan—began gaining market share in the U.S. by offering vehicles that were more fuel-efficient, reliable, and competitively priced than their American counterparts. The 1973 oil crisis only accelerated this shift, as consumers abandoned gas-guzzling American cars in favor of smaller, more efficient Japanese models. By 1981, Japanese automakers controlled more than 21% of the U.S. auto market, a sharp increase from just 5% in 1970.

A similar story played out in consumer electronics and semiconductors. Companies like Sony, Panasonic, and Toshiba took over global markets for televisions, cameras, and home appliances, pushing American firms to the sidelines. More concerning for Washington was Japan's dominance in semiconductors, the foundation of modern computing and defense technology. By 1985, Japanese firms controlled over 50% of the global semiconductor market, overtaking U.S. firms such as Intel and Texas Instruments.

For the United States, this was more than just an economic issue—it was a strategic one. If Japan's rise continued unchecked, America risked losing its technological and industrial edge. Calls for retaliation grew louder, leading to a series of aggressive U.S. trade policies aimed at curbing Japan's economic momentum.

The Plaza Accord: A Forced Currency Revaluation

As tensions escalated, Washington sought to weaken Japan's export advantage through currency intervention. The U.S. accused Japan of keeping the yen artificially low to make its goods cheaper in international markets, a charge that had been repeatedly leveled against China in more recent years. The widening trade imbalance, coupled with domestic political pressure, led to the Plaza Accord of 1985, a coordinated agreement between the United States, Japan, West Germany, France, and the United Kingdom.

The agreement's primary objective was to devalue the U.S. dollar against other major currencies, forcing Japan to allow the yen to appreciate. The impact was immediate and severe. Before the Plaza Accord, one U.S. dollar equaled 240 yen. Within just two years, the yen had strengthened dramatically, reaching 150 yen per dollar by 1987 and further appreciating to 120 yen per dollar by 1989. This marked a 50% increase in the value of the yen against the dollar, making Japanese exports significantly more expensive and dampening their global competitiveness.

The shift in exchange rates had a profound effect on Japan's economy. A Toyota Corolla that had been priced at 2.4 million yen—equivalent to $10,000 before the Plaza Accord—would now cost an American consumer $16,000 due to the stronger yen. This sudden loss of price competitiveness led to an economic slowdown, exactly as Washington had intended.

However, the Plaza Accord also triggered unintended consequences that ultimately destabilized Japan's economy. The sharp appreciation of the yen led to a surge of speculative capital into Japanese financial markets, fueling an unprecedented asset bubble. Stock prices and real estate values skyrocketed, with land in Tokyo's

Ginza district becoming so expensive that, at its peak, the Imperial Palace grounds in Tokyo were valued higher than all of California.

By the late 1980s, Japan's Nikkei 225 stock index had soared to 38,957 points, nearly three times its pre-Plaza Accord level. But when the bubble inevitably burst in the early 1990s, the consequences were devastating. By 1992, the Nikkei had collapsed to 14,000 points, wiping out trillions of dollars in wealth. Real estate prices followed, plunging by over 50% in the following years. The financial sector, burdened by bad loans, entered a prolonged crisis, setting the stage for Japan's "Lost Decades"—a period of economic stagnation, deflation, and slow growth that lasted well into the 2000s.

Lessons for Today: Japan Then, China Now

The U.S.-Japan trade war of the 1980s serves as a powerful warning about the unintended consequences of economic intervention. While the Plaza Accord temporarily alleviated U.S. concerns about Japan's growing trade dominance, it also set off a chain reaction that culminated in one of the most severe economic downturns in modern history.

Japan had been experiencing extraordinary economic growth before the 1985 agreement. Throughout the 1960s and 1970s, its GDP expanded at an average annual rate of 7-10%, with some years even reaching double-digit growth. This rapid expansion allowed Japan to establish itself as a global leader in automobiles, semiconductors, and electronics, surpassing many U.S. firms in key industries. However, the Plaza Accord, which pressured Japan into appreciating the yen, fueled an asset bubble that ultimately burst in the early 1990s. The aftermath was devastating—Japan's economic growth slowed to a mere 1% per year, a stagnation that would persist for decades.

One of the most crippling features of Japan's post-Plaza economic era was deflation. As asset values collapsed and consumer confidence evaporated, prices fell rather than rose. While moderate inflation erodes the real burden of debt over time, deflation has the opposite effect—it makes debt more expensive in real terms, discourages borrowing, and leads businesses and households to delay spending in anticipation of even lower prices. This deflationary cycle paralyzed Japan's economy, causing wages to stagnate, corporate investment to dry up, and domestic demand to collapse.

In response, the Japanese government dramatically increased public spending, resulting in one of the highest debt-to-GDP ratios in the world. Today, Japan's government debt exceeds 260% of GDP, a level that would likely trigger a financial crisis in most other economies. Yet, Japan has managed to avoid collapse largely due to ultra-low interest rates and an insular financial system in which domestic investors hold most of the debt.

However, this reliance on perpetual government stimulus underscores the extent to which Japan has struggled to regain its economic dynamism following the interventionist policies of the 1980s. Growth remains sluggish, and deflationary pressures continue to weigh on consumer spending and corporate investment. With an aging population and mounting fiscal burdens, Japan's economic model raises an important question: How long can a nation sustain excessive debt before structural weaknesses begin to surface?

Parallels and Divergences: China's Strategic Response

The lessons from this era are strikingly relevant to today's de-dollarization debate. In the 1980s, Japan was a rising economic power but remained deeply integrated into the U.S.-led financial order, even after facing direct economic pressure from Washington. Today, China finds itself in a similar position, having built an export-driven economy that has contributed to a massive U.S. trade deficit.

When China joined the World Trade Organization (WTO) in 2001, its trade surplus with the U.S. was just *$28 billion*. By 2010, that figure had surged to *$273 billion*, and by 2022, the U.S.-China trade deficit had surpassed *$380 billion*, exceeding even Japan's peak imbalance. Like Japan in the 1980s, China has faced repeated accusations of currency manipulation, with Washington arguing that Beijing has artificially suppressed the yuan's value to maintain its export competitiveness.

Yet, the key difference lies in how China has chosen to respond. Unlike Japan, which ultimately complied with U.S. demands and remained within the dollar-based financial system, China has pursued a far more aggressive strategy. Rather than passively adjusting to U.S. trade pressure, China is actively working to build an alternative financial architecture to reduce its dependence on the U.S. dollar. It has expanded the international use of the yuan, forged new trade alliances, and strengthened de-dollarization efforts in coordination with countries like Russia and India.

Echoes of the Past: Economic Competition in Key Industries

China's rise in key industries mirrors Japan's trajectory but on a much larger scale. In automobiles, semiconductors, and high-tech manufacturing, China is replicating Japan's past success. Chinese automakers, particularly in the electric vehicle (EV) sector, are rapidly gaining global market share, much like Toyota and Honda did in the 1980s. Meanwhile, Washington has imposed export bans on advanced semiconductor technology—an echo of past restrictions placed on Japanese firms to limit their dominance in microchips.

However, the scale and scope of China's economic challenge to the U.S. surpass anything Japan posed in the 1980s. While Japan remained heavily reliant on the U.S. market and financial system, China is actively diversifying its trade partnerships and reshaping the global economic landscape.

The Unintended Consequences of Economic Coercion

The U.S.-Japan trade war illustrates how economic intervention can yield unintended consequences. Japan's forced currency appreciation led to long-term stagnation, serving as a cautionary tale. Today, U.S. tariffs and sanctions on China risk not only short-term disruption but also the gradual erosion of the dollar's dominance. As China expands its global influence, these economic pressures may further incentivize de-dollarization efforts worldwide.

Unlike 1980s Japan, China and other emerging economies possess tools to resist financial coercion, building a multipolar financial system independent of the U.S. dollar. History suggests that aggressive U.S. economic policies aimed at preserving dominance may, ironically, accelerate its decline, fostering new financial alliances that bypass American influence.

4

THE FINANCIAL FRAGILITY OF THE U.S. DOLLAR

The U.S. dollar's status as the world's primary reserve currency has long been underpinned by trust in the stability of the American financial system. For decades, the strength of the U.S. economy, the liquidity of its capital markets, and the global dominance of U.S. Treasury bonds have reinforced the dollar's central role in global trade and finance. However, beneath this outward strength, a series of structural weaknesses have emerged, raising serious questions about the dollar's long-term viability.

Debt, Deficits, and the Fragility of U.S. Treasuries

At the core of these vulnerabilities lies an unprecedented accumulation of U.S. government debt. The United States has run persistent budget deficits for decades, but the scale of borrowing in recent years has reached levels once considered unthinkable. In 2000, the U.S. national debt stood at $5.6 trillion. By 2010, it had more than doubled to $13.5 trillion. Today, it exceeds $34 trillion, and projections indicate that the federal deficit will continue growing indefinitely. The ability of the U.S. to sustain such massive debt depends on continued demand for Treasury bonds. However, recent trends suggest that confidence in Treasuries as the world's safest asset is eroding.

Foreign central banks, which were once among the largest buyers of U.S. government debt, have been steadily reducing their holdings of Treasuries. China, once the largest foreign holder, has divested more than $500 billion in U.S. debt over the past decade, seeking to diversify its foreign reserves. Other major economies, including Russia, Saudi Arabia, and India, have followed suit, shifting a greater portion of their reserves into gold, commodities, and other non-dollar assets.

The U.S. faces a fundamental problem: as its debt burden continues to grow, it must attract ever-larger sums of capital to finance its deficits. Historically, this has been achieved through the issuance of new Treasury bonds, purchased by both domestic and foreign investors. However, if demand for Treasuries continues to weaken, the U.S. will be forced to offer higher interest rates to entice buyers, significantly increasing its debt servicing costs. With annual interest payments on the national debt already exceeding $1 trillion, a continued rise in borrowing costs would place an even greater strain on government finances.

Beyond the debt crisis, inflation and monetary policy missteps have further eroded confidence in the dollar. The Federal Reserve's response to economic crises over the past two decades has centered on aggressive monetary expansion, flooding financial markets with liquidity in an effort to stimulate growth. The most extreme example of this came during the COVID-19 pandemic, when the U.S. money supply increased by more than 40% in just two years, an expansion of liquidity without historical precedent.

While this massive stimulus initially stabilized the economy, it also set the stage for the highest inflation rates in four decades. By 2022, U.S. inflation had surged to 9.1%, forcing the Federal Reserve into a cycle of aggressive interest rate hikes to contain rising prices. Higher interest rates, while necessary to combat inflation, have created their own set of problems. As rates rise, debt becomes more expensive to service, and financial markets—particularly in emerging economies that hold dollar-denominated debt—face increased volatility.

De-Dollarization and the Rise of Alternatives

The structural weaknesses of the dollar extend beyond inflation and debt. De-dollarization efforts among major economies have begun accelerating precisely because of concerns about the long-term value of the greenback. Nations that once relied on the dollar for stability are now actively seeking alternatives. The proportion of global foreign exchange reserves held in U.S. dollars has steadily declined, falling from 70% in 2000 to less than 59% today. Central banks have increased their purchases of gold at record levels, signaling a loss of trust in traditional reserve assets such as Treasuries.

At the same time, the dominance of the U.S. financial system is increasingly being challenged by the rise of alternative payment mechanisms and digital currencies. China's digital yuan, for example, has already been integrated into cross-border transactions, providing an alternative to SWIFT-based settlements. Cryptocurrencies, once dismissed as speculative assets, are now being explored as a means of facilitating non-dollar trade, particularly in regions where access to traditional banking systems is restricted.

The growing reluctance of foreign nations to accumulate U.S. assets, combined with rising inflation, mounting debt, and the emergence of alternative financial systems, poses a serious challenge to the dollar's long-term viability. While the greenback remains the world's dominant currency for now, the forces undermining its stability are gaining momentum. If these trends continue, the dollar's future as the undisputed foundation of the global financial system may no longer be assured.

The erosion of a dominant reserve currency is never instantaneous, but history suggests that once confidence begins to wane, the decline can accelerate rapidly. The British pound, once the backbone of global finance, lost its supremacy not in a single moment, but through decades of economic strain, shifting trade patterns, and the rising dominance of the U.S. economy.

Similarly, while the dollar remains entrenched in global markets today, the growing diversification of reserves, the rise of alternative payment networks, and the strategic realignment of major economies indicate that the foundation of dollar hegemony is slowly weakening. If the U.S. continues to rely on debt-fueled growth, weaponize its financial system, and neglect the warning signs of de-dollarization, the global financial order could undergo a transformation that few in Washington are prepared to confront.

5

DE-DOLLARIZATION IN MOTION

The shift away from the U.S. dollar is no longer theoretical; it is actively reshaping global finance. Across multiple continents, nations are restructuring their trade and financial systems to reduce reliance on the dollar. This movement is not led by a single country or institution but by a diverse coalition of governments, central banks, and economic alliances that see reducing dollar dependence as a means of safeguarding financial sovereignty. From China's yuan push to BRICS trade agreements and the rise of digital currencies, these developments suggest a slow but irreversible transformation of the global financial order.

China's Push for Yuan Internationalization

China has emerged as the most determined challenger to the dollar's supremacy. Its de-dollarization strategy is not reactionary but deliberate, long-term, and multi-faceted. While Beijing has promoted the yuan as an alternative reserve currency for years, it has dramatically accelerated its efforts in response to U.S. sanctions on Russia and broader geopolitical tensions.

One of China's most effective tools has been the establishment of bilateral currency swap agreements, allowing trade between China and partner nations to bypass the dollar entirely. Over 30 countries, including Brazil, Argentina, Russia, Pakistan, and several African nations, have signed such agreements with the People's Bank of China (PBOC). These agreements allow businesses and governments to settle transactions directly in yuan, eliminating the need to hold or convert dollars. In 2023, China and Brazil finalized an agreement to conduct all bilateral trade in their own currencies, marking a major milestone in Latin America's shift toward de-dollarization.

China's approach extends beyond financial agreements. The Belt and Road Initiative (BRI), its vast infrastructure project spanning Asia, Africa, and Europe, is designed not only to enhance China's trade influence but also to reduce reliance on the dollar in cross-border transactions. Many of the loans and contracts under BRI are now denominated in yuan rather than dollars, binding recipient countries more closely to the Chinese financial system.

A particularly disruptive move has been China's attempt to dethrone the petrodollar system by persuading major oil-exporting nations to accept yuan for energy sales. For decades, the global oil trade has been conducted almost exclusively in dollars, reinforcing the currency's status as the world's dominant reserve. But in 2022, Saudi Arabia signaled that it was open to pricing oil sales in yuan, particularly in trade with China, its largest buyer. If the world's largest oil exporters begin to accept multiple currencies instead of relying solely on the dollar, it would mark a profound shift in global financial markets.

Further reinforcing the yuan's role in global trade, China has developed an alternative to the SWIFT banking system. The Cross-Border Interbank Payment System (CIPS) was designed to facilitate international yuan transactions without requiring a U.S. intermediary. Although still in its early stages, CIPS usage has grown rapidly, particularly among sanctioned nations like Russia and Iran, which have found themselves cut off from U.S.-dominated financial channels. If this system gains broader international adoption, it could significantly weaken the dollar's role in cross-border payments.

These coordinated moves illustrate how China is not merely advocating for de-dollarization but actively building an alternative system. If China succeeds in creating a parallel global financial structure, it could trigger a more rapid acceleration away from the dollar than many analysts currently anticipate.

The Rise of the BRICS Currency Bloc

While China has taken the lead in internationalizing its currency, it is not alone in its efforts. The BRICS alliance—Brazil, Russia, India, China, and South Africa—has increasingly coordinated economic policies to reduce dependence on the dollar. Once primarily a diplomatic organization, BRICS is now emerging as an economic bloc intent on reshaping the global monetary order.

One of the most significant steps toward de-dollarization within BRICS has been the expansion of non-dollar trade settlements. In

2022, Russia and India began conducting oil trade in rubles and rupees, bypassing the dollar altogether. Similarly, Brazil and China finalized a trade agreement allowing their central banks to directly exchange yuan and reais for cross-border transactions. These moves demonstrate a growing willingness among major economies to experiment with alternative currency arrangements.

The most ambitious BRICS proposal to date is the development of a new reserve currency that could compete with the dollar on a global scale. While still in the planning stages, BRICS nations have openly discussed creating a currency backed by a basket of commodities or a mix of their national currencies. Such a reserve currency would provide an alternative store of value that is less influenced by U.S. monetary policy, reducing the need for countries to hold large dollar reserves.

Russia, facing severe financial sanctions from the West, has become an even more vocal proponent of de-dollarization within BRICS. The Kremlin has aggressively expanded bilateral trade in rubles and yuan, particularly with China and India. Moscow has also been instrumental in pushing for greater cooperation among BRICS nations to establish financial mechanisms that do not rely on Western banks.

In response to these shifts, other regional economic blocs have also begun exploring similar strategies. The Association of Southeast Asian Nations (ASEAN) has initiated discussions on reducing the region's reliance on the dollar by promoting settlements in local currencies. Similarly, the African Union and Latin American trade groups are increasingly exploring ways to conduct trade outside the dollar system.

The rise of BRICS as an economic counterweight to Western financial institutions underscores the reality that de-dollarization is no longer a theoretical discussion—it is actively shaping the policies of some of the world's largest economies. If BRICS successfully implements a viable alternative financial system, it could accelerate the dollar's decline as the world's default currency.

The Role of Digital Currencies and Cryptocurrencies

Beyond geopolitical maneuvering and economic alliances, technological innovation is also playing a critical role in de-dollarization. The rise of Central Bank Digital Currencies (CBDCs) and cryptocurrencies has the potential to bypass traditional dollar-dominated financial channels, further undermining the dollar's role in international transactions.

China has been at the forefront of this shift with the digital yuan, the world's most advanced state-backed digital currency. Unlike traditional payment systems that rely on U.S.-controlled financial infrastructure, the digital yuan is designed to facilitate direct transactions between nations without the need for an intermediary. The People's Bank of China has already conducted cross-border digital yuan transactions with Hong Kong, the United Arab Emirates, and Thailand, demonstrating its potential as a tool for international trade.

Other nations, including Russia, India, and Brazil, are also developing their own digital currencies to reduce their dependence on dollar-based banking systems. In Africa, Nigeria and South Africa have launched pilot programs for CBDCs, reflecting the growing interest in alternative digital financial infrastructure.

Cryptocurrencies, though still a relatively small part of global finance, have also emerged as an unofficial de-dollarization tool. Bitcoin, Ethereum, and stablecoins are increasingly being used for cross-border transactions in countries facing U.S. sanctions, such as Iran, Venezuela, and Russia. While traditional financial institutions dismiss cryptocurrencies as too volatile for large-scale trade, the growing crypto adoption among developing economies suggests they may play a role in a more decentralized global financial system.

The combination of CBDCs, digital payment systems, and cryptocurrencies presents a long-term structural threat to the dollar's dominance. While it remains to be seen how widely these alternatives will be adopted, their mere existence signals that the world is no longer dependent on a single currency for international trade.

6

THE ROAD AHEAD: DE-DOLLARIZATION

The movement toward de-dollarization is no longer a theoretical possibility—it is already underway. As nations increasingly explore alternatives to the U.S. dollar in trade, financial reserves, and investment flows, the fundamental question is no longer whether the dollar will remain dominant, but whether its dominance is sustainable in its current form. The answer lies in understanding the forces at play: the dollar's vulnerabilities, the strategic response of the United States, and the nature of the new financial system that could emerge in the coming decades.

Is the Dollar's Collapse Inevitable?

The idea of the U.S. dollar collapsing entirely is often discussed in alarmist circles, but history suggests that reserve currencies do not disappear overnight. Instead, they gradually lose relevance as economic realities shift. The best historical parallel is the decline of the British pound as the world's dominant reserve currency in the early-to-mid 20th century.

For over a century, the pound sterling was the foundation of global finance, underpinned by Britain's vast colonial empire and its role as the world's leading industrial power. London was the center of international banking, and trade was primarily settled in sterling. However, by the early 20th century, Britain's economic strength had begun to wane. The cost of two world wars left the British economy heavily indebted, and its trade dominance was eroded by the rise of the United States and other emerging powers. The final blow came in 1944 with the Bretton Woods Agreement, which officially established the U.S. dollar as the world's primary reserve currency.

The United States today is not in the same position as post-war Britain, but some parallels are emerging. The U.S. economy remains the largest in the world, but its share of global GDP has declined significantly—from nearly 40 percent in 1960 to around 24 percent today. Meanwhile, the United States has accumulated a national debt exceeding $34 trillion, a level that, relative to GDP, is comparable to some of the debt burdens that historically led to the decline of reserve currencies.

One of the key risks to the dollar's future is confidence. A currency maintains its dominance not just because of economic fundamentals, but because global markets and policymakers believe in its stability. If confidence in the dollar erodes, a feedback loop could emerge, in which nations and investors increasingly diversify into other assets, further weakening the dollar's position. The erosion of confidence in the British pound followed this pattern—a slow loss of trust that eventually made way for a new financial order.

Unlike Britain in the early 20th century, the United States is not facing imminent economic collapse. However, the persistence of high inflation, unsustainable fiscal deficits, and the weaponization of the dollar as a geopolitical tool could accelerate de-dollarization beyond what most policymakers expect. If major economies—such as China, India, and the European Union—continue to develop alternative financial infrastructure, the process could accelerate to a tipping point.

For now, the dollar is unlikely to experience a sudden collapse. However, the real danger lies in a slow erosion of its influence, where other currencies and financial structures gradually take its place, leaving the U.S. economy vulnerable to external constraints that it has not faced in decades.

Can the U.S. Stop De-Dollarization?

The United States has a strategic window to slow or manage the process of de-dollarization, but doing so will require a fundamental shift in policy. The dollar's dominance is not solely a product of market forces; it is also a result of strategic decisions made by the U.S. government and financial institutions. Just as Washington actively built the post-World War II economic order to enshrine the dollar at the center of global finance, it can take steps to reinforce confidence in the greenback and dissuade nations from seeking alternatives.

One of the most effective ways to slow de-dollarization would be to restore confidence in U.S. economic fundamentals. A key reason why central banks and sovereign wealth funds are diversifying away from the dollar is concern over inflation and debt sustainability. If the U.S. government can demonstrate serious commitment to fiscal discipline—either by controlling spending, reforming entitlement programs, or implementing responsible monetary policy—it would reassure investors that the dollar remains a stable store of value.

Another critical factor is trade policy. One of the paradoxes of the U.S. approach to de-dollarization is that protectionist policies—such as tariffs and trade restrictions—have pushed other countries to bypass the dollar in trade settlements. If the United States reverses this trend and strengthens global trade alliances, it could reduce the incentive for nations to create alternative payment systems.

Similarly, the overuse of financial sanctions has been a major driver of de-dollarization. The freezing of Russian central bank reserves in 2022 served as a warning to many countries that dollar assets could become liabilities in a geopolitical crisis. While sanctions are an important tool of U.S. foreign policy, excessive reliance on them could accelerate the push toward alternative financial systems. Washington must strike a balance between maintaining its influence and ensuring that the dollar remains a neutral instrument of trade, rather than a geopolitical weapon.

The United States also needs to consider how digital finance is reshaping global monetary flows. The rise of central bank digital currencies (CBDCs), particularly China's digital yuan, could challenge the dollar's role in international trade settlements. To counter this, the Federal Reserve could take a more active role in developing a digital dollar, ensuring that the U.S. remains at the forefront of financial innovation. Failure to adapt to this shift could accelerate the decline of dollar dominance, as more countries and businesses opt for alternative digital payment systems that bypass traditional U.S.-controlled financial networks.

While the U.S. cannot fully prevent de-dollarization, it can influence the pace and scale of the transition. By addressing the economic vulnerabilities that make alternative currencies attractive, reducing reliance on financial sanctions, and modernizing its financial infrastructure, the United States can maintain the dollar's relevance in a changing world. Strategic diplomacy and economic partnerships will also play a crucial role in reinforcing confidence in the dollar's stability and long-term viability.

A Multipolar Financial System

Even if the United States takes decisive action, the long-term trajectory appears to be toward a multipolar financial system, in which no single currency dominates global trade and investment. This shift is not necessarily a catastrophe for the U.S., but it will require a fundamental rethinking of how the American economy operates.

Historically, the global financial system has been structured around dominant reserve currencies. Before the British pound, the Dutch guilder served as the world's primary trade currency in the 17th and early 18th centuries. However, the transition from one dominant currency to another has always been accompanied by periods of financial instability. If the dollar loses its role as the sole global reserve currency, it could introduce greater volatility in financial markets as global capital flows adjust to a new reality.

A multipolar system would likely involve a basket of major currencies—the dollar, euro, yuan, and possibly digital currencies issued by central banks. The IMF's Special Drawing Rights (SDRs) could also gain a more prominent role as a neutral international reserve asset. While the dollar would still be important, it would no longer enjoy the "exorbitant privilege" of being the undisputed global medium of exchange.

For the United States, this means adjusting to a world in which it can no longer finance deficits as easily as it has in the past. The ability to issue debt without worrying about foreign exchange constraints has been a major advantage of dollar dominance. If global investors diversify their holdings, U.S. borrowing costs could rise, forcing Washington to adopt more responsible fiscal policies.

A multipolar system could also reshape global trade patterns. Regional trade agreements—such as those being developed by BRICS nations, ASEAN, and the European Union—could increasingly settle transactions in local currencies, reducing the need for dollar liquidity. This would make the world economy less reliant on Federal Reserve policy, reducing the influence of U.S. monetary decisions on global markets.

The transition to a multipolar system is already happening, but the speed and nature of this shift remain uncertain. If managed carefully, it could lead to a more balanced and stable financial system.

However, if the transition is disorderly, it could create major disruptions in global markets, particularly for countries that remain heavily dependent on dollar-based trade and finance.

The challenge for the United States is clear: adapt to a changing financial landscape, or risk losing the strategic advantages that have defined its global economic dominance for nearly a century. Clinging to outdated financial hegemony without recalibrating to new economic realities may accelerate the very decline it seeks to avoid. The coming years will test whether the U.S. can embrace a more flexible, cooperative approach—or whether its grip on global finance will continue to erode.

CHAPTER 6

CURRENCY DEPRECIATION'S DOOM LOOP

This chapter exposes the high-stakes reality of a world trapped in a relentless cycle of dollar dependence and economic fragility. It unravels the complex web of forces that compel nations to hoard U.S. dollars, even as this reliance deepens their financial vulnerabilities. The chapter examines the 2022 currency crisis as a stark warning sign of the perils that await economies tethered to the dollar. As the narrative unfolds, it poses a critical question: Could the very currency that nations cling to for stability become a victim of its own dominance? Delving into the geopolitical ramifications, it highlights how dollar dependency shapes global alliances and economic strategies. Finally, it confronts the looming reckoning that such reliance may bring, as mounting debt, inflation, and geopolitical fractures threaten the dollar's position. This chapter challenges readers to consider whether the global financial system is locked in a doom loop from which escape seems increasingly elusive.

1

WHY NATIONS ARE FORCED TO ACCUMULATE DOLLARS

The global economy runs on dollars. From trade settlements to sovereign debt issuance and financial market stability, the U.S. dollar has long been the undisputed medium of exchange and store of value in international finance. Yet, for many nations, this reliance on dollars is more of a necessity than a choice, creating a system of structural dependence that exposes economies to extreme volatility whenever global liquidity conditions tighten. This dependency often results in a recurring cycle—the dollar doom loop—where countries struggling to secure enough dollars to meet their obligations experience financial distress, leading to capital flight, weakening currencies, and deeper economic crises.

The Structural Trap of Dollar Dependency

Most global transactions—whether for oil, industrial goods, or manufactured exports—are priced and settled in U.S. dollars. This reality forces countries to hold large dollar reserves, not only to facilitate trade but also to service external debt and support their own financial systems. As of 2023, approximately 60% of global foreign exchange reserves were held in U.S. dollars, and nearly 50% of all global trade invoices were dollar-denominated, even when neither the buyer nor seller was based in the United States.

This structure means that most economies, particularly emerging markets, must continuously acquire and maintain dollar reserves to avoid disruptions. Countries with high levels of dollar-denominated external debt are particularly vulnerable because they must repay loans in dollars, regardless of fluctuations in their own national currencies. If their local currency weakens against the dollar, the cost of servicing these debts surges, forcing governments and corporations to seek even more dollars—often at a time when access to dollar liquidity is tightening.

The risk is even greater for economies that run persistent trade deficits, meaning they import more than they export. These countries are forced to borrow in dollars to finance the difference, making them dependent on global capital markets. If dollar liquidity tightens — whether due to U.S. monetary policy, a financial shock, or a sudden loss of investor confidence — these nations find themselves in a dollar shortage crisis that can quickly spiral out of control.

The Doom Loop: A Self-Reinforcing Crisis

The cycle typically begins when the Federal Reserve raises interest rates in response to inflationary pressures in the United States. Because U.S. monetary policy affects global liquidity conditions, higher interest rates immediately impact capital flows to emerging markets. Investors, seeking safer and higher-yielding assets, pull funds from riskier economies and redirect them toward U.S. Treasuries and dollar-denominated assets, causing capital flight from developing nations.

As capital outflows accelerate, local currencies depreciate against the dollar, making dollar-denominated debts more expensive to repay. Governments and corporations in emerging markets scramble to secure dollars, either by tapping into their foreign exchange reserves or by raising domestic interest rates to stabilize their currency and attract investors. But higher local interest rates slow economic growth, increasing the risk of a downturn or recession.

For countries that lack sufficient reserves or have high debt levels, this cycle can quickly turn into a full-blown financial crisis. Faced with dwindling foreign exchange reserves, governments may be forced to seek emergency IMF loans, which often come with harsh austerity measures that further depress economic activity and increase social unrest. In extreme cases, central banks are forced to impose capital controls to stop the outflow of dollars, as seen in Argentina, Turkey, and Sri Lanka in recent years.

This doom loop has played out in repeated financial crises across different eras. In the 1980s, the Latin American debt crisis was triggered by rising U.S. interest rates, which made it nearly impossible for countries like Mexico, Brazil, and Argentina to service their dollar-denominated debts. Similarly, the 1997 Asian Financial Crisis erupted when investors lost confidence in Southeast Asian economies, leading to mass capital flight and a collapse of currencies such as the Thai baht, Indonesian rupiah, and South Korean won. More recently, the 2013 taper tantrum saw emerging markets struggle as the Federal Reserve signaled an end to its quantitative easing program, leading to a sharp tightening of global liquidity conditions.

Developed vs. Emerging Economies

While the doom loop primarily affects emerging markets, developed economies are not entirely immune from its effects. The euro, yen, and British pound have all faced episodes of depreciation under dollar strength, particularly in times of financial stress. The Eurozone debt crisis (2010–2012) saw European nations struggle under the weight of dollar funding pressures, leading to soaring bond yields in countries such as Greece, Spain, and Italy.

Even Japan, which has one of the most stable reserve currencies in the world, saw the yen weaken to a 32-year low in 2022 as investors sought higher yields in U.S. assets. The United Kingdom, which faced its worst currency crisis in decades following the controversial 2022 tax cut plans under former Prime Minister Liz Truss, also saw a surge in borrowing costs and capital flight, exposing the vulnerabilities of even advanced economies when investor sentiment shifts toward the dollar.

For developed nations, the consequences of a strong dollar are typically contained within financial markets, whereas for emerging economies, the effects extend into severe economic and political crises. The key difference is that reserve currency economies—such as the Eurozone, Japan, and the UK—have central banks with deep financial tools to absorb shocks. Emerging markets, on the other hand, often lack the monetary and fiscal flexibility to respond effectively, making their crises more acute and difficult to resolve.

The Role of U.S. Monetary Policy in Perpetuating the Doom Loop

The irony of the global financial system is that the U.S. Federal Reserve—whose mandate is to manage domestic inflation and employment—has an outsized influence on global financial stability. When the Fed tightens monetary policy, it is primarily concerned with conditions in the United States. Yet, its actions dictate liquidity conditions for the entire world, disproportionately affecting economies that rely on dollar funding.

This dynamic has led some policymakers in emerging markets to call for a more predictable, globally coordinated approach to monetary policy—one where the Fed takes into account the international consequences of its decisions. However, no such framework currently exists, meaning that each cycle of tightening and loosening in the U.S. creates waves of instability in economies that have little control over their fate.

The recurring nature of this doom loop suggests that it is not simply a byproduct of bad economic management in individual countries, but rather a systemic feature of the global monetary order. As long as the dollar remains the dominant global reserve currency, nations will continue to be trapped in cycles of capital flight, inflationary shocks, and financial crises whenever dollar conditions tighten.

Looking Ahead: Is There a Way Out?

For many nations, the challenge is finding a way to reduce their dependence on the dollar without causing immediate financial instability. Some countries have attempted to build stronger foreign exchange reserves to protect against future dollar shortages, while others have sought alternatives, such as currency swap agreements or regional trade blocs that reduce the need for dollar settlements.

Yet, escaping the doom loop is easier said than done. Most nations cannot avoid borrowing in dollars due to the structure of global finance, and de-dollarization efforts have thus far been incremental rather than transformative. Until a viable alternative emerges—or the U.S. fundamentally reshapes its monetary policy to account for global spillover effects—the global economy will remain subject to the recurring cycles of dollar-driven instability.

2

THE 2022 CURRENCY CRISIS:
A WARNING SIGN?

The global economy has witnessed numerous currency crises over the past several decades, each following a familiar pattern: a strengthening U.S. dollar, rising interest rates, capital flight from emerging markets, and the eventual collapse of weaker currencies.

Yet, the events of 2022 stood apart—not only in scale but in how deeply they affected both developed and emerging economies alike. As the Federal Reserve embarked on its most aggressive rate-hiking cycle in over four decades, the ripple effects were swift and severe. Major currencies plummeted, sovereign debt burdens soared, and entire economies teetered on the brink of default.

The crisis underscored a harsh reality: when the dollar strengthens too much, it can wreak havoc across global financial markets, reinforcing the very doom loop that has destabilized nations time and time again. As capital flees to the safety of the dollar, indebted economies face surging repayment costs, deepening financial distress and fueling broader instability.

The Federal Reserve's Rate Hikes and Global Market Fallout

By early 2022, inflation in the United States had surged to its highest levels since the early 1980s, forcing the Federal Reserve to abandon its loose monetary policy and embark on a rapid tightening cycle. Over the course of the year, the Fed raised interest rates by *425 basis points*, the sharpest increase in decades. The impact was immediate: higher U.S. yields attracted global capital, strengthening the dollar and triggering a wave of capital flight from emerging markets. The sudden shift in monetary policy sent shockwaves through financial markets, exposing structural weaknesses in heavily indebted economies.

The U.S. dollar index (DXY), which measures the dollar's value against a basket of major currencies, surged over 20% between mid-

2021 and late 2022, reaching levels not seen since the early 2000s. This rapid appreciation placed extreme pressure on economies that relied on dollar funding. Currencies across the world, from the euro and yen to the British pound and Brazilian real, experienced steep declines. For nations that had borrowed heavily in dollars, the consequences were devastating. Soaring debt service costs forced governments to either deplete foreign reserves or risk financial crises, deepening economic instability.

Sri Lanka's Sovereign Default – A Case Study in Dollar Dependency

Few nations experienced the effects of the 2022 crisis as acutely as Sri Lanka, which became one of the first sovereign casualties of the dollar's rise. Years of excessive borrowing, coupled with economic mismanagement, left the country highly vulnerable to external shocks. By mid-2022, Sri Lanka had nearly $51 billion in external debt, with more than 50% of it dollar-denominated. As global interest rates rose, the cost of rolling over its debt became prohibitive.

By April 2022, the country had exhausted its foreign exchange reserves, leaving it unable to pay for critical imports such as food, fuel, and medicine. Inflation soared above 70%, and essential goods became scarce. The Sri Lankan rupee collapsed, losing over 80% of its value against the dollar, further exacerbating the crisis. Social unrest erupted, culminating in the storming of the presidential palace in July 2022 and the eventual resignation of President Gotabaya Rajapaksa.

In a desperate attempt to stabilize its economy, Sri Lanka turned to the International Monetary Fund (IMF) for emergency assistance. In early 2023, the IMF approved a $2.9 billion bailout package, but as with past IMF interventions, the aid came with strict conditions. The government was forced to implement austerity measures, including higher taxes, cuts to public spending, and the privatization of state-owned assets. These reforms, while intended to restore financial stability, deepened the economic hardship for millions of Sri Lankans, underscoring the painful trade-offs that accompany IMF rescues.

Turkey's Inflation Crisis and the Erosion of the Lira

While Sri Lanka's crisis was largely driven by a lack of foreign exchange reserves, Turkey's collapse was a textbook case of policy mismanagement colliding with global monetary tightening. Turkey had long relied on low interest rates to fuel economic growth, even in the face of rising inflation. President Recep Tayyip Erdoğan's government resisted raising rates, despite warning signs that its economic policies were unsustainable.

As the Federal Reserve raised rates, capital fled Turkey at an alarming pace. The Turkish lira, which had already been under pressure, plunged to record lows, losing over 40% of its value in 2022 alone. Inflation surged past 85%, wiping out household savings and making basic goods unaffordable for millions. Unlike Sri Lanka, Turkey had ample foreign exchange reserves, but its refusal to implement conventional economic policies worsened the situation.

The Turkish government was forced to intervene by spending billions in foreign reserves to prop up the lira and imposing a series of unconventional monetary measures, including a controversial deposit protection scheme that attempted to shield savers from currency fluctuations. While these short-term interventions helped stabilize the lira temporarily, they did little to address the fundamental issue: a rapidly deteriorating economic environment driven by excessive borrowing and an overreliance on loose monetary policy.

The Eurozone's Unexpected Dollar Problem

Unlike Sri Lanka or Turkey, the Eurozone was not facing a sovereign debt crisis, yet it still found itself caught in the global dollar storm of 2022. The euro, which had long been viewed as a stable alternative to the dollar, experienced its sharpest decline in decades. By mid-2022, the currency had fallen below parity with the dollar for the first time in nearly 20 years. The euro's collapse was fueled by multiple factors: a severe energy crisis sparked by Russia's invasion of Ukraine, weakening economic growth, and the Federal Reserve's aggressive rate hikes.

For European companies that relied on dollar-denominated imports—particularly for energy—the decline in the euro's value dramatically increased costs. Importing liquefied natural gas (LNG), oil, and raw materials became significantly more expensive, worsening inflationary pressures across the continent. The European Central Bank (ECB), which had been hesitant to raise interest rates in previous years, was forced to abandon its accommodative stance and implement its first rate hikes in over a decade.

The Eurozone's struggles in 2022 highlighted a key dynamic in global finance: even economies with strong currencies and deep financial markets are not immune to the effects of a surging dollar. When the world's dominant reserve currency appreciates too rapidly, the consequences reverberate far beyond emerging markets, affecting even the most developed economies. The euro fell to parity with the dollar for the first time in two decades, exacerbating inflationary pressures across the region as the cost of dollar-denominated imports soared. Meanwhile, European central banks were forced to strike a delicate balance between tightening monetary policy to curb inflation and preventing further economic contraction, underscoring the global ripple effects of Fed-driven dollar strength.

The IMF and Global Emergency Assistance

As the dollar continued to strengthen throughout 2022, multiple nations turned to the International Monetary Fund (IMF) and other financial institutions for emergency assistance. In addition to Sri Lanka, countries such as Pakistan, Egypt, and Argentina sought IMF bailouts as they struggled to secure enough foreign reserves to meet their obligations.

The IMF approved a $3 billion bailout package for Egypt, which had faced mounting external debt pressures due to a weakening Egyptian pound. Argentina, which had already received multiple rounds of IMF assistance, was forced to renegotiate its existing debt arrangements, as inflation soared past 100% and the peso collapsed. The strain on these economies highlighted how rising U.S. interest rates and a strong dollar intensified financial vulnerabilities, making external support critical but more complex.

While the IMF's role in stabilizing distressed economies is well-established, its interventions often come with controversial conditions. Many of the bailout packages in 2022 required austerity measures, currency devaluations, and structural reforms that, while necessary for long-term stability, exacerbated short-term economic pain. In Argentina's case, IMF-imposed fiscal tightening led to widespread protests, with many citizens blaming the fund for worsening economic hardship.

Lessons from the 2022 Currency Crisis

The 2022 crisis underscored a fundamental reality of global finance: when the Federal Reserve tightens monetary policy, the effects are felt worldwide, particularly in economies dependent on dollar funding. Whether through capital flight, inflationary pressures, or sovereign defaults, the world's reliance on the dollar exposes nations to financial volatility whenever U.S. monetary conditions shift.

This crisis also showed that the doom loop is no longer confined to emerging markets. While past crises—such as the 1980s Latin American debt crisis and the 1997 Asian Financial Crisis—primarily hit developing economies, 2022 proved that even major currencies like the euro and yen are susceptible to extreme dollar strength.

Going forward, the question is whether nations will reduce their exposure to dollar volatility or remain trapped in a system that leaves them vulnerable to future financial distress. One thing is clear: the 2022 crisis was not an isolated event—it was a preview of the recurring risks embedded in a global economy built on dollar dependency.

3

COULD THE DOLLAR ITSELF BE A FUTURE VICTIM?

For decades, the U.S. dollar has been the foundation of global finance, playing a central role in trade, investment, and sovereign debt markets. Its dominance has been sustained by the sheer scale of U.S. financial markets, the liquidity of U.S. Treasuries, and, above all, the belief that the dollar is the safest and most stable currency in the world.

However, history suggests that no currency maintains its supremacy indefinitely. The forces that have made the dollar indispensable to the global economy may also be laying the groundwork for its vulnerability. If cracks begin to form in investor confidence, the same doom loop that has destabilized countless emerging market currencies could one day ensnare the dollar itself.

A Currency of Privilege—and Growing Risk

The dollar's dominance stems from its role as the world's primary reserve currency. As of 2023, nearly 60% of global foreign exchange reserves were held in dollars, and over 80% of international trade transactions were settled in dollars. U.S. Treasuries have long been considered the safest and most liquid assets in the world, making them the preferred reserve asset for central banks and institutional investors alike.

Yet, the privilege of reserve currency status also comes with obligations. Because the global economy runs on dollars, the U.S. must supply enough liquidity to meet international demand. This has historically been achieved through persistent trade deficits, in which the U.S. imports more than it exports, allowing surplus dollars to circulate abroad. However, if confidence in U.S. debt sustainability begins to wane, the very mechanism that has upheld the dollar's dominance could turn into a liability.

A shifting geopolitical and economic landscape is now putting this privilege under increasing strain. As rising U.S. debt levels fuel concerns over fiscal stability, foreign central banks—particularly in emerging markets—are diversifying their reserves away from the dollar. Meanwhile, alternative financial systems, such as China's Cross-Border Interbank Payment System (CIPS) and Russia's SPFS, are gaining traction, offering nations an escape from dollar dependence. If these trends continue, the ability of the U.S. to finance deficits cheaply and exert influence through monetary policy may erode, accelerating a transition toward a more fragmented global financial order.

The Looming Risk of a U.S. Treasury Sell-Off

At the heart of global dollar liquidity is the U.S. Treasury market, the single most important financial asset underpinning the world economy. Foreign central banks and investors hold over $7.6 trillion in U.S. Treasury securities, viewing them as risk-free assets. However, if investors begin to doubt Washington's ability to manage its rising debt burden, a sell-off of U.S. Treasuries could trigger a destabilizing feedback loop.

The warning signs are already appearing. The U.S. national debt surpassed $34 trillion in early 2024, and the country's fiscal deficit remains on an unsustainable trajectory. Debt servicing costs are rising rapidly, exceeding $659 billion in 2023 and projected to surpass $1 trillion annually by the end of the decade. As the Federal Reserve raises interest rates to combat inflation, the cost of borrowing is becoming a growing burden on the U.S. economy.

Foreign central banks, historically the largest buyers of U.S. debt, are reducing their exposure. China, once the largest foreign holder of Treasuries, has cut its holdings from over $1.3 trillion in 2013 to less than $800 billion by 2023. Japan, the second-largest holder, has also been divesting U.S. bonds to defend the yen from depreciation. If this trend continues, the U.S. Treasury will be forced to offer higher yields to attract buyers, increasing borrowing costs and raising concerns about debt sustainability.

A major sell-off of Treasuries would place the Federal Reserve in a difficult position. If the Fed allows bond yields to rise naturally, borrowing costs across the U.S. economy could surge, slowing growth and triggering financial instability. If the Fed intervenes by buying Treasuries to stabilize markets, it would be forced to expand the money supply—potentially weakening the dollar and fueling inflation. This is precisely the type of doom loop that has caused investor flight in emerging market currencies for decades.

What Happens When Confidence in the Dollar Fades?

For most of modern financial history, the dollar has been viewed as the default safe haven currency. During economic downturns or geopolitical crises, global investors rush to buy dollars, reinforcing its strength. But what happens if the next financial crisis originates in the U.S. itself?

If global confidence in the dollar weakens, the first signs would appear in the Treasury market. A decline in foreign demand for Treasuries would force yields higher, placing greater strain on the U.S. government's ability to finance its deficits. This would spill over into broader financial markets, driving up borrowing costs for corporations and households alike. A weaker dollar would make imports more expensive, worsening inflationary pressures, and leading to capital outflows from U.S. markets.

Unlike emerging markets, which often suffer from currency depreciation due to external shocks, a U.S.-driven dollar crisis would have far greater consequences for the global financial system. The dollar's decline would undermine confidence in global trade settlements, disrupt commodity markets, and destabilize central bank reserve portfolios. In short, a crisis centered around the dollar would not just affect the U.S.—it would shake the foundations of the global monetary order.

History has shown that no currency remains dominant forever. The fall of the British pound was a slow process, shaped by mounting debt and shifting global power dynamics. Today, similar warning signs are emerging for the dollar—though whether its decline will be gradual or sudden remains an open question.

A Gradual Decline or a Sudden Crisis?

The future of the dollar's role in the global economy depends largely on whether these shifts occur gradually or through a sudden loss of confidence. If the transition is slow, the world could move toward a multipolar currency system, where the dollar continues to play a key role but coexists with other reserve currencies such as the euro, yuan, and potentially a BRICS-backed financial alternative.

However, a sudden crisis—perhaps triggered by a major U.S. fiscal crisis, a geopolitical shock, or a rapid loss of investor confidence—could accelerate the process dramatically. In such a scenario, the U.S. would find itself facing many of the same challenges that have plagued emerging markets in past crises: a plunging exchange rate, surging inflation, and policymakers scrambling to restore confidence in the currency.

For now, the dollar remains the dominant force in global finance, but the warning signs are clear. If the U.S. fails to manage its fiscal trajectory while global economic players continue to build alternatives to the dollar, its role as the world's undisputed reserve currency may gradually erode. The question is no longer whether the global financial order will change, but how quickly and how dramatically that change will occur.

4

THE GEOPOLITICS OF A DOLLAR DOOM LOOP

The economic turmoil created by dollar-driven financial crises rarely remains confined to currency markets and debt restructuring programs. When entire economies are destabilized due to the inability to secure dollars, the ripple effects often spill over into politics, geopolitics, and global power dynamics. The currency doom loop is not merely an economic phenomenon—it is also a catalyst for political instability, shifting alliances, and the reordering of global influence.

Currency Crises and Political Instability

History has shown that currency collapses and debt crises often precipitate major political upheavals. The 1997 Asian Financial Crisis led to widespread economic turmoil across Southeast Asia, triggering the resignation of Indonesian President Suharto, who had ruled for more than three decades. In Argentina's 2001 default, a deepening economic crisis led to mass protests, bank runs, and a rapid turnover of five presidents within just a few weeks. More recently, Sri Lanka's 2022 currency collapse, fueled by a shortage of dollars, resulted in violent protests, the storming of the presidential palace, and the forced resignation of the government.

The pattern is clear—when countries cannot obtain the dollars they need to service debt or pay for essential imports, domestic inflation surges, wages collapse, and public unrest follows. In weaker states, financial distress can lead to state failure, while in middle-income economies, it often results in sweeping political transitions that alter foreign policy and economic strategy. If future currency crises—particularly in large, systemically important economies—follow this pattern, the global power landscape could shift dramatically.

Chapter 6: Currency Depreciation's Doom Loop

The U.S. Dollar and the Global Balance of Power

The dominance of the U.S. dollar is not just an economic advantage for the United States—it is also a central pillar of its geopolitical influence. The dollar's role as the world's reserve currency gives Washington the ability to impose devastating financial sanctions, cut adversaries off from global financial networks, and shape the economic policies of allied nations through dollar liquidity control. However, as financial distress linked to dollar dependency becomes more widespread, the United States risks losing part of this leverage.

One of the clearest examples of this shift is Russia's response to Western financial sanctions following its 2022 invasion of Ukraine. When the U.S. and European allies froze over $300 billion in Russian foreign exchange reserves, Moscow responded by accelerating de-dollarization efforts and pushing for alternative payment systems with China, India, and the Middle East. Similarly, China has been working to build financial structures that bypass U.S. influence, such as the Cross-Border Interbank Payment System (CIPS), which provides an alternative to the SWIFT network.

If multiple nations continue to experience repeated cycles of financial distress linked to dollar shortages, they may push for more aggressive monetary realignment efforts, which could weaken the dollar's political and economic hegemony over time.

A Multipolar Financial Order?

As currency crises triggered by the dollar doom loop become more frequent, countries may seek to create a multipolar financial system that is less reliant on any single currency. The BRICS bloc has already discussed creating a shared reserve currency or a system for settling trade in non-dollar assets, though no such system has yet reached widespread adoption.

If the United States continues to use its currency dominance as a foreign policy weapon, and if emerging markets continue to suffer from periodic crises due to Federal Reserve policy shifts, the incentives to diversify away from the dollar will only intensify. Over time, these shifts could gradually reshape the global financial landscape. Regional reserve currencies such as the yuan and the euro may take on a greater role in international trade and capital markets, particularly if an expanded BRICS currency system gains traction. At the same time, gold-backed trade settlements could become more common as nations look for ways to insulate themselves from the volatility of the dollar and the uncertainties of U.S. monetary policy.

The rise of sovereign digital currencies, or CBDCs, could accelerate this transformation by enabling direct cross-border transactions that bypass traditional dollar-based financial channels altogether. While none of these developments are likely to dethrone the dollar overnight, their cumulative impact could weaken its grip on global finance and push the world toward a more multipolar monetary system. This shift would become even more pronounced if major commodity exporters—such as Saudi Arabia, Brazil, and Russia—gradually reduce their reliance on dollar settlements in trade, paving the way for alternative financial networks to emerge.

The Political Risks for the United States

If dollar volatility contributes to economic and political instability abroad, the United States may eventually face a blowback effect. If key strategic allies—such as India, Brazil, and ASEAN economies— face financial turmoil tied to excessive reliance on dollar financing, they may begin to rethink their alignment with U.S. economic institutions.

Additionally, if the Federal Reserve is forced to dramatically adjust monetary policy to stabilize global markets, it may find itself increasingly constrained by external economic pressures. In the worst-case scenario, a sudden shift away from the dollar as the primary global reserve currency could lead to higher borrowing costs for the U.S. government, a weaker ability to finance deficits, and the erosion of U.S. financial supremacy.

While the dollar remains dominant, recurring crises, political instability, and efforts to build alternatives suggest its absolute supremacy may be fading. Whether the shift is gradual or abrupt remains uncertain, but one thing is clear: nations are watching closely and actively seeking to reduce their reliance on dollar-based finance.

5

THE DOLLAR'S INEVITABLE UNRAVELING

The cycle is familiar. The U.S. Federal Reserve tightens monetary policy, the dollar surges, and economies around the world scramble to secure enough liquidity to meet their obligations. It happens time and time again, and with each repetition, the consequences grow more severe. The events of 2022 were not an anomaly but a warning—an unmistakable sign that the global financial system remains dangerously fragile, trapped in a recurring crisis driven by dollar dependency.

For emerging markets, the doom loop of currency depreciation, capital flight, and debt distress has become an unavoidable reality. Sri Lanka's collapse, Turkey's inflation spiral, and Argentina's ongoing financial struggles all highlight the risks faced by economies that borrow in dollars but earn in their own weaker currencies. Even developed economies were not spared in 2022. The euro's decline to parity with the dollar, the yen's record-breaking plunge, and the turmoil in the UK bond market demonstrated that the fallout from excessive dollar strength is no longer confined to fragile emerging markets.

At the heart of this crisis is the structure of the global monetary order itself. Nations are forced to accumulate dollars, often at great cost, to protect their economies from future shocks. Yet, the very system that compels them to do so is what makes them vulnerable. The Federal Reserve sets policy based on domestic U.S. conditions, but its decisions send shockwaves across the world, triggering financial instability in places far beyond Washington's immediate concerns.

The irony is that even the dollar itself is not immune to the forces it unleashes. The very factors that have made the U.S. currency indispensable—its role in trade, its dominance in sovereign debt markets, its perception as the safest store of value—are now exposing its vulnerabilities. The warning signs are clear. Foreign central banks are reducing their reliance on U.S. Treasuries. Countries like China and Russia are building financial systems that operate outside of dollar control. The United States itself is on an unsustainable fiscal trajectory, piling up debt at a rate that may one day shake investor confidence in what was once considered the ultimate risk-free asset.

History has shown that no global currency remains dominant forever. The British pound ruled international finance for over a century before it was displaced. The same forces that undermined sterling—mounting debt, declining economic influence, shifting geopolitical alliances—are beginning to chip away at the dollar's supremacy. The world is not yet ready to abandon the dollar entirely, but the first cracks are beginning to show.

The question is not whether another crisis will come, but how severe it will be when it does. Will it be another wave of emerging market defaults, another eurozone currency crisis, another period of economic turmoil in developing nations? Or will it be something more profound—an event that finally forces the world to reconsider whether the dollar should remain the backbone of global finance? The answers are still uncertain, but one truth is becoming impossible to ignore: the era of unquestioned dollar supremacy is coming under strain, and with each new crisis, the possibility of change grows stronger.

CHAPTER 7

THE RISE OF REGIONAL ECONOMIC BLOCS

As the global financial order fractures, regional economic blocs are emerging as powerful alternatives to the U.S.-led system. This chapter examines how trade agreements increasingly bypass the dollar, accelerating the shift toward a multipolar world. China plays a central role in this transformation, leveraging its economic influence to redefine trade dynamics and expand the yuan's acceptance in global markets. Historical parallels offer insight into past reserve currency transitions, raising the question: Can China's financial system function as a true alternative to the dollar? The final section examines the broader implications for global trade, exploring whether these developments signal the end of the dollar's uncontested dominance or the dawn of a more fragmented financial landscape. As economic alliances reshape the flow of capital and goods, the world stands at a crossroads—one where the future of global commerce may no longer be dictated by a single currency

1

TRADE AGREEMENTS THAT BYPASS THE DOLLAR

For much of the twentieth and early twenty-first centuries, the U.S. dollar was the undisputed backbone of global trade. From oil transactions to manufactured goods, the greenback was the medium of exchange that lubricated international commerce. But as geopolitical tensions rise and economic priorities shift, nations are beginning to reevaluate their dependence on the dollar. The result is an accelerating movement toward regional trade agreements that settle transactions in local currencies, gradually reducing the dollar's role in global finance.

The Rise of Regional Currency Agreements

This transformation is most visible in regional economic blocs, where member countries are increasingly conducting trade without routing through U.S. financial institutions. What began as a pragmatic effort to lower transaction costs and currency risks has now evolved into a deliberate strategy to reduce exposure to U.S. economic policies. Over the past decade, these agreements have quietly gained traction, and today, a significant share of international commerce within some of the world's largest economic blocs is conducted in alternative currencies.

In Southeast Asia, the Association of Southeast Asian Nations (ASEAN) has made substantial progress in reducing dollar reliance. Trade within ASEAN reached $850 billion in 2023, and an increasing portion of it is settled in regional currencies such as the Indonesian rupiah, the Thai baht, and the Malaysian ringgit. While dollar transactions still dominate, the share of intra-ASEAN trade settled in local currencies rose from 10% in 2015 to over 25% in 2023. China's push for yuan-based settlement mechanisms has further accelerated this shift, with the People's Bank of China extending swap lines to facilitate regional transactions outside the dollar system.

A similar pattern is unfolding in Latin America. Brazil and Argentina, two of the region's largest economies, have expanded bilateral trade settlements in their own currencies, cutting out the dollar as an intermediary. Brazil, the largest economy in South America, now settles nearly 30% of its trade with China in yuan, a dramatic shift from just a decade ago when dollar-based transactions accounted for nearly all of it. In 2023, Argentina also announced a new mechanism to pay for Chinese imports in yuan, sidestepping the dollar entirely to conserve foreign exchange reserves.

Africa, a continent historically dependent on dollar transactions, is also moving toward de-dollarization. The African Continental Free Trade Area (AfCFTA), which officially launched in 2021, represents a significant milestone. Covering 54 countries and 1.3 billion people, AfCFTA is designed to boost intra-African trade, which historically hovered at a mere 16% of total African trade due to over-reliance on dollar-settled transactions with external partners. With the introduction of the Pan-African Payment and Settlement System (PAPSS), central banks across the continent now have the infrastructure to settle cross-border payments in local currencies, reducing exposure to exchange rate volatility tied to the dollar.

Cracks in the Petrodollar System

The Middle East, traditionally a stronghold of dollar-denominated transactions due to the petrodollar system, is also seeing cracks in its reliance on the greenback. The Gulf Cooperation Council (GCC) states, led by Saudi Arabia and the United Arab Emirates, are expanding the use of the Chinese yuan in oil and trade deals. Saudi Arabia, the world's largest oil exporter, made headlines in 2023 when it announced that it was open to accepting yuan for oil sales to China, a development that would have been unthinkable just a decade ago. While the petrodollar system remains intact, the growing willingness of major energy exporters to accept alternative currencies is a strong signal that the global monetary order is evolving.

This shift is not just about oil but also about broader financial autonomy. The UAE has expanded financial agreements with China and India to conduct trade settlements in yuan and rupees rather than dollars. Even Iraq and Iran, two historically dollar-dependent economies, have begun experimenting with non-dollar energy transactions. If major oil producers continue diversifying their settlement currencies, the long-standing link between global energy markets and the dollar could weaken, further eroding its dominance.

A Shifting Global Financial Order

The rise of regional trade blocs is not merely about convenience. It is increasingly a response to the risks associated with dollar hegemony—risks that became evident when the U.S. used the dollar as a financial weapon. Sanctions on Russia in the wake of the Ukraine conflict in 2022 provided a stark reminder to nations worldwide: the dollar's dominance gives the United States unparalleled leverage, which it is willing to wield when geopolitical interests demand it. In response, more nations are pursuing financial autonomy, seeking to reduce their reliance on a system that leaves them vulnerable to U.S. economic decisions.

Although the dollar remains dominant in global trade, the evidence is clear: its hold is gradually loosening. The share of global trade conducted in U.S. dollars declined from 70% in 2000 to around 58% in 2023, a significant drop in just two decades. Meanwhile, regional currencies and alternative payment systems are gaining traction, marking the early stages of a shift that could redefine global commerce in the years ahead.

The question now is not whether regional trade blocs will continue to move away from the dollar but how quickly and to what extent this process will accelerate. If current trends persist, the twenty-first century may witness the emergence of a fragmented financial world, where multiple currencies share the stage rather than a single, dominant global reserve currency.

2

CHINA'S PLAYBOOK:
REWRITING GLOBAL TRADE RULES

For decades, the global financial system has been structured around the U.S. dollar, ensuring that most international trade transactions — whether for oil, raw materials, or consumer goods — flowed through American banks and financial institutions. Even as China rose to become the world's second-largest economy, it remained deeply embedded in this dollar-based order. Beijing, despite its growing economic might, was heavily dependent on dollar reserves, as nearly all its international trade was settled in U.S. currency. But the past decade has marked a turning point in global finance. Through deliberate policy shifts, trade realignment, and infrastructure investments, China has been gradually reshaping the financial landscape, expanding the role of the yuan and challenging dollar hegemony in ways that were unthinkable two decades ago.

The shift is not occurring in isolation. A combination of economic pressures, U.S. financial sanctions, and Washington's increasingly confrontational approach toward global trade has accelerated de-dollarization efforts worldwide. Many emerging economies, once bound by necessity to the U.S. financial system, are now exploring alternatives, and China has positioned itself as the key enabler of this transition. While the yuan is still far from replacing the dollar outright, the mechanisms China has built for a parallel financial system are now too large to ignore.

The Belt and Road Initiative: China's Strategic Playbook

A major pillar of China's challenge to the dollar is the Belt and Road Initiative (BRI), an expansive global infrastructure project designed to connect Asia, Africa, and Europe through a vast network of roads, ports, and railways. Since its launch in 2013, Beijing has funneled over $1 trillion into BRI-related projects across more than 150 countries, ranging from highways in Kenya to ports in Sri Lanka and energy grids in Central Asia. But beyond its infrastructure ambitions, the BRI has served another, more strategic function—as a tool for expanding the use of the yuan in global trade and finance.

Initially, most BRI loans were denominated in dollars, reflecting China's own reliance on the greenback for international transactions. However, that dynamic has been shifting. In recent years, Beijing has actively pushed for BRI-related financing to be conducted in yuan rather than dollars. This change has been most evident in Central Asia and parts of Africa, where a growing number of loan agreements and trade settlements are now structured in yuan.

Consider Kazakhstan, a major transit hub for China's BRI infrastructure projects. Ten years ago, nearly all of Kazakhstan's cross-border trade with China was settled in dollars. Today, over 25% of Kazakhstan-China trade is conducted in yuan, a figure that continues to rise. Similar patterns can be seen in Pakistan, where the China-Pakistan Economic Corridor (CPEC)—a $60 billion investment in roads, power plants, and ports—has been increasingly structured around yuan-denominated transactions.

The shift is not limited to infrastructure financing. In BRI-participating nations, local businesses are now opting to trade in yuan rather than convert to dollars first, reducing currency risks and transaction costs. This is particularly visible in African economies, where countries like Nigeria, Egypt, and South Africa have seen a surge in yuan-based transactions for imports and exports. As these nations become more economically linked to China, the shift away from dollar-based trade is likely to deepen.

CIPS: China's Answer to SWIFT

For decades, the global financial system has been anchored by SWIFT, the international messaging network that enables banks to execute cross-border payments. SWIFT's reach is unparalleled, handling more than $150 trillion in transactions annually, with the vast majority flowing through dollar-based correspondent banking networks. But SWIFT is also heavily controlled by Western financial authorities, which means that Washington wields extraordinary power over the system. The United States has weaponized SWIFT in the past—most notably when it cut off Iran from global finance and when it sanctioned Russia following the invasion of Ukraine. These moves alarmed Beijing, reinforcing the need for a parallel system that could shield China and its trade partners from Western financial pressure.

Enter CIPS (Cross-Border Interbank Payment System), Beijing's direct response to SWIFT. While it remains much smaller in scale, CIPS is expanding rapidly, with more than 1,300 financial institutions across over 100 countries now connected to the system. Unlike SWIFT, which only facilitates messaging between banks, CIPS allows for direct settlement of transactions in yuan, eliminating the need for dollars in international trade.

Russia's experience provides a clear example of how CIPS is reshaping global trade flows. When the West froze Russia's foreign reserves and cut its banks off from SWIFT, Moscow dramatically increased its reliance on CIPS. By 2023, more than half of Russia's total trade with China was being settled in yuan, a stunning reversal from just a few years earlier when nearly all transactions were conducted in dollars. This shift was not merely a political necessity — it also demonstrated how China's financial infrastructure was now capable of sustaining large-scale trade outside of the Western financial system.

Beyond Russia, other nations facing U.S. financial pressure — such as Iran and Venezuela — have also turned to CIPS as a lifeline. Meanwhile, BRI partner countries have increasingly begun using CIPS to facilitate trade directly in yuan, reducing their dependence on dollar-based transactions that pass through Western financial institutions.

Beijing's Currency Swaps: Bypassing the Dollar

Another mechanism China has employed to increase yuan adoption is its bilateral currency swap agreements, which allow countries to trade directly in their own currencies without using the dollar as an intermediary. Since the mid-2010s, the People's Bank of China (PBOC) has signed swap agreements with more than 40 central banks worldwide, covering economies as diverse as Argentina, Indonesia, Turkey, and the UAE. The goal is simple: make it easier for countries to conduct trade with China in yuan rather than first converting their local currencies into dollars.

A striking example is Argentina, which, facing a severe dollar shortage in 2023, turned to China for financial relief. Instead of depleting its dwindling dollar reserves to pay for Chinese imports, Argentina activated its swap line with the PBOC, allowing it to settle nearly $1 billion in trade with China using yuan. This move not only alleviated pressure on Argentina's economy but also reinforced the idea that reliance on the dollar is not inevitable.

Similar trends are emerging in the Middle East, where China has persuaded Gulf states to explore oil sales denominated in yuan. Saudi Arabia, long one of the pillars of the petrodollar system, has publicly discussed pricing some of its oil exports to China in yuan. While the bulk of global energy transactions are still settled in dollars, even incremental shifts toward yuan-based oil trade represent a significant erosion of U.S. financial dominance.

A Slow but Steady Transformation

China's efforts to build a parallel financial system are not about replacing the dollar overnight. The U.S. currency remains deeply embedded in global trade and finance, and the yuan still lacks full convertibility and deep liquidity in global markets. But the trend is unmistakable. Through BRI infrastructure investments, alternative payment systems like CIPS, bilateral currency swaps, and energy trade deals, China has created a financial ecosystem that operates increasingly outside the reach of U.S. control.

The question is no longer whether China can build a parallel financial system—it already has. The real question is how quickly it will scale, how many countries will join, and whether the U.S. will adapt to a world where financial hegemony is no longer absolute.

3

THE YUAN'S RISING GLOBAL ROLE

For much of modern history, global trade has revolved around a single dominant currency. The U.S. dollar has not only functioned as the world's primary medium of exchange but has also served as the preferred store of value and reserve asset for central banks, corporations, and financial institutions worldwide. This dominance, however, has been gradually challenged by China's growing economic influence and its deliberate efforts to expand the international role of the yuan.

Despite its rapid economic rise, China has historically lagged in financial globalization. The yuan remained largely a domestic currency, tightly controlled by Beijing, while global trade continued to function in dollars. However, over the past decade, a series of economic, geopolitical, and structural shifts have begun altering this dynamic. What was once a slow, incremental process of yuan internationalization has now accelerated, particularly as a growing number of nations seek alternatives to the dollar amid increasing geopolitical tensions.

The Yuan's Expanding Role in Trade Settlements

One of the clearest indicators of the yuan's growing acceptance is its rising share in global trade settlements. While the dollar still dominates global transactions, the yuan has made significant inroads, particularly in Asia, Latin America, and among BRICS nations.

In 2010, the yuan accounted for less than 1% of global foreign exchange transactions. By 2023, that figure had risen to over 7%, making the yuan the fourth most traded currency worldwide, surpassing the Japanese yen. This is a remarkable shift for a currency that, until recently, had little presence beyond China's borders.

Nowhere is this shift more evident than in China's trade with key partners. In 2023, more than 50% of China's total trade with Russia was settled in yuan, a dramatic increase from less than 3% in

2014. Similar trends are emerging with Brazil, Argentina, and the Gulf states, where yuan-based transactions are growing.

In Southeast Asia, where China is the dominant trading partner, the yuan's adoption has outpaced all other non-dollar currencies. The Association of Southeast Asian Nations (ASEAN) has steadily increased yuan-based trade settlements, reflecting China's deepening economic ties with the region. Countries like Indonesia, Thailand, and Malaysia have actively encouraged local currency settlements with China, reducing their dependence on dollar transactions.

A key factor driving this shift is China's aggressive use of currency swap agreements. Through these arrangements, Beijing provides liquidity in yuan to foreign central banks, allowing them to conduct trade without first acquiring dollars. By 2023, China had signed over 40 bilateral swap agreements, covering economies as diverse as Nigeria, Pakistan, Argentina, and the UAE.

These agreements are not just technical adjustments to global finance. They represent a strategic effort to embed the yuan into global trade networks, making it easier and more cost-effective for countries to trade directly with China.

Russia's Pivot to the Yuan: A Case Study in De-Dollarization

The most striking example of the yuan's rise can be found in Russia's post-sanctions economy. In response to U.S. and European financial restrictions following the 2022 invasion of Ukraine, Russia faced an urgent need to reduce its reliance on the dollar. As Western banks severed ties and the Russian central bank was frozen out of international markets, Moscow dramatically increased its use of the yuan for trade, investments, and even savings.

By mid-2023, over 75% of Russia-China trade was conducted in yuan, a staggering transformation from previous years when the dollar dominated. Russian energy giants Gazprom and Rosneft began pricing a significant portion of their oil and gas exports to China in yuan, bypassing dollar-based financial systems entirely.

The shift wasn't just limited to government and corporate transactions. Russian businesses and individuals, faced with limited access to Western banking, started holding savings in yuan. By the end of 2023, yuan deposits in Russian banks had surged over 800% compared to pre-sanctions levels. The Moscow Stock Exchange even adopted the yuan as the most actively traded foreign currency, reflecting its newfound importance in Russia's financial system.

While Russia's pivot to the yuan was driven by necessity rather than preference, the long-term impact is clear: it provided China with a powerful case study demonstrating that an alternative to dollar-based trade is both viable and scalable.

The Yuan and Energy Trade: Cracks in the Petrodollar

Since the 1970s, the petrodollar system has been a cornerstone of U.S. financial dominance. Under this arrangement, oil-exporting nations — led by Saudi Arabia — have priced and sold oil exclusively in dollars, ensuring a steady global demand for the U.S. currency. However, recent developments suggest that this system is beginning to erode, with the yuan emerging as a potential alternative.

China, now the world's largest importer of crude oil, has been actively pushing energy producers to accept yuan for oil and gas sales. The biggest breakthrough came in December 2022, when Saudi Arabia's Crown Prince Mohammed bin Salman confirmed that Riyadh was open to accepting yuan for Chinese oil purchases. While most Saudi oil exports are still priced in dollars, even the possibility of yuan-based transactions represents a fundamental shift in the energy market. If adopted on a larger scale, such a move could weaken the petrodollar system, reducing global demand for U.S. dollars in energy trade. Additionally, it would expand China's financial influence by increasing the yuan's role in global commodity markets, signaling a broader shift toward a multipolar currency landscape.

Other energy exporters have already moved in this direction. The United Arab Emirates and Iran now conduct a significant portion of their energy sales to China in yuan. Meanwhile, Beijing has established the Shanghai International Energy Exchange (INE), where crude oil futures are priced in yuan rather than dollars, creating an alternative pricing mechanism for global energy markets.

While the dollar remains the dominant currency in global oil transactions, the gradual expansion of yuan-based settlements is chipping away at Washington's grip on the energy trade. If this trend accelerates — especially if Saudi Arabia and other Gulf states deepen their use of yuan — it could mark the beginning of a broader shift away from the petrodollar system, reshaping the foundations of global finance.

Challenges to the Yuan's Global Expansion

Despite these advances, the yuan still faces significant barriers to becoming a fully-fledged global currency. Unlike the dollar, which is freely traded and backed by deep, liquid capital markets, the yuan remains tightly controlled by the Chinese government.

One of the biggest obstacles is capital controls. Beijing maintains strict regulations on currency flows, limiting the ability of foreign investors to freely convert and repatriate yuan holdings. This lack of full convertibility dampens demand for the yuan as a global reserve currency, as financial institutions prefer the stability and openness of dollar-based markets.

There is also the issue of trust and transparency. The U.S. financial system, despite its vulnerabilities, operates under a predictable legal and regulatory framework. China's financial system, by contrast, remains highly opaque, with state intervention playing a major role in markets. For the yuan to truly rival the dollar, Beijing would need to increase transparency, deepen its capital markets, and allow greater financial liberalization—steps that remain politically sensitive for the Chinese leadership.

The Yuan's Rise in a Multi-Currency World

The rise of the yuan represents one of the most profound financial shifts of the 21st century, but it does not signal the immediate end of dollar dominance. Instead, what is emerging is a multi-currency world, where the yuan plays an increasingly significant role in global trade and finance, particularly in Asia, Latin America, and resource-exporting economies.

As more countries adopt yuan-based trade settlements, and as China continues to build alternative financial infrastructure, the long-standing assumption that the dollar will remain the sole pillar of global finance is increasingly being challenged. The key question is whether Beijing will embrace the financial reforms necessary to accelerate yuan adoption, or whether its continued restrictions on capital flows will limit the yuan's full potential as a global reserve currency. One thing is certain—the yuan is no longer just China's currency; it is becoming a key player in the global financial order.

The implications of this shift extend far beyond trade. As central banks diversify their foreign exchange reserves, many are increasing their yuan holdings to hedge against dollar volatility and geopolitical risks. The expansion of China's Cross-Border Interbank Payment System (CIPS) as an alternative to SWIFT, along with growing currency swap agreements, is further embedding the yuan into global finance. While significant barriers remain—such as China's tight capital controls and the lack of full yuan convertibility—the momentum toward a more multipolar financial system is undeniable.

Whether the yuan ultimately rivals the dollar or simply becomes one of several major currencies in a fragmented system, its growing role marks the beginning of a new era in global finance.

4

HOW RESERVE CURRENCIES RISE AND FALL

For centuries, global trade and finance have been shaped by the dominance of a single reserve currency. Today, the U.S. dollar sits at the center of the international monetary system, underpinning cross-border transactions, sovereign reserves, and global investment. But history makes one thing clear: no currency holds this position indefinitely. The Dutch guilder once reigned as the backbone of international commerce before giving way to British sterling.

For more than a century, the pound was the undisputed global currency—until the weight of war, debt, and shifting economic power tilted the scales in favor of the U.S. dollar. Each transition seemed improbable at the time, yet each followed a familiar pattern. The question now is whether the dollar, after decades of dominance, is beginning its own slow descent, with the yuan and other rising currencies positioning themselves as alternatives.

While the dollar remains entrenched, the past offers a valuable roadmap for understanding how reserve currency transitions unfold. These shifts do not happen overnight. They emerge over decades, driven by economic imbalances, geopolitical realignments, and financial instability. The forces at play today—rising U.S. debt, China's growing financial influence, and the steady erosion of trust in the dollar-led system—echo past transitions that reshaped the global economy.

Patterns of Reserve Currency Decline: A Recurring Cycle

The decline of a dominant reserve currency is rarely sudden. It is a slow unraveling, a process that begins quietly before momentum builds, often culminating in an irreversible shift. History shows that reserve currencies follow a cycle. First, the issuing country enjoys economic primacy, providing the world with a stable and liquid currency for trade and investment. Its financial markets attract capital, reinforcing trust in the system. But over time, rising fiscal burdens and growing economic competition begin to strain this dominance. Debt accumulates, deficits widen, and new financial centers emerge, offering alternatives that challenge the existing order. Eventually, confidence weakens, and once the tipping point is reached, the shift accelerates.

This pattern has played out before. The Dutch guilder dominated the 17th and early 18th centuries, powered by the Netherlands' vast trading empire and the financial innovations of the Bank of Amsterdam. But military conflicts, rising debt, and Britain's economic expansion undermined the guilder's supremacy. The British pound took its place, becoming the foundation of global finance for more than a century. Sterling's dominance, in turn, was eroded by the immense costs of two world wars, Britain's economic stagnation, and the ascent of the United States as the world's leading industrial and financial power. By the mid-20th century, the global monetary order had shifted, and the dollar had taken center stage

.

From Sterling to the Dollar: The Last Great Transition

Of all past reserve currency shifts, the most relevant parallel to today's landscape is the decline of the British pound and the rise of the U.S. dollar. For much of the 19th and early 20th centuries, the British economy was the engine of global commerce, and London was the world's financial capital. The pound sterling was the currency of international trade, used to settle transactions across Europe, Asia, and the Americas. Central banks held their reserves in sterling, and British banks extended credit across continents. At its peak, nearly 70% of global foreign exchange reserves were held in pounds.

Yet, as Britain's economic position weakened, so too did confidence in its currency. The enormous costs of World War I, followed by the Great Depression and the economic devastation of World War II, left Britain heavily indebted and struggling to maintain its financial standing. Meanwhile, the United States had emerged as the world's largest economy and primary creditor, with a deep and liquid financial system that attracted global capital. The decisive moment came with the Bretton Woods Agreement in 1944, which formally established the U.S. dollar as the world's reserve currency, backed by gold at a fixed rate of $35 per ounce. The pound, once the pillar of global finance, began its long descent.

Even after Bretton Woods, the transition was not immediate. The pound remained relevant in global finance throughout the 1950s and 1960s, and Britain still held considerable influence. But as trust in British economic stability eroded, countries and investors slowly shifted their reserves into dollars, recognizing the superior strength of the U.S. financial system. What began as a gradual decline eventually reached a point of no return. By the time Britain was forced to devalue the pound in 1967, the process was all but complete.

The question now is whether the dollar is on a similar path. The forces that led to the pound's decline—rising debt, shifting economic power, and the rise of financial alternatives—are increasingly evident today.

The Dollar at a Crossroads

Much like Britain in the early 20th century, the United States now faces a convergence of pressures that threaten to weaken its financial dominance. The national debt has surpassed $34 trillion and continues to climb. Fiscal deficits are expanding at an unsustainable pace. The Federal Reserve's credibility has been tested by prolonged periods of loose monetary policy, followed by aggressive tightening cycles to control inflation. Meanwhile, China's economic rise mirrors the way the United States once eclipsed Britain—offering a growing alternative to the existing monetary order.

The global financial landscape is also evolving in ways that could accelerate a shift. The emergence of alternative trade agreements, central bank digital currencies, and non-dollar payment networks signals a world that is no longer bound exclusively to the dollar. China has been steadily expanding its financial influence through bilateral currency swaps, yuan-denominated trade settlements, and the development of CIPS, an alternative to the U.S.-controlled SWIFT payment system. As in previous reserve currency transitions, these changes start small but gain momentum over time.

Still, the U.S. holds significant advantages that Britain lacked in the early 20th century. The dollar remains the most liquid and widely used currency in the world. U.S. capital markets are deeper and more sophisticated than any of their competitors. The petrodollar system continues to reinforce global demand for the dollar, ensuring its relevance in energy trade. These factors make an immediate collapse of the dollar's status unlikely. But history suggests that reserve currency transitions happen not through sudden displacement but through gradual erosion, as trust in alternatives builds and old structures become increasingly fragile.

A Slow Shift or a Sudden Break?

The decline of a global reserve currency is usually a long, drawn-out process—until it isn't. The shift from sterling to the dollar took decades, but once confidence in the pound weakened past a critical threshold, the transition accelerated. If the dollar follows the same trajectory, the early signs may already be in place. The growing reluctance of foreign governments to hold U.S. debt, the expansion of non-dollar trade settlements, and the development of financial systems outside Washington's control all point to a slow but inevitable rebalancing of global finance.

The real question is whether this transition will be *gradual or abrupt*. A slow decline would see the dollar maintain a key role in a multipolar currency system, sharing global influence with the yuan, the euro, and other emerging currencies. A sudden crisis—perhaps triggered by a major fiscal shock, geopolitical instability, or a loss of investor confidence—could accelerate the process dramatically. If the U.S. fails to manage its debt burden and maintain the credibility of its financial system, what was once an unthinkable shift could happen far sooner than expected.

No currency remains dominant forever. The guilder gave way to the pound. The pound yielded to the dollar. Now, the forces reshaping global finance suggest that the world may be entering another period of transition. The U.S. still commands immense financial power, but the foundations of dollar supremacy are beginning to shift. If history is any guide, future generations may look back at the 21st century as the moment when the world moved from a dollar-centric system to a truly multipolar financial order.

5

CAN CHINA DETHRONE THE DOLLAR?

The rapid expansion of China's financial infrastructure and the yuan's growing role in global trade raise a critical question: Can China's financial system truly function as an alternative to the dollar-dominated global order? While Beijing has taken significant steps to build yuan-based trade networks, alternative payment systems, and bilateral financial arrangements, a full-scale transition away from the dollar faces serious structural and political challenges.

Unlike previous reserve currency transitions, which were largely driven by market forces and shifting economic fundamentals, the rise of China's financial system is highly state-driven. This presents both opportunities and obstacles. On one hand, China's centralized control allows it to rapidly implement financial reforms and expand its influence in targeted markets. On the other, strict capital controls, lack of full currency convertibility, and transparency concerns limit the yuan's ability to function as a truly global currency.

The question is not whether China wants to challenge the dollar—it clearly does—but whether the rest of the world is ready to embrace the yuan on a large enough scale to create a viable alternative financial order.

The Deep Structural Advantage of the U.S. Dollar

To understand the challenges facing China's financial ambitions, it is essential to recognize why the dollar remains dominant. The U.S. dollar is not just a currency; it is deeply embedded into the global financial system. Nearly 60% of global foreign exchange reserves are held in dollars, and over 85% of global trade transactions are still settled using the greenback. Even as China has expanded its trade footprint, most of its own international transactions remain dollar-denominated, reflecting the inertia and stability of the existing system.

A key factor reinforcing the dollar's supremacy is the unparalleled depth and liquidity of U.S. financial markets. The U.S. Treasury market alone is worth over $26 trillion, offering a scale and security that no other financial system can match. In times of crisis, investors flock to U.S. government bonds, strengthening the dollar's status as the world's ultimate safe-haven asset.

China's financial system, by contrast, remains heavily controlled by the state, limiting its ability to attract large-scale international capital. The lack of a fully open capital account means that investors cannot freely move money in and out of China, reducing trust in the yuan as a store of value. Even countries that trade with China in yuan often convert their holdings back into dollars rather than keeping them as reserves.

Capital Controls: The Yuan's Biggest Barrier

One of the biggest challenges to the yuan's rise as a global reserve currency is China's strict capital controls. Unlike the U.S., which allows free movement of capital, China maintains heavy restrictions on currency exchange and capital flows to prevent financial instability.

Foreign investors, for example, face limits on how much money they can take in and out of China, while domestic Chinese companies are subject to government-imposed restrictions on overseas investment. This reduces trust in the yuan as a global financial asset because investors know that their ability to access or liquidate their holdings is ultimately subject to Beijing's political discretion.

The 2015 Chinese stock market crisis serves as a case study in how capital controls undermine confidence in the financial system. That year, a massive selloff in Chinese equities triggered panic capital outflows, prompting Beijing to tighten foreign exchange restrictions and impose new limits on cross-border transactions. The move, while stabilizing China's markets in the short term, damaged long-term investor confidence, reinforcing the perception that the yuan remains a tightly controlled currency rather than a freely tradable global asset.

For China to fully challenge the dollar, it would need to loosen these capital controls, allowing the yuan to flow freely across borders and be held by foreign institutions without government intervention. However, such a move would expose China to potential financial volatility, creating a dilemma for policymakers who prioritize economic stability over financial liberalization.

China's Financial Achilles' Heel

Beyond capital controls, another significant challenge facing China's financial ambitions is the issue of trust and transparency. The U.S. dollar's dominance is not just about economic size, but also about credibility. Investors and central banks trust the rule of law in the U.S., the independence of the Federal Reserve, and the depth of American capital markets.

China, by contrast, operates a highly opaque financial system, where state intervention plays a central role. The Chinese Communist Party (CCP) exerts strong influence over monetary policy, banking regulations, and corporate governance. While this level of control allows for stability in times of crisis, it also creates uncertainty for investors who fear arbitrary policy shifts, government intervention, or political crackdowns.

For example, Beijing's recent crackdown on major tech firms—including Alibaba, Tencent, and Ant Group—sent shockwaves through financial markets, wiping out hundreds of billions of dollars in market value and raising concerns about the unpredictability of China's regulatory environment. Such actions make foreign investors hesitant to commit large-scale capital to China, further limiting the yuan's role as a global financial anchor.

China's Financial System: A Trust Issue?

Another key barrier to the yuan's expansion is geopolitical alignment. While many emerging markets are deepening financial ties with China, most still hesitate to fully replace the dollar with the yuan. Many of China's largest trading partners, including Germany, Japan, and India, remain deeply integrated with the U.S.-led financial order, making a complete shift away from the dollar economically impractical.

Even within the BRICS alliance, member nations are divided on how far they are willing to push de-dollarization. While Russia and China have embraced yuan-based trade, Brazil and India remain more cautious, balancing their economic relationships with both

China and the U.S. This division limits the speed and scale of the yuan's adoption in global finance.

The U.S., meanwhile, actively pressures allies to maintain dollar-based trade, leveraging its control over institutions like the IMF and World Bank to reinforce dollar dominance. Many nations still rely on dollar-denominated financing, making a full transition to yuan-based trade both risky and costly.

Can the Yuan and Dollar Coexist?

While China's financial system is not yet capable of fully replacing the dollar, what is emerging is a multi-currency world, where the yuan plays a much larger role than before. Instead of outright replacing the dollar, Beijing's strategy appears to be focused on creating financial alternatives, allowing countries to diversify their monetary holdings and reduce dependence on U.S.-led institutions. In this scenario, the yuan coexists alongside the dollar, euro, and other major currencies, with different regions adopting different financial frameworks based on their economic interests.

China's Belt and Road Initiative (BRI) and Cross-Border Interbank Payment System (CIPS) will continue expanding, providing financial options outside of U.S. control. Meanwhile, the petrodollar system faces increasing competition from yuan-based energy trade, particularly as China deepens its oil and gas partnerships with the Gulf states.

While Beijing still has significant reforms to undertake, the foundation of an alternative financial order is already in place. The key question is not whether China can build a rival system—it already has—but whether it can earn the trust of global markets and scale its financial infrastructure to truly challenge the dollar.

A Slow and Uncertain Path to Monetary Multipolarity

China's financial system is growing in influence but remains far from a full-fledged alternative to the dollar. Strict capital controls, limited financial transparency, and geopolitical skepticism all present serious obstacles. However, the trajectory is clear—the world is moving toward a more diversified monetary system, where multiple currencies, including the yuan, compete for global influence.

The dollar's absolute dominance may be fading, but its position as the world's primary reserve currency is still firmly intact. Whether China can break through these barriers and establish a fully functional alternative financial order remains one of the most critical questions in global economics today.

A true shift to monetary multipolarity requires more than just economic size—it demands deep, liquid, and trustworthy financial markets capable of absorbing global capital flows without excessive state intervention. While China has taken steps to internationalize the yuan through swap agreements, digital currency initiatives, and expanding trade settlement in its currency, its reluctance to allow free capital movement undermines broader adoption. Global investors remain wary of Beijing's ability to impose sudden policy shifts, as evidenced by crackdowns on major domestic corporations and abrupt regulatory overhauls.

Moreover, trust in a currency is as much about perception as it is about policy. The dollar's dominance has been built on decades of legal predictability, institutional stability, and a robust financial ecosystem supported by deep capital markets. China, by contrast, faces skepticism from many international investors and policymakers, who see its financial system as opaque and its government's monetary decisions as unpredictable. While the yuan will continue to grow in influence, its trajectory will likely be incremental rather than revolutionary—gradually carving out a space in global trade and finance but falling short of replacing the dollar outright.

6

THE NEW TRADE ORDER

The rise of China's financial system and the growing use of the yuan in global trade are not just economic developments; they are fundamental shifts that will reshape international trade dynamics for decades to come. As China expands its economic influence and more nations seek to reduce their reliance on the dollar, the global trading system is slowly transitioning from a unipolar to a multipolar monetary order. This transition brings both opportunities and risks, with profound implications for emerging markets, multinational corporations, financial institutions, and global economic stability.

At the heart of this shift is a deepening fragmentation of the global financial system. While the U.S. dollar still dominates world trade, alternative trade networks, regional economic blocs, and currency diversification strategies are challenging the old order. The question is no longer whether de-dollarization will occur, but how quickly and to what extent it will reshape the trade landscape.

The Decline of Dollar-Based Trade in Emerging Markets

For decades, emerging markets have been forced to conduct trade in dollars, even when their primary trading partners were non-U.S. nations. This dependency on the dollar has long been seen as a double-edged sword. On one hand, it provides access to the world's most stable and liquid financial system. On the other, it exposes countries to currency risks, U.S. monetary policy decisions, and financial sanctions.

This dynamic is now shifting. With the expansion of yuan-based trade agreements, local currency settlements, and alternative financial systems, many emerging markets are actively reducing their exposure to dollar volatility.The India-UAE trade agreement, signed in 2023, is a clear example of this trend. The deal allows for bilateral trade to be settled in Indian rupees and UAE dirhams rather than dollars, reducing foreign exchange costs and minimizing dependency on U.S. financial networks. Similarly, Brazil and Argentina have explored using a common currency for trade, reflecting broader efforts in South America to move away from dollar-based commerce.

In Africa, where China has established deep economic ties through infrastructure projects and commodity trade, yuan-based settlements are increasing. The Nigerian central bank has expanded its yuan reserves, while South African and Egyptian banks have begun conducting more trade settlements in yuan rather than dollars. These shifts, while still incremental, weaken the dollar's hold over global trade and investment flows.

One major consequence of this shift is reduced vulnerability to U.S. interest rate hikes and monetary policy changes. Historically, when the Federal Reserve raises interest rates, emerging markets suffer capital outflows, currency depreciation, and rising debt burdens. A more diversified currency landscape means that countries will be less exposed to the ripple effects of U.S. economic policies, allowing for greater financial independence.

China's Trade and Alternative Payment Systems

China is not only increasing yuan-based trade; it is actively restructuring trade networks to support a non-dollar-based system. Through initiatives like the Belt and Road Initiative (BRI) and the Regional Comprehensive Economic Partnership (RCEP), China is creating a network of trading partners that can function outside the traditional U.S.-led financial system.

The BRI, now spanning over 150 countries, has already facilitated the expansion of yuan-based transactions across Asia, Africa, and parts of Europe. In Central Asia, where China has become the dominant economic player, over 25% of trade is now conducted in yuan—a figure that was virtually zero a decade ago. Similarly, the China-Pakistan Economic Corridor (CPEC) has led to a growing share of Pakistan's imports being settled in yuan rather than dollars.

Meanwhile, China's Cross-Border Interbank Payment System (CIPS) is expanding as an alternative to SWIFT, allowing countries to process transactions without relying on U.S.-controlled payment networks. By 2023, CIPS had more than 1,300 financial institutions across 103 countries, with usage growing rapidly in sanctioned economies like Russia and Iran.

For multinational corporations, these developments mean new strategic considerations in supply chain financing and international trade settlements. Companies that operate in China and other emerging markets will increasingly have to weigh the benefits of conducting trade in yuan versus the security of using dollar-based systems. This dual-track system—one dominated by the dollar and another driven by alternative currencies—could reshape global supply chains and lead to new financial alliances based on currency preferences.

Can the World Function Without the Dollar?

Despite these shifts, the dollar remains the backbone of global finance, and replacing it entirely would require a fundamental restructuring of the global economy. The reality is that most central banks, multinational corporations, and institutional investors still overwhelmingly prefer dollar-based transactions due to its liquidity, stability, and trust in U.S. financial markets. For now, the world is not moving toward a single alternative currency, but rather a more diversified system, where the yuan, euro, and other regional currencies play a greater role in international trade.

However, there are two key scenarios that could accelerate the shift away from dollar dominance. The *first* is geopolitical instability and financial sanctions. As the U.S. increasingly uses its financial system as a tool of foreign policy, more countries may seek protection from potential sanctions by reducing their reliance on dollar-based transactions. Russia's rapid transition to yuan-based trade after being cut off from SWIFT serves as a warning sign for other nations that wish to avoid economic vulnerabilities tied to U.S. policy decisions.

The *second* scenario is the weakening of U.S. financial stability. If fiscal deficits, rising debt burdens, and inflationary pressures erode confidence in U.S. monetary policy, countries may accelerate their diversification into alternative currencies and assets. While this is not an immediate risk, history suggests that currency dominance is ultimately tied to economic strength and geopolitical stability— factors that could shift in the coming decades. Central banks are already boosting gold reserves and forging bilateral trade deals in non-dollar currencies, signaling that a shift toward a more multipolar currency system could accelerate if these trends strengthen.

A Fragmenting Global Trade System

The rise of alternative trade systems and currency settlements is one of the most significant financial transformations of the 21st century. While the dollar remains dominant, it is no longer unchallenged. The emergence of regional trade blocs, bilateral currency agreements, and non-dollar payment networks signals a shift toward a more fragmented monetary order, where multiple financial centers compete rather than a single currency dictating global trade.

For emerging markets, this shift offers greater financial sovereignty, reducing exposure to U.S. monetary policy shocks. For multinational corporations, it means adapting to a world where currency considerations are no longer one-size-fits-all.

The implications for global trade are profound. If current trends persist, the next decade could see a transformation in how nations conduct business, settle transactions, and store financial reserves. Whether this results in a cohesive multi-currency system or a fractured economy remains to be seen. What is clear, however, is that the old order is fading, and a new era of trade and finance is taking shape.

The transition from dollar dominance will not be immediate or linear. Economic crises may temporarily reinforce the dollar's safe-haven status, while geopolitical events could accelerate the use of regional currencies. Much will depend on how the U.S. responds — whether it adapts to the changing system or resists, driving more nations toward alternatives. A cooperative approach could help sustain the dollar's influence, while economic pressure and sanctions may only weaken its long-term role.

Even if the dollar remains central, its monopoly is fading. The rise of alternative payment systems, regional trade settlements, and digital currencies suggests a more competitive financial future. Policymakers, businesses, and investors must recognize this shift and navigate an evolving system where financial power is increasingly decentralized.

PART IV

THE U.S. AT A CROSSROADS
The Fragile Future of Dollar Hegemony

"If you do not change direction,
you may end up where you are heading."
— Lao Tzu

The era of unchallenged dollar dominance is fading. As global financial shifts accelerate, the U.S. faces mounting pressure to adapt or risk losing its economic supremacy. Part IV examines the forces reshaping the international monetary order, from the hidden vulnerabilities behind the dollar's short-term surges to the broader structural decline of U.S. financial influence. Through three pivotal chapters, this section explores the gradual erosion of dollar hegemony, the rise of competing financial systems, and the critical choices that will determine whether the U.S. leads in the new multipolar era or falls behind.

CHAPTER 8

THE DOLLAR SURGE: A FRAGILE STRENGTH

The dollar's dominance is often seen as a sign of U.S. economic resilience, but what if its strength is an illusion? This chapter examines the paradox of a surging dollar—how investors rush to it in times of crisis, even as its long-term stability weakens. It explores why global uncertainty fuels dollar demand, how a stronger dollar undercuts U.S. exports and corporate earnings, and the ripple effects on emerging markets drowning in dollar-denominated debt. As history has shown, rapid appreciation can precede an equally dramatic collapse. Could the dollar's recent surge be a prelude to its own decline? The final section grapples with the larger question: How much time remains before the world starts to move beyond the dollar?

1

THE PARADOX OF DOLLAR STRENGTH

Throughout history, financial crises have often forced investors to reassess the stability of currencies and financial systems. But in almost every major upheaval, one currency has repeatedly defied expectations: the U.S. dollar. Whether it was the 2008 financial meltdown, the pandemic-driven turmoil of 2020, or the inflation shock of 2022, the dollar has surged in value when global markets were at their most fragile. The conventional wisdom holds that this pattern is a testament to the dollar's resilience—a confirmation of its status as the ultimate safe-haven asset. Yet, beneath the surface, this recurring cycle is not a sign of lasting strength. It is a distortion—one that masks deeper vulnerabilities within the global financial system and accelerates the very forces working against the dollar's long-term dominance.

The 2022 Crisis: A Turning Point for Dollar Dependence?

The mechanics behind crisis-driven dollar surges are well understood. When global financial uncertainty spikes, investors instinctively seek refuge in assets that are liquid, universally trusted, and perceived as safe. U.S. Treasuries, backed by the full faith and credit of the U.S. government, fit that description better than any other financial instrument in the world. The unmatched depth of the U.S. Treasury market ensures that, in moments of distress, global capital floods into dollars, pushing up their value.

But 2022 was different. The dollar's surge that year was not simply a reflexive flight to safety; it was fueled by one of the most aggressive monetary tightening cycles in modern history. As the Federal Reserve moved to tame inflation, the U.S. Dollar Index (DXY)—which measures the dollar against a basket of major currencies—soared over 20%, reaching its highest level in two decades. Unlike past crises, where dollar strength reflected economic confidence, the 2022 surge exposed systemic vulnerabilities in global financial markets.

The impact was immediate. The Japanese yen collapsed to levels unseen since 1990, forcing the Bank of Japan to intervene in foreign exchange markets for the first time in nearly 25 years. The euro, once seen as the dollar's primary competitor, fell below parity—an extraordinary reversal for a currency that had long positioned itself as a stable counterweight to U.S. monetary dominance. But it was emerging markets that suffered the worst consequences.

More than $13 trillion in emerging-market debt was denominated in U.S. dollars, meaning that every uptick in the dollar's value made debt servicing more expensive for nations already struggling with inflation and depleted reserves. Sri Lanka defaulted on its external obligations for the first time since independence. Argentina, long accustomed to financial crises, saw its peso collapse, forcing inflation beyond 100%—a level that turned daily life into a struggle for survival. Egypt and Pakistan found themselves scrambling for increasingly expensive dollars to pay for essential imports, reinforcing a cycle of economic distress.

Yet, this time, the response was different. Instead of merely enduring the pressure of another dollar-driven crisis, governments, central banks, and financial institutions began taking proactive steps to reduce their exposure to the greenback. The 2022 crisis did not just trigger short-term volatility; it accelerated a global rethink of dollar dependence.

Beyond Crisis: The Search for Alternatives Gains Momentum

Unlike past cycles, where the dollar's dominance was reinforced in the aftermath of crises, the 2022 dollar surge led to a renewed sense of urgency in de-dollarization efforts. Central banks, particularly in Asia and the Middle East, responded by diversifying their reserves at an unprecedented pace.

The share of global reserves held in dollars had already been in steady decline, falling from 71% in 1999 to 58% by 2022, but the events of that year added fuel to the shift. China, long the most vocal advocate of de-dollarization, doubled down on its push to settle trade agreements in yuan, particularly with energy-exporting nations like Russia and Saudi Arabia. India introduced a rupee-based international trade settlement mechanism, allowing foreign partners to bypass the dollar for select transactions. Even European policymakers, historically aligned with the U.S. financial system, began exploring alternative payment structures to reduce reliance on dollar-based transactions.

A striking consequence of the 2022 crisis was the record surge in gold purchases by central banks. Facing heightened exchange-rate volatility, nations from Turkey to Brazil ramped up gold reserves as a hedge against dollar fluctuations. Unlike previous cycles, where central banks increased their holdings of U.S. Treasuries in response to uncertainty, this time, they actively sought alternatives.

The Fragility of the Dollar's Strength

The paradox is clear. The dollar's ability to rise above all others during financial crises has historically been its greatest strength. But in an era where global finance is becoming increasingly multipolar, that same strength is becoming a liability. Each time the dollar surges, it triggers economic distress in nations heavily reliant on dollar funding, forcing them to explore alternative financial arrangements. What was once an abstract discussion about reducing dependence on the U.S. financial system has, for many economies, become an existential necessity.

This is what separates today's world from previous decades. In the past, when crises strengthened the dollar, there were few viable alternatives. But as financial technology, geopolitical alliances, and trade structures evolve, each new crisis provides fresh momentum to the search for alternatives. What was once a system of necessity — where nations had little choice but to rely on the dollar — has now become a system of preference, and that preference is steadily eroding as viable alternatives emerge.

While the dollar remains the world's dominant currency, the 2022 crisis marked a turning point. Instead of reinforcing trust in the system, it reinforced the need to hedge against it. The crisis didn't just expose vulnerabilities in emerging markets; it exposed vulnerabilities in the very structure of a global economy dependent on a single currency. Each new shock now accelerates a gradual but unmistakable shift toward a more fragmented financial order.

How Long Can the Cycle Continue?

Every crisis reaffirms the dollar's role as the dominant global currency—but for how much longer? Each dollar surge extracts a cost from the global economy, forcing governments, financial institutions, and multinational corporations to reconsider their dependence on the greenback.

The question is no longer whether the next crisis will trigger another dollar spike—it almost certainly will. The real question is whether the world's response to that surge will push it closer to a breaking point. In previous crises, dollar dominance was reinforced because there were no serious alternatives. But today, as we explore in the next section, the very mechanisms of global finance are shifting. The world may not be on the brink of abandoning the dollar, but it is no longer unquestioningly bound to it.

2

WHY INVESTORS RUSH TO THE DOLLAR

There is an old saying in financial markets: when the world is in crisis, the safest place to be is in U.S. dollars. Time and again, when uncertainty grips the global economy—whether through recession, geopolitical turmoil, or financial meltdowns—investors reflexively turn to the dollar. This behavior has been so deeply ingrained that it often goes unquestioned, treated as an immutable law of global finance. But while this instinct has repeatedly reinforced the dollar's dominance, there is growing evidence that the mechanisms behind it may be weakening. Each wave of crisis-driven dollar appreciation increases global dependence on a single currency—raising the question of how much longer this cycle can continue before cracks emerge.

The Shrinking Margin of Safety in U.S. Treasuries

At the heart of the dollar's safe-haven appeal is the market for U.S. Treasury securities. No other asset offers the same combination of liquidity, perceived safety, and depth. In times of crisis, global investors—whether foreign central banks, hedge funds, or multinational corporations—turn to Treasuries because they can be bought and sold instantly. During the 2008 financial crisis, U.S. bond yields collapsed as investors scrambled for safety, despite the fact that the crisis itself had originated in American financial markets. The same pattern unfolded in 2020 during the COVID-19 pandemic and again in 2022 as the Federal Reserve's aggressive interest rate hikes pushed the U.S. Dollar Index (DXY) to a two-decade high.

Yet beneath the surface, warning signs are emerging. The U.S. national debt has surged past $34 trillion, and Washington is issuing Treasuries at an unprecedented rate to finance growing deficits. Foreign central banks—historically among the largest buyers of U.S. debt—are scaling back their holdings. China has reduced its exposure to Treasuries by over $500 billion in the last decade, and Japan, the second-largest foreign holder, has been offloading U.S. bonds to defend the yen. If confidence in the sustainability of U.S. debt erodes, the traditional reflex of seeking safety in Treasuries could weaken, forcing the Federal Reserve into increasingly interventionist policies to maintain market stability.

Global Trade Still Tied to the Dollar—For Now

Beyond financial markets, the dollar retains its dominance in global trade, reinforcing its status as the world's reserve currency. As of 2023, the dollar accounted for 88% of global foreign exchange transactions, underscoring its unparalleled role in international commerce. Commodities—particularly oil, gas, and industrial metals—are overwhelmingly priced in dollars, compelling nations to maintain substantial dollar reserves. Even as some governments explore alternative currencies, the sheer inertia of the system keeps the dollar firmly entrenched.

But there are signs of erosion. Saudi Arabia, long a cornerstone of the petrodollar system, has publicly stated that it is open to settling oil trades in currencies other than the dollar—an unthinkable prospect just a few years ago. Russia, in response to Western sanctions, has redirected much of its trade toward China, settling transactions in yuan and rupees instead of dollars. Even Brazil and Argentina have explored bypassing the dollar in regional trade agreements, signaling a broader shift. While these changes are incremental, they point to a slow-moving yet fundamental transformation in global trade dynamics.

The Dollar Debt Trap: A Crisis in the Making

One of the greatest reinforcements of the dollar's global role has been its centrality in sovereign and corporate debt markets. Over $13 trillion in emerging-market debt is denominated in dollars, making it the lifeblood of global credit markets. When the Federal Reserve tightens monetary policy—as it did aggressively in 2022—borrowing costs surge, forcing nations to secure additional dollars just to service existing debt. This creates a dangerous feedback loop: a rising dollar increases debt burdens, which then fuels greater demand for dollars, further strengthening the currency at the expense of fragile economies.

This pattern was evident in Sri Lanka, Argentina, and Turkey in 2022, where mounting dollar-denominated debts triggered currency collapses and inflationary spirals. Even major economies struggled— India's rupee fell to record lows, while Pakistan and Egypt faced severe dollar shortages that led to import restrictions and economic instability. The lesson from these crises is clear: while the dollar remains the world's go-to currency in moments of panic, each surge in its value amplifies the risks for countries heavily reliant on it, reinforcing the long-term incentive to build alternative financial structures.

The Unraveling of a Financial Paradox

For decades, the dollar has served as both a shield and a weapon—a stabilizing force in global markets while simultaneously increasing the world's vulnerability to its movements. Yet the very factors that make it indispensable in times of crisis are also pushing nations to seek ways to reduce their reliance on it. Central banks, wary of the risks of overexposure to the dollar, have steadily shifted their reserves away from the greenback, increasing their holdings of gold and alternative currencies. The share of global reserves held in dollars, which once stood at 71% in 1999, has now declined to 58% as of 2022.

The question is no longer whether the dollar will continue to be the world's safe haven in the next crisis—it almost certainly will. The real question is whether one of these crises will be the last, the moment when enough nations decide that continued dependence on the dollar is a risk they can no longer afford. If that moment comes, the flight to the dollar that has defined global finance for decades may not just weaken—it may unravel entirely.

3

WHY A STRONG DOLLAR HURTS AMERICA

For years, a rising dollar has been hailed as a symbol of American economic strength. Political leaders, financial analysts, and even the average citizen have long equated a stronger dollar with a more powerful United States. On the surface, this logic appears sound. A surging greenback reflects confidence in the U.S. economy, attracts capital inflows, and keeps borrowing costs low. But beneath this outward strength lies a contradiction—one that becomes more pronounced each time the dollar enters an extended period of appreciation. A stronger dollar, far from being an unqualified economic benefit, carries profound consequences for American businesses, trade competitiveness, and even the government's long-term fiscal sustainability.

The very forces that make the dollar a magnet for global capital in times of crisis also make it an obstacle to growth for the U.S. economy. While the currency's dominance benefits financial markets and provides unmatched liquidity, it also undermines the competitiveness of American exports, widens trade deficits, erodes corporate profits, and intensifies fiscal pressures. At a time when globalization is shifting supply chains and foreign economies are diversifying away from dollar-based trade, the costs of dollar overvaluation are becoming harder to ignore.

The Export Squeeze: Why U.S. Goods Become Unaffordable

One of the most immediate and visible effects of a strong dollar is its impact on U.S. exports. When the dollar appreciates against other currencies, American-made goods and services become more expensive for foreign buyers. This, in turn, reduces demand for U.S. products abroad, making it harder for domestic manufacturers, agricultural producers, and tech firms to compete on the global stage. The effects of this dynamic were on full display in 2022, when the dollar's surge sent shockwaves through the export sector. The manufacturing industry, a key pillar of the U.S. economy, felt the brunt of this shift. Major American exporters such as Boeing and Caterpillar saw overseas demand weaken, as foreign buyers opted for cheaper alternatives from European or Asian competitors. The agriculture sector faced similar challenges, with American farmers struggling to sell soybeans, corn, and wheat in global markets where currencies such as the euro and yuan had depreciated, making U.S. agricultural exports comparatively expensive.

Even industries that rely on intangible exports—such as technology and entertainment—have suffered under dollar strength. Apple, whose iPhones and MacBooks are sold in nearly every major economy, reported that foreign exchange fluctuations wiped out $5 billion in revenue in a single quarter in 2022. Other multinational giants, from Microsoft to McDonald's, have cited the strong dollar as a key headwind to their international earnings. By some estimates, the top 50 U.S. multinational corporations derive more than 40% of their total revenue from overseas markets, making them highly sensitive to dollar appreciation.

The Widening Trade Deficit: A Hidden Economic Drag

A persistently strong dollar also exacerbates one of the most entrenched structural issues in the U.S. economy: the trade deficit. For decades, the United States has imported more than it exports, running a trade deficit that has widened considerably during periods of dollar strength. The logic is straightforward—when the dollar is strong, it becomes cheaper for American consumers and businesses to purchase foreign goods, while making U.S. exports less attractive abroad.

This imbalance was particularly evident in 2022, when the U.S. trade deficit ballooned to a record $948 billion, driven in large part by a soaring dollar that made imports more affordable relative to domestic production. The trade deficit with China alone exceeded $400 billion, a reflection of the structural forces that have made the U.S. increasingly reliant on foreign manufacturing.

The long-term implications of a widening trade deficit extend beyond simple numbers. A persistent deficit means that more dollars are flowing out of the U.S. economy to pay for imported goods and services than are coming in through exports. Over time, this weakens domestic production capacity, discourages investment in American manufacturing, and further entrenches the reliance on offshore supply chains.

A strong dollar, in effect, fuels further offshoring by making it more cost-effective for U.S. companies to shift production overseas rather than compete with cheaper imports at home. As this cycle continues, the U.S. risks losing critical industries, increasing its vulnerability to global supply chain disruptions and eroding long-term economic resilience.

Corporate America's Profit Squeeze

For multinational corporations, currency fluctuations can make or break profitability. While a weaker dollar often provides a tailwind — boosting earnings as overseas revenue translates into more dollars — a stronger dollar does precisely the opposite. In 2022, the currency's appreciation wiped out billions in corporate profits across industries ranging from technology to consumer goods. As the dollar remains volatile, companies must navigate an increasingly uncertain currency environment, hedging their exposure to mitigate further financial losses.

Microsoft, a company whose cloud services and software products are used in virtually every economy, saw more than $6 billion in lost revenue due to unfavorable exchange rates that year. Similarly, Procter & Gamble, which operates in over 180 countries, estimated that currency fluctuations cost it $3.3 billion in lost earnings in the same period. These figures are not anomalies — they are part of a broader pattern in which a rising dollar translates into shrinking profit margins for U.S. corporations with significant foreign exposure. For businesses with extensive global operations, managing currency risk has become as critical as supply chain management or market expansion.

The impact is not limited to corporate earnings; it also ripples through stock markets. When a strong dollar weakens revenue growth, investors react by selling off shares in multinational firms, dragging down major stock indices such as the S&P 500. This cycle was evident in 2022, when some of the largest U.S. companies issued downward revisions to their earnings forecasts due to currency-related losses, triggering market corrections. As exchange rate pressures persist, market volatility could intensify, forcing investors to reassess their strategies in an increasingly unpredictable financial landscape.

The Strong Dollar Paradox: A Growing Liability

Perhaps the most overlooked consequence of dollar strength is its impact on the U.S. government's debt obligations. At first glance, a strong dollar appears to be beneficial for debt sustainability—after all, it keeps borrowing costs lower by maintaining demand for U.S. Treasuries. However, this advantage is counterbalanced by the sheer size of America's fiscal deficit and the growing burden of servicing its debt in an environment of rising interest rates.

As of 2023, the U.S. national debt had surpassed $33 trillion, with interest payments alone projected to exceed $1 trillion annually within the next decade. While a strong dollar keeps foreign demand for U.S. bonds high, it also creates a conundrum: to sustain demand, the Federal Reserve must maintain tight monetary conditions, which in turn raises the cost of borrowing for the U.S. government itself.

This feedback loop—where the very policies that prop up the dollar also make debt servicing more expensive—has put policymakers in an increasingly precarious position. Rising borrowing costs mean that a larger share of the federal budget must be allocated to debt interest payments, crowding out spending on infrastructure, education, and defense. The stronger the dollar, the harder it becomes to manage the long-term sustainability of the U.S. fiscal position.

The Illusion of Strength

For all the benefits that come with a dominant currency, the costs of an overvalued dollar are becoming harder to ignore. From shrinking exports and widening trade deficits to corporate earnings pressure and rising debt burdens, the effects of persistent dollar strength pose long-term challenges that extend beyond immediate market fluctuations.

Beyond these economic strains, an overvalued dollar also exacerbates global financial instability. Emerging markets, which rely heavily on dollar-denominated debt, face mounting repayment pressures as the greenback strengthens. This dynamic has triggered multiple financial crises in the past, from the Latin American debt crisis of the 1980s to currency collapses in Asia and beyond. As the dollar continues to act as both a stabilizer and a disruptor, the risk of another crisis fueled by dollar volatility remains ever-present.

Each crisis-driven surge in the dollar may create temporary stability, but it also accelerates the structural imbalances that make future crises more likely. If the pattern continues—where each successive surge in the dollar weakens the very foundations of the U.S. economy—then the so-called strength of the greenback may turn out to be an illusion, a temporary phenomenon masking the growing vulnerabilities beneath.

Financial markets often mistake dollar strength for U.S. economic resilience, but this assumption ignores the long-term consequences. A persistently strong dollar discourages domestic manufacturing, fuels asset bubbles, and strains global liquidity— forcing central banks worldwide to react. As foreign governments and institutions seek to reduce their dependence on the dollar, the global financial system may become more fragmented, further challenging the stability that dollar dominance once ensured.

At some point, the U.S. will have to confront an uncomfortable reality: an economy that relies too heavily on a perpetually strong dollar is one that risks undermining its own future. The next section explores whether this cycle can continue indefinitely—or if the forces accumulating against the dollar's dominance will eventually bring about its reckoning.

4

WILL A DOLLAR SURGE LEAD TO A CRASH?

For decades, the U.S. dollar has defied conventional expectations. Time and again, as the global economy has faced crises, the dollar has surged, reaffirming its position as the world's dominant currency. From the financial meltdown of 2008 to the pandemic-driven turmoil of 2020 and the inflation shock of 2022, each period of uncertainty has sent investors rushing into the relative safety of U.S. assets, driving up demand for the greenback. Yet, for all its resilience, the question lingers: could one of these surges be the precursor to an eventual collapse?

The notion of a dollar crash seems almost unthinkable, particularly given the currency's entrenched role in global trade and finance. But history is littered with examples of dominant monetary systems that ultimately gave way to new financial orders. The British pound, once the undisputed global reserve currency, saw its influence wane over the course of the 20th century. The same fate befell the Dutch guilder before it. The assumption that the dollar is somehow immune to such a decline may be more a matter of habit than inevitability.

A currency does not collapse overnight. It erodes over time, as structural weaknesses compound and confidence slowly gives way to alternatives. And while the dollar's immediate trajectory remains one of strength, the very factors that propel it upward during crises may be the same ones that accelerate its eventual decline.

The Fragile Foundation Beneath the Dollar's Strength

To understand why the dollar could face an unexpected reversal, it is necessary to examine what drives its surges in the first place. The primary mechanism is the flight to safety—when investors fear financial instability, they seek the security of U.S. Treasuries and dollar-denominated assets. This phenomenon has been particularly pronounced in the past decade, with crises prompting unprecedented capital inflows into the United States.

The trouble, however, is that these surges are not rooted in fundamental economic strength but rather in the perceived weakness of alternatives. The euro, for example, has struggled with persistent sovereign debt crises, while the Japanese yen has been weighed down by decades of stagnation and ultra-loose monetary policy. Emerging market currencies, for all their potential, remain vulnerable to capital flight whenever economic uncertainty spikes. The dollar, by default, becomes the safe haven—not because it is flawless, but because no viable competitor has yet emerged to replace it.

But what happens when the assumptions underpinning this system begin to crack? The Federal Reserve's aggressive tightening in 2022 and 2023 exposed a key vulnerability: when U.S. interest rates rise, the costs of servicing dollar-denominated debt globally skyrocket. This creates a domino effect—foreign borrowers must scramble for dollars, central banks must defend their currencies, and liquidity tightens across global markets. As the strain builds, faith in the system weakens, and the very institutions that have long depended on dollar stability begin to question its sustainability.

A Shifting Global Order: The Rise of Alternatives

A key difference between past dollar surges and the present environment is the growing effort by major economies to reduce dependence on the greenback. Unlike previous cycles, where countries largely accepted dollar dominance as a given, today's geopolitical landscape is one of active diversification.

China has taken the lead in this regard, forging currency swap agreements with dozens of countries and increasing the use of the yuan in international trade. Russia, following its financial isolation from Western markets, has embraced alternative payment systems that bypass the dollar entirely. Even Saudi Arabia—long a cornerstone of the petrodollar system—has signaled openness to pricing oil sales in currencies other than the dollar.

These developments, while incremental, represent a fundamental shift in global financial behavior. The assumption that every crisis will reinforce the dollar's dominance is no longer guaranteed. If enough countries succeed in building parallel financial systems, the next dollar surge could be followed not by another cycle of renewed confidence, but by a growing realization that alternatives are increasingly viable.

Debt, Deficits, and the Burden of Dollar Dominance

Beyond geopolitical shifts, the greatest threat to the dollar's long-term stability may come from within the United States itself. While the U.S. economy remains the world's largest, it is also one of the most indebted. The national debt, which stood at $33 trillion in 2023, continues to grow at an unsustainable pace, with interest payments projected to exceed $1 trillion annually within the next decade.

For now, demand for U.S. Treasuries remains strong, thanks in part to the very crisis cycles that drive investors toward dollar-denominated assets. But if confidence in U.S. fiscal management begins to erode—whether due to political dysfunction, rising debt levels, or an unexpected market shock—the consequences could be severe. If major foreign holders of Treasuries, such as China and Japan, decide to meaningfully reduce their exposure, the dollar's status as the world's safe-haven currency could come under serious pressure.

In such a scenario, the dollar would not necessarily collapse overnight. Instead, it would face a more gradual decline, with reduced demand leading to higher borrowing costs for the U.S. government, increased inflationary pressures, and a potential loss of purchasing power. The real risk is not a sudden collapse, but a prolonged erosion of confidence—one that accelerates as global markets adjust to a world where the dollar is no longer the unquestioned pillar of financial stability.

The Unraveling of a Safe Haven?

The past has shown that no currency remains dominant forever. The British pound, once the foundation of global finance, saw its influence wane as the realities of a shifting economic landscape took hold. The Dutch guilder, which dominated trade during the 17th century, eventually faded as Dutch global influence declined. The U.S. dollar, despite its unparalleled reach, is not immune to the same forces.

If global markets begin to view the dollar's dominance as a source of fragility rather than strength, the shift away from the greenback could accelerate. The question, then, is not whether the dollar will continue to surge in times of crisis—it almost certainly will. The real question is whether those surges will eventually be met with diminishing returns, signaling the moment when global confidence in the dollar begins to unravel.

At some point, the world may stop rushing back to the dollar when trouble arises. When that moment comes, the forces that have long sustained its dominance will no longer be enough to hold it up. The next sectionr will explore what happens when that shift is no longer theoretical—but reality.

5

THE COUNTDOWN TO DOLLAR DECLINE

For generations, the U.S. dollar has been the bedrock of the global financial system, the ultimate safe haven in times of turmoil. Whenever crisis struck—whether in the form of banking collapses, sovereign debt crises, or geopolitical shocks—investors instinctively turned to the dollar as the one asset they could trust. This cycle has repeated itself so often that it has become ingrained in the fabric of global finance, a near-automatic response to uncertainty. Yet history has shown that financial orders do not last forever. What was once unchallenged eventually faces competition, and what once seemed permanent can erode over time.

The paradox of the dollar's strength is that each crisis-driven surge creates the very conditions that weaken its long-term dominance. Every time the greenback soars, emerging markets struggle under the weight of dollar-denominated debt, global trade imbalances widen, and U.S. exports become less competitive. These forces, in turn, incentivize foreign governments and financial institutions to diversify away from the dollar—not as a political statement, but as a necessary safeguard against economic instability.

This shift is no longer theoretical; it is happening in real time. Central banks have steadily reduced the share of their foreign exchange reserves held in dollars, from 71% in 1999 to 58% in 2022, replacing some of those holdings with gold, yuan, and other assets. China has spearheaded new payment mechanisms designed to bypass the dollar, while major energy exporters such as Russia and Saudi Arabia have begun exploring non-dollar transactions for oil sales. Even within traditional U.S. allies, the idea of a multipolar financial system—one where no single currency reigns supreme—is gaining traction.

For now, the dollar's structural advantages remain formidable. The sheer size of U.S. financial markets, the liquidity of Treasuries, and the overwhelming use of the dollar in global trade ensure that no immediate replacement is on the horizon. But the long-term trajectory is shifting. Each successive crisis may still produce a short-term rush into the dollar, but the strength of that rush is already showing signs of diminishing. The safety net that has protected the dollar in the past is fraying—slowly, but visibly.

The Danger of Complacency

The real threat to the dollar's future is not a sudden collapse, but *complacency*. If U.S. policymakers continue to assume that crisis-driven dollar surges validate American financial supremacy, they risk ignoring the underlying weaknesses these surges expose. Rising fiscal deficits, political dysfunction, and over-reliance on the dollar's safe-haven status have all contributed to a fragile equilibrium—one that remains intact only because no major alternative has yet emerged. But history suggests that alternatives develop slowly, then all at once.

Consider the British pound, which once held the same dominance that the dollar enjoys today. At its peak, the pound sterling accounted for the majority of global trade settlements and foreign exchange reserves. But as Britain's economic position weakened in the early 20th century, global investors gradually shifted toward the emerging power of the U.S. dollar. The tipping point did not come in one sudden moment of collapse, but through a slow erosion of confidence—an erosion that, once it reached critical mass, became irreversible. It is not difficult to imagine a similar scenario playing out with the dollar. The question is not whether such a shift could happen, but whether the U.S. will recognize the warning signs before it is too late.

At some point, there will be a crisis that does not follow the usual script. A moment when investors, instead of instinctively pouring into the dollar, begin looking elsewhere. A moment when central banks, instead of boosting dollar reserves, accelerate their diversification. A moment when global markets begin adjusting to a world in which the dollar is no longer the unquestioned pillar of financial stability. That moment is not here yet—but it is coming. And when it arrives, the forces that have long sustained the dollar's dominance will no longer be enough to hold it up.

The unraveling of dollar hegemony will not be an isolated financial event—it will reshape global geopolitics, trade relationships, and economic policymaking. As nations diversify their reserves and expand trade in alternative currencies, the U.S. will face growing limits on its ability to wield financial influence as a geopolitical tool. Sanctions, once a formidable instrument of economic coercion, may lose their impact as parallel financial systems develop beyond Washington's reach. Meanwhile, emerging financial hubs—from Shanghai to Dubai—are strengthening their role in global markets, gradually eroding Wall Street's dominance. What was once an unquestioned economic hierarchy is becoming a multipolar financial landscape, with regional power centers gaining ground.

Yet the greatest challenge may not come from abroad, but from within. The dollar's strength has long been tied to global confidence in U.S. governance and economic stability. Persistent fiscal deficits, political gridlock, and the unchecked expansion of debt are beginning to strain that confidence. Historically, reserve currency shifts have not been dictated by a single crisis, but by a slow erosion of trust—until a tipping point is reached. The dollar's future will depend not just on external forces, but on whether Washington recognizes the urgency of restoring fiscal discipline, strengthening trade relationships, and embracing financial innovation. The question is no longer whether the global monetary order is shifting, but whether the U.S. will act before the forces of change make the decision for it.

CHAPTER 9

THE EROSION OF U.S. FINANCIAL POWER

For decades, U.S. financial dominance has been anchored by the unrivaled status of the dollar and the deep liquidity of Treasury bonds. But cracks in this foundation are beginning to show. This chapter explores how the declining global appetite for U.S. debt signals a shift in confidence. It then examines whether a multi-currency world is an inevitability or a challenge the U.S. can still counter. The unintended consequences of financial weaponization and trade policies are accelerating this shift raising a critical question: How should the U.S. respond? The final section considers whether American policymakers will evolve with the changing landscape—or cling to a fading hegemony at great economic cost.

1

THE DECLINING ROLE OF U.S. TREASURY BONDS

For much of the past century, U.S. Treasury bonds stood as the undisputed foundation of the global financial system. They were more than just debt instruments; they were the bedrock of international reserves, the ultimate safe haven, and the benchmark for risk-free assets worldwide. Central banks, sovereign wealth funds, and institutional investors accumulated them with unwavering confidence, trusting in the creditworthiness of the U.S. government and the unparalleled liquidity of its financial markets. Holding U.S. Treasuries was not merely an investment decision; it was an economic necessity in a world where trade, commodities, and capital flows were overwhelmingly denominated in dollars.

When America Becomes the Buyer of Last Resort

Yet, this long-standing dynamic is beginning to unravel. Over the past decade, foreign appetite for U.S. government debt has weakened, exposing fault lines that were once unthinkable. The numbers tell a striking story: in 2013, China held more than $1.3 trillion in U.S. Treasury securities, a position built over decades as Beijing recycled its massive trade surpluses into American debt markets. By 2023, China's holdings had fallen below $860 billion, marking a deliberate shift in Beijing's financial strategy. Japan, historically the largest foreign creditor to the United States, has also been trimming its exposure. Together, these two economic powerhouses—the anchors of foreign Treasury demand—are no longer accumulating U.S. debt at the pace they once did.

The reasons behind this retreat vary. For China, the decision is as much about geopolitical risk as it is about financial prudence. The weaponization of the U.S. financial system—most visibly seen in the freezing of Russian central bank reserves after the invasion of Ukraine—sent shockwaves through capitals around the world. If Washington could effectively erase hundreds of billions of dollars from a sovereign nation's balance sheet overnight, what guarantee did other nations have that their own reserves would remain untouchable? Beijing has taken no chances. It has ramped up its purchases of gold, increased holdings of alternative assets, and accelerated efforts to internationalize the yuan.

For Japan, the shift reflects a different calculus. As the Bank of Japan grapples with rising domestic inflation and an aging population, its need for yen stability has grown more pressing. Diversifying away from Treasuries has become a necessary tool in managing exchange rate volatility, particularly in the face of persistent Federal Reserve tightening that sent the yen tumbling to multi-decade lows. The global landscape for fixed-income securities is also evolving. For years, U.S. Treasuries offered superior yields compared to European or Japanese government bonds, making them an obvious choice for foreign investors. But with rising interest rates across multiple regions, the relative attractiveness of U.S. debt is no longer as compelling.

The Waning Global Appetite for U.S. Debt

This shift is not confined to China and Japan. Across emerging markets, a quiet but decisive move away from dollar-denominated debt is taking shape. Countries once reliant on U.S. Treasuries to back their currencies are exploring alternatives. Saudi Arabia, long a pillar of petrodollar recycling, has signaled a willingness to price oil in non-dollar currencies, a move that would have been unthinkable even a decade ago. Meanwhile, the broader BRICS bloc—Brazil, Russia, India, China, and South Africa—is actively working to develop an alternative financial infrastructure that reduces dependence on U.S. capital markets.

The declining appetite for U.S. Treasuries is not happening in isolation. It is part of a broader transformation in global finance—one that goes beyond government debt markets and extends to the very foundation of international trade and settlement. As nations seek alternatives to holding U.S. debt, many are also looking for ways to reduce their dependence on the dollar itself. The result is a world inching toward a multi-currency financial system, where the dollar may no longer be the unchallenged medium of exchange.

As these trends accelerate, the implications for the United States are profound. For decades, America's ability to finance its debt at low interest rates depended on the unquestioned global demand for Treasuries. If that demand erodes, borrowing costs will rise, placing new pressures on fiscal policy. Already, the numbers are flashing warning signs. In 2023, U.S. interest payments surpassed $1 trillion for the first time, a figure that now rivals annual military spending.

With a national debt exceeding $34 trillion and a deficit trajectory that shows no signs of reversal, the stakes have never been higher. If foreign investors continue to scale back, Washington may soon find itself trapped in a cycle of rising debt costs, forcing difficult choices between fiscal restraint and even greater reliance on the Federal Reserve.

The Fed as Buyer of Last Resort

The Federal Reserve, once merely a regulator of liquidity, has been forced to assume a new and uncomfortable role: that of buyer of last resort for U.S. debt. With foreign central banks scaling back their Treasury purchases, the Fed has been absorbing a growing share of the issuance, effectively monetizing portions of the national debt. While this has provided short-term stability, it raises a more unsettling question: *what happens when the largest buyer of U.S. government bonds is no longer the world, but America itself?*

The decline in foreign Treasury demand is not an overnight crisis, nor is it a catastrophic collapse. Rather, it is a slow-burning transformation, one that is reshaping the very structure of global finance. For much of the post-war period, Treasuries functioned as the world's reserve asset, providing liquidity, stability, and security. That assumption is now being tested. The process may take years, even decades, but the trajectory is unmistakable. The world is no longer accumulating U.S. debt with the same enthusiasm, and Washington may soon find itself facing a reality it has not had to contend with in generations: the cost of borrowing is rising, and the world's appetite for American debt is no longer guaranteed.

2

A MULTI-CURRENCY WORLD: INEVITABLE OR NOT?

For much of the modern era, the U.S. dollar has operated as the central artery of global finance. It has been more than just a currency; it has been the language of international trade, the unit of account for commodities, and the safe haven asset in times of crisis. The world, by necessity rather than choice, has arranged itself around the dollar, with financial systems structured to ensure seamless dollar liquidity. Governments hold reserves in U.S. Treasuries, corporations settle cross-border transactions in dollars, and even crises in far-flung corners of the world lead to capital flight into the greenback.

Yet, that dominance is no longer absolute. A fundamental shift is underway, one that has been gathering momentum for years but is now becoming unmistakable. Countries are diversifying their reserve holdings, settling trade in alternative currencies, and actively reducing their exposure to U.S. financial dominance. This is no longer theoretical—it is happening in real-time. In 2000, the dollar accounted for roughly 72 percent of global foreign exchange reserves; by 2023, that figure had slipped to just 58 percent, a steady decline that signals the slow but undeniable fragmentation of global finance.

The Weaponization of Finance: A Catalyst for Change

For some, the move away from dollar dependence is a deliberate strategy of self-preservation. The United States' increasing willingness to use its financial power as a geopolitical weapon has raised alarm bells in capitals across the world. The freezing of $300 billion in Russian central bank assets after the invasion of Ukraine was a watershed moment. If Washington could unilaterally strip a country of its reserves with the flick of a bureaucratic pen, who was to say it wouldn't do the same to others? The message was clear: reliance on the dollar meant vulnerability to the political whims of the U.S. government. The response was immediate and far-reaching.

China, already the loudest advocate for a multipolar financial system, accelerated its efforts to challenge dollar hegemony. Its Belt and Road Initiative (BRI) began incorporating yuan-denominated trade settlements, allowing recipient countries to bypass the dollar entirely. At the same time, Beijing entered into currency swap agreements with over 40 nations, ensuring that critical trade partners had access to yuan liquidity rather than relying on U.S. dollars. By 2023, more than 70 percent of trade between China and Russia was conducted in yuan and rubles, a dramatic reversal from the previous decade when nearly all transactions were dollar-based.

The trend is not confined to China and Russia. Across the BRICS bloc, de-dollarization efforts are intensifying. Discussions around a common reserve currency—potentially backed by gold, commodities, or a basket of BRICS currencies—are gaining traction. Brazil and Argentina have explored mechanisms to settle trade in local currencies, reducing reliance on the dollar for bilateral commerce. The African Continental Free Trade Agreement (AfCFTA), the most ambitious economic integration project on the continent, has openly debated the creation of a regional currency framework that could bypass the dollar in intra-African trade.

Even among the Gulf states, which have historically been pillars of the petrodollar system, shifts are occurring. Saudi Arabia, the world's largest oil exporter, has openly considered pricing a portion of its oil sales in yuan, a move that would have been inconceivable a decade ago. The UAE has strengthened financial ties with China, agreeing to settle a growing portion of its trade in yuan, dirhams, and other regional currencies. India, another major global player, has expanded its rupee-based trade settlements with Russia and the UAE, further reducing dollar dependency.

Technology and the Rise of Alternative Payment Systems

At the same time, technological advancements are accelerating the push toward a multi-currency world. The rise of Central Bank Digital Currencies (CBDCs) is offering countries a direct alternative to the dollar-based financial system. China's digital yuan (e-CNY), already operational in domestic transactions, is expanding into cross-border settlements, providing an alternative payments infrastructure that bypasses U.S.-controlled networks like SWIFT. Russia and Iran have explored using gold-backed digital currencies for trade settlements, while other nations are experimenting with blockchain-based financial instruments to reduce reliance on traditional banking intermediaries.

Beyond CBDCs, regional payment systems are developing outside the U.S.-centric financial order. The Association of Southeast Asian Nations (ASEAN) has launched initiatives to integrate local currency settlement systems, allowing cross-border trade without requiring dollar conversion. Latin American nations are exploring a digital regional currency to streamline intra-bloc transactions. If these systems gain traction, they could erode the automatic preference for dollar-based settlements over time.

Despite these shifts, the dollar remains deeply embedded in global finance. It still accounts for the majority of global reserves, dominates 88 percent of all foreign exchange transactions, and remains the primary medium of exchange for most international trade. The global financial system is deeply interconnected, and unwinding decades of dollar dominance is neither simple nor immediate. Even nations pushing for de-dollarization continue to hold substantial U.S. assets, knowing that sudden, aggressive moves could destabilize their own economies.

Yet, the trend lines are clear. A true multi-currency world is no longer a speculative scenario; it is emerging in slow, deliberate steps. The dollar will not be replaced overnight, nor is it likely to vanish as the world's primary currency anytime soon. However, its unchallenged supremacy is fading, and the notion of a single, dominant global reserve currency is being replaced by a more fragmented system of competing financial networks.

For the United States, this transformation presents a serious dilemma. The dollar's status has long provided Washington with an unparalleled strategic advantage—one that allowed it to finance deficits at low cost, exert influence over global trade, and impose economic pressure on adversaries with near-total control. If the world moves toward a genuine multi-currency system, those advantages will erode, leaving the U.S. facing a new and uncertain financial landscape.

The shift away from dollar dominance is not just a financial event—it is a strategic realignment of global power. The very institutions that shaped post-war economic order, from the IMF to the

World Bank, may see their influence wane as new financial architectures emerge. The geopolitical consequences of this shift are profound, potentially altering the balance of power between the West and the Global South.

The next question is whether this shift is inevitable—or if the United States has the means to halt or reverse it. Some policymakers argue that Washington still has time to reassert the dollar's dominance by strengthening trade alliances, modernizing its financial infrastructure, and avoiding the overuse of economic sanctions that alienate allies. Others believe that the transition to a multi-currency world is already past the point of no return.

Regardless of which side of the debate one takes, one thing is certain: the forces reshaping global finance are in motion. Whether the United States can adapt to this new reality or will defiantly resist it remains to be seen.

3

THE UNINTENDED FALLOUT FOR THE U. S.

For decades, America's unrivaled financial power was taken as a given. The U.S. dollar's dominance provided the country with unparalleled benefits—cheap borrowing, economic leverage over adversaries, and the ability to run persistent deficits without the usual constraints faced by other nations. The global financial system, structured around U.S. Treasuries and the Federal Reserve's liquidity network, allowed Washington to dictate the rules of international finance. But as the rest of the world takes deliberate steps to reduce its dependence on the dollar, the long-term consequences for the United States are beginning to emerge.

Rising Borrowing Costs and the End of Easy Money

One of the most immediate and tangible effects of declining global demand for U.S. Treasuries is the rising cost of borrowing. For years, foreign governments and central banks absorbed vast quantities of U.S. debt, effectively subsidizing American spending and keeping interest rates artificially low. That dynamic is shifting. With major holders like China and Japan trimming their Treasury holdings and BRICS nations actively pursuing alternatives, the U.S. is being forced to offer higher yields to attract buyers.

The numbers tell the story. In 2023, U.S. interest payments surpassed $1 trillion for the first time, a staggering figure that now rivals annual defense spending. The country's national debt, which exceeded $34 trillion, continues to expand with no structural reforms in sight. As foreign buyers retreat, the burden increasingly falls on domestic institutions, pension funds, and—most notably—the Federal Reserve itself. The Fed's role as the buyer of last resort has grown significantly since the quantitative easing programs of the 2008 financial crisis and the COVID-19 stimulus era. While this provides short-term stability, it raises an unsettling question: how sustainable is a system where the U.S. government essentially lends to itself to finance its deficits?

The long-term fiscal trajectory is even more alarming. According to projections from the Congressional Budget Office (CBO), by 2033, U.S. interest payments could exceed $1.5 trillion annually, making debt servicing one of the largest line items in the federal budget. If foreign demand for Treasuries continues to decline, Washington will be forced to choose between deep spending cuts, higher taxes, or an even heavier reliance on domestic debt monetization—each of which carries significant economic and political risks.

Higher borrowing costs will eventually spill over into the broader economy. With interest rates elevated, corporate borrowing becomes more expensive, mortgage rates rise, and consumer debt burdens increase. A debt-fueled economy that has relied on low rates for decades may struggle to adjust to a world where financing comes at a much steeper price. This is not just a theoretical concern—it is already unfolding. The U.S. housing market has been rattled by mortgage rates climbing above 7 percent, while corporate debt refinancing at higher rates threatens to squeeze profitability across multiple industries.

The Erosion of U.S. Financial Leverage

Beyond fiscal constraints, a weakening dollar-based system undermines Washington's ability to project power through financial means. Sanctions, a tool that has been used with increasing frequency, rely on the primacy of the dollar. The ability to freeze assets, restrict access to U.S. capital markets, and cut adversaries off from the SWIFT network has given Washington an unparalleled instrument of coercion. But as alternative financial channels emerge, the effectiveness of these measures is eroding.

Russia, faced with crippling Western sanctions after its invasion of Ukraine, has demonstrated the limits of dollar-based financial punishment. Forced to operate outside the Western banking system, Moscow pivoted quickly—settling trade in yuan and rubles, utilizing alternative payment systems, and engaging in gold-based transactions. Despite its financial isolation from the West, Russia managed to stabilize its currency, maintain energy exports, and keep its economy afloat. Other nations are taking note.

China has long viewed financial dependence on the U.S. as a strategic vulnerability. The creation of CIPS (Cross-Border Interbank Payment System), an alternative to SWIFT, reflects Beijing's determination to build a parallel financial infrastructure that is insulated from American influence. Meanwhile, countries under varying degrees of U.S. sanctions—including Iran, Venezuela, and North Korea—have found ways to circumvent dollar-based restrictions, either through cryptocurrency, barter trade, or deepening ties with China and Russia.

The more the U.S. wields financial restrictions as a weapon, the greater the incentive for nations to develop alternatives. This is the paradox facing Washington: the very strategies used to maintain global financial dominance are accelerating the push toward a decentralized system that reduces the country's leverage.

A Weaker Dollar and the Risk of Inflationary Pressure

If the world gradually moves away from dollar dependency, the implications for U.S. inflation dynamics could be profound. Historically, America has enjoyed the unique ability to export inflation, as global demand for dollars kept the currency strong and allowed the country to import goods cheaply. A world in which more trade is settled in local currencies and central banks reduce their dollar reserves means fewer dollars held abroad. Over time, this could lead to a weaker dollar, making imports more expensive and raising inflationary pressures domestically.

The effects of a weaker dollar would be most acutely felt in commodity markets. If major oil producers diversify their pricing mechanisms away from the dollar, energy costs in the U.S. could become far more volatile. The shift away from petrodollar dominance—already underway in small but meaningful steps—could translate into structurally higher fuel prices, placing additional strain on household budgets and corporate profit margins.

The effects would not be felt immediately, but they would be persistent. In a multi-currency world, demand for dollars would shrink, reducing the U.S. government's ability to fund deficits with minimal repercussions. A weaker dollar could also lead to higher energy and commodity prices, especially if oil-producing nations continue to explore pricing mechanisms that move away from the petrodollar system. If energy costs become more volatile in dollar terms, the Federal Reserve may find itself in a difficult position — forced to balance inflationary pressures with the need to support economic growth.

The Illusion of Unquestioned Economic Strength

For now, the dollar remains the dominant global currency, and U.S. assets are still seen as a safe haven during periods of uncertainty. But the long-term forces at play suggest that the landscape is changing. The confidence that underpinned dollar hegemony for decades is no longer absolute. Nations are hedging their bets, diversifying their holdings, and building contingency plans for a future in which the U.S. does not dictate the terms of global finance.

Washington's ability to adjust to this new reality will determine whether the transition is gradual and manageable or chaotic and destabilizing. If policymakers recognize the shifting tides and make strategic adjustments — strengthening trade alliances, modernizing financial infrastructure, and ensuring that dollar-based markets remain attractive — then the erosion of U.S. financial hegemony may be a slow and controlled process. But if the response is one of denial, complacency, or overreliance on coercive measures, the decline could accelerate in ways that leave the U.S. struggling to regain its footing.

The slow erosion of financial supremacy is not just about currency markets or debt ratios — it is about power, influence, and America's place in the global order. The question is no longer whether change is happening. The question is whether the United States is prepared for what comes next.

4

THE ROAD AHEAD – ADAPT OR RESIST?

The United States stands at a crossroads. For decades, it has enjoyed the unrivaled benefits of financial hegemony, reaping the rewards of a system that placed the dollar at the center of global commerce. The ability to finance deficits at low cost, exert influence through financial sanctions, and serve as the world's economic anchor gave Washington a position of extraordinary power. But as the world moves toward a more fragmented financial landscape, that position is no longer unchallenged. The choices the U.S. makes in the coming years will determine whether it can adapt to this shifting reality or whether it will resist the inevitable, risking an accelerated loss of influence.

The Case for Adaptation: A Controlled Transition

If the U.S. acknowledges the shifting economic order and takes proactive steps to reinforce its role within it, the transition to a multi-currency world could be managed without significant destabilization. This would require Washington to rethink its approach to global finance, trade alliances, and monetary policy.

First, strengthening economic partnerships beyond traditional Western allies is critical. While the U.S. has historically relied on Europe, Japan, and other developed economies as its primary trade and financial partners, the emerging economies of the Global South are increasingly shaping global markets. Ignoring this shift risks pushing these nations further toward financial structures that exclude the U.S. Instead of assuming continued dollar loyalty, Washington could deepen its engagement with regions that are actively exploring alternatives, ensuring that American financial markets remain attractive and accessible.

Second, modernizing the U.S. financial infrastructure is essential to maintaining relevance in a rapidly evolving digital economy. While China has led the charge in developing Central Bank Digital

Currencies (CBDCs) and alternative payment systems, the U.S. has remained hesitant. The slow progress on a digital dollar risks leaving Washington behind in the next phase of global finance. If new financial architectures emerge that facilitate trade in multiple currencies outside of the U.S. banking system, the dollar's reach will continue to shrink. Actively developing competitive digital financial tools, improving transaction efficiency, and integrating with global blockchain-based settlement systems would ensure that the U.S. remains at the forefront of financial innovation.

Third, Washington must reconsider its overreliance on financial coercion as a tool of geopolitical strategy. The excessive use of sanctions, trade restrictions, and financial exclusion has accelerated efforts by other nations to bypass the dollar system. While these measures have been effective in the short term, they have ultimately incentivized global players to seek alternative frameworks, eroding Washington's long-term leverage. A more restrained and strategic approach to economic diplomacy—one that balances security concerns with maintaining global trust in U.S. financial leadership— would slow the pace of de-dollarization and reinforce the stability of American financial markets.

Furthermore, policymakers must address the structural imbalances in U.S. fiscal policy. Persistent deficit spending, rising debt-servicing costs, and an unsustainable reliance on foreign capital inflows have made the American financial system increasingly vulnerable. While the U.S. can still borrow at lower rates than most nations, this privilege is not infinite. Restoring fiscal discipline, ensuring debt sustainability, and reducing dependence on monetary interventions to stabilize markets would signal to global investors that the U.S. remains a credible financial leader.

The Risk of Resistance: A Disruptive Decline

If Washington chooses instead to ignore these shifts, doubling down on an outdated model of financial dominance, the consequences could be severe. The assumption that the world will always need the dollar, no matter how aggressively the U.S. wields its financial power, is proving increasingly flawed.

A resistance strategy—where the U.S. attempts to forcibly maintain its financial hegemony through economic pressure, geopolitical confrontation, and protectionist policies—would likely backfire. Countries already exploring alternative systems would accelerate their transition away from U.S.-centric financial structures. Trade alliances among BRICS nations, de-dollarization initiatives in oil markets, and the rise of regional financial networks would all intensify. A growing number of nations, wary of U.S. political influence over the global financial system, would actively reduce their exposure to dollar-based transactions.

This shift would not necessarily happen gradually. A major geopolitical event—such as a Taiwan crisis, a severe U.S.-China economic decoupling, or a prolonged debt ceiling crisis—could accelerate capital flight from the dollar. A U.S. credit rating downgrade, similar to the ones seen in 2011 (S&P) and 2023 (Fitch), could erode investor confidence further, pushing more global capital into alternative assets like gold, yuan reserves, or digital currencies backed by multiple nations. If such an event were to coincide with rising U.S. fiscal deficits and higher Treasury yields, the resulting instability could trigger a disorderly shift away from U.S. financial markets.

Such a scenario would leave the U.S. with fewer economic tools to manage its fiscal challenges. If foreign demand for Treasuries continues to decline and deficits remain unchecked, interest rates will be forced higher, increasing debt-servicing costs and straining economic growth. The Federal Reserve may find itself in an untenable position—either allowing borrowing costs to spiral upward, or intervening with large-scale purchases of U.S. debt, effectively monetizing deficits and risking a loss of confidence in the dollar itself.

Furthermore, if the U.S. is perceived as unwilling to adjust to global shifts, trust in its financial system could weaken. Investors and central banks do not shift reserve strategies overnight, but confidence erodes in gradual steps. As alternative financial systems mature, a moment of crisis—whether a major debt standoff, a geopolitical flashpoint, or a financial market disruption—could accelerate the move away from the dollar in unpredictable ways.

The 20th-century decline of British financial supremacy offers a cautionary parallel. The pound sterling remained a dominant currency long after Britain's economic and geopolitical influence waned, but once markets fully adjusted to the reality of a U.S.-led world, sterling lost its reserve currency status in dramatic fashion.

A Future Not Yet Decided

The coming years will be pivotal in determining whether the U.S. navigates the shifting economic landscape with foresight and pragmatism or clings to a fading status quo, risking a disruptive transition. The move toward a multipolar financial world is not a question of if, but when and how. The U.S. remains in a position of considerable strength—it still issues the world's most liquid assets, operates the deepest capital markets, and holds a level of institutional credibility unmatched by emerging competitors. But these advantages will not last forever without adaptation.

The ability to shape the future of the global financial order lies in Washington's response. A deliberate, measured adjustment to a changing world could preserve U.S. influence for decades to come. A strategy of resistance, denial, and coercion could accelerate the very decline that policymakers hope to avoid. The shift toward a multipolar financial world is no longer a theoretical possibility—it is unfolding in real-time. While the U.S. still enjoys enormous structural advantages, including deep capital markets and strong institutional credibility, those strengths are eroding at the margins.

If Washington adapts, it can preserve much of its global financial influence. If it resists, it risks turning an orderly transition into a disruptive realignment—one that could permanently weaken America's economic standing. The clock is ticking, and the world will not wait.

CHAPTER 10

AMERICA AT A CROSSROADS

As economic uncertainty deepens, the United States stands at a pivotal moment that will define its role in the global order. The choices ahead are stark: retreat into protectionism and economic nationalism or embrace strategic adaptation to sustain its leadership. This chapter explores the risks of isolationist policies and the long-term consequences of restricting global trade and investment. At the same time, it examines the case for renewed global engagement, arguing that economic strength comes not from closing doors but from innovation, flexibility, and collaboration. Policy decisions made today will shape America's future—will the nation reinforce its global influence through foresight and adaptation, or will it risk decline by resisting inevitable change? In an era of shifting power dynamics, this chapter poses a critical question: Can the U.S. reclaim its economic edge, or is it destined to retreat from global leadership?

1

THE FUTURE OF U.S. ECONOMIC LEADERSHIP

For decades, the United States shaped the global economy through a combination of trade dominance, financial innovation, and strategic alliances. The post-World War II order, built on the pillars of the Bretton Woods system, an open trade framework, and a robust financial market, placed the U.S. at the center of global commerce. The dollar became more than just a currency; it was a symbol of economic strength and stability, a store of value for investors worldwide, and the linchpin of international trade.

But the foundations of this dominance are now under strain. The rise of economic nationalism, the erosion of trade alliances, and the growing appeal of alternative financial systems are changing the landscape. The United States no longer holds the unquestioned position it once did. Challenges from China, the shifting trade preferences of emerging markets, and a growing effort to bypass the dollar in global transactions have made it clear that the status quo is no longer guaranteed.

Now, the country stands at a crossroads. The decisions made over the next decade will determine whether the U.S. retains its leadership role in global finance and trade or gradually cedes influence to rising powers. The issue is not merely one of maintaining prestige; it is about securing long-term economic stability and ensuring that America's financial system remains central to the functioning of global markets. The forces at play are complex, but the overarching question is simple: will the U.S. adapt to the evolving global order, or will it resist change at its own peril?

The pathway forward is not predetermined. The policies enacted today will either fortify America's economic leadership or accelerate its decline. The challenge is twofold—internally, the country must address structural weaknesses that threaten its global competitiveness, while externally, it must reaffirm its role as a trusted partner in international trade and finance. There is no time for complacency. In a world where economic alliances are shifting and competitors are advancing, maintaining a position of strength requires proactive strategy, not nostalgia for a past era.

The path the U.S. chooses will shape the financial architecture of the 21st century. If it embraces forward-thinking economic policies, strengthens its trade relationships, and invests in critical industries, it will retain its role as the world's economic leader. If it turns inward, retreats from global engagement, and ignores the rising competition, it will find itself navigating a future where financial power is more dispersed, and its own influence diminished. The stakes could not be higher.

A Slow Decline or a Bold Rebirth?

The erosion of U.S. economic leadership would not happen in a single, dramatic moment, but rather through a slow accumulation of missed opportunities, policy missteps, and external shifts beyond Washington's control. Nations that were once unquestioning allies in the dollar-led financial system are now hedging their bets, diversifying reserves, and forging trade agreements that sidestep the U.S. banking network.

The expansion of alternative financial infrastructure—whether through China's yuan-based payment systems, the rise of central bank digital currencies, or regional trade blocs—illustrates that the global economy is evolving in ways that no longer depend exclusively on the dollar. If the U.S. fails to recognize these changes and adjust accordingly, it risks becoming a spectator rather than a shaper of the future financial order.

Ultimately, the question is not whether America will face economic challenges—it already does. The real question is whether it will lead through adaptation or decline through inertia. History has shown that economic leadership is never guaranteed, nor is it owed to any nation, no matter how powerful. The United States still has unparalleled advantages: deep capital markets, technological innovation, and a highly productive workforce. But these strengths alone are not enough. The future of U.S. economic leadership will be determined not by past achievements, but by the choices made today.

2

THE DANGERS OF CONTINUED PROTECTIONISM

The impulse to turn inward is as old as economic competition itself. Protectionist policies have long been framed as a way to shield domestic industries, preserve jobs, and strengthen national self-sufficiency. The rhetoric is appealing: reduce reliance on foreign imports, impose tariffs to curb unfair competition, and bring back manufacturing to American soil. It promises security, economic revival, and a return to a golden age of industrial dominance. But history has repeatedly shown that the consequences of protectionism rarely align with its promises.

When Protectionism Backfires: Lessons from the Past

Over a century ago, the United States relied heavily on tariffs to fund its government and protect its industries, but the global economy was vastly different. The world was not as deeply interconnected, supply chains were local rather than global, and trade was not the economic lifeblood it is today. By the early 20th century, as the U.S. emerged as an industrial powerhouse, the reliance on protectionism was already showing cracks. The Smoot-Hawley Tariff Act of 1930, often cited as one of the policies that exacerbated the Great Depression, demonstrated the dangers of excessive trade barriers. Designed to protect American farmers and businesses, it triggered retaliatory tariffs from trading partners, sending global trade into a downward spiral. The result was not economic revival but contraction, rising costs, and an acceleration of economic decline.

Fast forward nearly a century, and the lessons remain unchanged. The modern iteration of protectionism—whether through tariffs on steel and aluminum, restrictions on technology exports, or punitive trade policies—has set off a chain reaction. When the U.S. imposed tariffs on Chinese goods in 2018, the effects rippled across industries. American businesses faced higher input costs, farmers lost key export markets, and multinational corporations restructured supply chains to minimize their exposure to U.S. tariffs. China responded by imposing its own tariffs, targeting American agriculture, industrial goods, and technology firms.

Beyond direct economic costs, protectionism has a more insidious effect: it strengthens competitors rather than weakening them. The tariffs imposed on China did not curb its rise; they accelerated Beijing's efforts to forge new trade partnerships and reduce reliance on the U.S. market. While American firms scrambled to navigate the shifting trade landscape, China deepened ties with Southeast Asia, Africa, and Latin America. The Regional Comprehensive Economic Partnership (RCEP), the world's largest trade agreement, was signed in 2020, with China at its center. The U.S. was notably absent.

Europe, too, adapted. As the U.S. retreated from multilateral trade agreements, the European Union solidified its economic ties with Asia, Latin America, and Africa. While Washington prioritized tariffs and economic restrictions, Brussels focused on deepening its trade footprint. The consequence is that America, once the architect of the global trade system, increasingly finds itself playing defense.

The Cost of Tariffs: Who Really Pays?

The belief that tariffs and trade barriers will force global partners to bow to U.S. economic dominance misunderstands the new reality. The world is no longer unipolar, and economic influence is no longer guaranteed. Countries today have alternatives, and when faced with an unpredictable trading partner, they will seek stability elsewhere. The more America weaponizes trade policy, the more it pushes allies and adversaries alike to develop alternative financial structures, bypassing the dollar and minimizing their exposure to U.S. economic leverage.

The economic cost of the U.S.-China trade war was tangible. Studies estimated that U.S. businesses paid over $80 billion in additional import costs as a direct result of tariffs. The agricultural sector, once heavily reliant on Chinese demand, saw a $24 billion decline in exports to China between 2018 and 2020. American consumers, despite reassurances that tariffs were being paid by foreign producers, faced price increases in everything from household goods to automobiles. Tariffs were not an economic shield—they were a hidden tax, ultimately borne by the very people they were supposed to protect.

The dangers of continued protectionism extend beyond economics. They erode trust, weaken alliances, and diminish U.S. leadership in global affairs. A country that prioritizes isolation over engagement loses influence, not gains it. The question is no longer whether the U.S. can afford to retreat from global trade—it is whether it can afford the consequences of doing so.

3

THE CASE FOR STRATEGIC ADAPTATION

If protectionism is not the answer, then what is? The United States cannot afford to turn inward at a time when the global economy is undergoing a fundamental transformation. Trade relationships are being redefined, financial power is becoming more decentralized, and geopolitical shifts are reshaping economic alliances. The question is no longer whether the U.S. should engage with the world, but rather how it can do so in a way that reinforces its economic leadership.

Retreating from the global stage would only accelerate the rise of alternative trade and financial systems that diminish U.S. influence. The only viable path forward is to engage strategically—leveraging America's unique advantages while modernizing its economic approach to meet the challenges of the 21st century. That means rethinking trade policy, reinvesting in domestic competitiveness, and securing the long-term stability of the U.S. dollar.

Strengthen Trade Alliances, Don't Undermine Them

For much of the postwar period, America's strength was built on a global network of economic alliances that ensured stability, expanded markets, and cemented the dollar's role as the world's reserve currency. The institutions and agreements that emerged from this era—the General Agreement on Tariffs and Trade (GATT), the World Trade Organization (WTO), and regional trade partnerships—were not just tools of economic expansion; they were instruments of U.S. strategic influence. But over the past decade, Washington's willingness to abandon these alliances in favor of unilateral action has eroded its credibility as a reliable economic partner.

Nowhere was this more evident than in the withdrawal from the Trans-Pacific Partnership (TPP) in 2017. The agreement was designed to counterbalance China's growing influence in Asia by creating a free trade zone that linked the U.S. with some of the world's most dynamic economies. Walking away from it did not weaken China—it strengthened it. In the absence of U.S. leadership, Beijing quickly moved to consolidate its regional economic ties, culminating in the signing of the Regional Comprehensive Economic Partnership (RCEP), a trade deal that now dominates Asia's economic landscape.

Rebuilding trust and influence in global trade requires more than just rhetoric; it requires tangible commitments. The U.S. must reinvest in regional trade agreements, particularly in Asia and Latin America, where China has aggressively expanded its economic reach. A renewed U.S. presence in trade negotiations could help stabilize supply chains, prevent overreliance on Chinese manufacturing, and reestablish the United States as the key partner for emerging markets. But that requires consistency. If the U.S. continues the pattern of withdrawing from agreements and re-entering them only when politically expedient, it risks losing credibility permanently.

Beyond formal trade agreements, the U.S. must also modernize its approach to economic diplomacy. Strengthening ties with Europe through a revitalized transatlantic trade agreement could serve as a counterweight to China's expanding influence in Africa and Latin America. Deepening economic engagement with India—one of the fastest-growing consumer markets—could offer a long-term alternative to dependence on China. The goal should not be to return to the old trade order but to build a more resilient and diversified network of economic partnerships that reinforce U.S. leadership rather than isolate it.

Investing in Domestic Competitiveness

Global engagement is only effective if it is backed by domestic strength. No amount of trade agreements or diplomatic maneuvering can compensate for a decline in America's ability to compete in the industries of the future. For decades, the U.S. was at the forefront of technological innovation, manufacturing prowess, and workforce development. Today, those advantages are eroding. A lack of investment in infrastructure, an aging industrial base, and a skills gap in the labor force have left the U.S. vulnerable to competition from China, Europe, and emerging economies.

Reversing this trend requires a renewed commitment to industrial strategy. That does not mean government-managed economic planning, but it does mean targeted investment in the sectors that will define global competitiveness in the coming decades. The semiconductor industry, for example, is a critical battleground. While the U.S. remains a leader in chip design, much of the world's manufacturing capacity has shifted to Taiwan and South Korea. Recent supply chain disruptions exposed the risks of over-reliance on foreign production. Strengthening domestic chip production through initiatives like the CHIPS and Science Act is a necessary step, but it must be part of a broader strategy to ensure U.S. technological independence.

Infrastructure investment is another key pillar. Roads, ports, and energy grids built for the 20th century are ill-equipped to support the demands of a modern, digitally connected economy. China's Belt and Road Initiative is not just an infrastructure program—it is an economic strategy designed to secure influence in global trade routes. The U.S. must counter this by reinvesting in its own infrastructure, ensuring that it remains the world's most efficient and competitive economy.

The skills gap presents an equally urgent challenge. While U.S. universities continue to produce world-class engineers and researchers, there is a widening divide between high-skilled and low-skilled labor. Addressing this requires a national strategy to modernize workforce training, focusing on fields like artificial intelligence, cybersecurity, and advanced manufacturing. Without a skilled workforce, even the best trade policies will fall short of securing long-term economic strength.

Securing the Dollar's Global Role

At the heart of America's economic power is the dollar. As long as the dollar remains the world's dominant reserve currency, the U.S. enjoys an unparalleled advantage—its debt is in demand, its financial system is central to global trade, and its ability to influence global markets remains intact. But the privilege of dollar dominance is not guaranteed. The rise of alternative financial systems, China's push for yuan internationalization, and the growing use of digital currencies all pose challenges to the dollar's supremacy.

Maintaining the dollar's global role requires a multifaceted approach. *First*, the U.S. must reinforce confidence in its financial system. That means addressing the growing national debt and ensuring that fiscal policy does not undermine long-term stability. While deficit spending can be a necessary tool for economic growth, an unchecked rise in debt-to-GDP ratios risks eroding trust in U.S. Treasuries—the backbone of the global financial system. A measured approach to fiscal discipline, combined with policies that encourage domestic investment and economic expansion, can help preserve the dollar's role as the world's safe-haven currency.

Second, the U.S. must embrace innovation in global finance. The emergence of central bank digital currencies (CBDCs) represents a potential paradigm shift in international payments. China has already introduced its digital yuan as an alternative to the dollar in trade settlements. If the U.S. lags behind in digital financial infrastructure, it risks ceding ground to competitors. Developing a digital dollar backed by the Federal Reserve could modernize the global financial system while reinforcing America's role at the center of it.

Finally, maintaining the dollar's dominance requires a recommitment to international economic institutions. The postwar financial order was built on American leadership in organizations like the International Monetary Fund and the World Bank. Over the past decade, as U.S. engagement has waned, China has stepped in to reshape these institutions to serve its own interests. The U.S. must reclaim its role in setting global financial rules, ensuring that the system continues to function in a way that upholds stability rather than fragmentation.

The future of the dollar is inseparable from the future of U.S. economic leadership. A strong, stable, and globally trusted dollar is one of America's most powerful tools. Letting that status erode through inaction or mismanagement would be an irreversible mistake.

The United States does not need to choose between protectionism and passivity. The real path forward lies in *strategic adaptation*—leveraging trade partnerships, reinvesting in domestic competitiveness, and securing the financial system against emerging threats. The world is shifting, but that does not mean the U.S. must surrender its leadership. It simply means that leadership must evolve.

4

POLICY INNOVATION AND THE FUTURE

The global economy is undergoing rapid transformation, and the United States stands at a pivotal moment. The economic models that sustained American dominance in the past are no longer sufficient in an era of shifting trade alliances, technological disruption, and rising geopolitical competition. To maintain its leadership, the U.S. must do more than react to global changes—it must actively shape the next phase of economic evolution. This requires a shift from short-term policy fixes to long-term strategic planning, from defensive measures to proactive leadership.

A strong economy is not built on nostalgia for past successes but on the ability to innovate, adapt, and lead. The policies that guided the U.S. through the late 20th century—a reliance on financial globalization, the offshoring of manufacturing, and laissez-faire economic management—must be reevaluated in light of the new global realities. The next era of U.S. economic strength will not be defined by a return to old models, but by a bold approach to policy innovation, investment in emerging industries, and a commitment to shaping international financial architecture rather than merely reacting to it.

Digital Finance: The Next Frontier of Monetary Power

The dominance of the U.S. dollar in global finance has been a cornerstone of American economic power, but that dominance is no longer unchallenged. The rise of digital finance is reshaping the way international transactions are conducted, and if the U.S. does not take the lead, others will. China's rollout of its central bank digital currency (CBDC), the digital yuan, is already positioning itself as an alternative to the dollar in trade settlements, particularly among countries wary of U.S. financial sanctions. Other nations, including members of the European Union, India, and Brazil, are exploring similar alternatives.

A Federal Reserve-backed digital dollar could modernize the global financial system while reinforcing the U.S. as the hub of international finance. By creating a seamless, secure, and globally accepted digital currency, the U.S. could preempt efforts by rival economies to displace the dollar's role in trade. But beyond simply issuing a digital currency, Washington must ensure that the global payments infrastructure remains centered around American institutions rather than fragmenting into competing systems. The world's financial architecture should not be shaped by reactionary policies but by forward-thinking leadership.

The risks of falling behind in digital finance extend beyond currency competition. The rise of decentralized finance (DeFi) platforms, blockchain technology, and alternative payment networks has the potential to bypass traditional banking institutions. If American regulators continue to approach these developments with hostility rather than innovation, the financial center of gravity could shift away from the U.S. to regions that embrace new financial technologies. The next decade will determine whether America retains its financial primacy or loses it to more agile economies that recognize the strategic importance of digital finance.

Energy & Tech: Securing Independence

Economic leadership in the 21st century is not just about trade and finance—it is about controlling the industries that will define the future. The global economy is undergoing a transition, and the nations that lead in key technological and energy sectors will set the terms of global competition for decades to come. For the United States, this means prioritizing investment in clean energy, artificial intelligence, semiconductor manufacturing, and biotechnology—the industries that will form the backbone of economic growth and geopolitical influence.

The shift toward renewable energy is more than an environmental imperative; it is an economic necessity. While the U.S. has historically been a dominant force in global energy markets, the rise of renewable energy technologies is altering the balance of power. China has already positioned itself as the world leader in solar panel and battery production, securing supply chains that will dictate the future of global energy. If the U.S. fails to make comparable investments, it risks ceding control over one of the most strategically important industries of the future.

Artificial intelligence is another key battleground. AI is rapidly transforming industries, from healthcare and finance to defense and logistics. China has explicitly stated its ambition to lead the world in AI by 2030, and it is investing heavily in research, development, and infrastructure to achieve that goal. The U.S. must counter this with equally ambitious policies that promote innovation, fund cutting-edge research, and ensure that American firms remain at the forefront of AI development.

Semiconductors—the backbone of the digital economy—are another area where the U.S. must secure its strategic independence. While American companies lead in semiconductor design, much of the manufacturing capacity has shifted to Taiwan and South Korea. Recent geopolitical tensions have underscored the risks of relying on foreign supply chains for critical technology. The passage of the CHIPS and Science Act was a step in the right direction, but securing long-term semiconductor dominance will require sustained investment in domestic production capabilities.

Economic leadership is no longer just about having the largest economy—it is about controlling the infrastructure, supply chains, and technological platforms that will shape the future. If the U.S. fails to lead in these industries, it will be forced to compete on terms set by others.

Reasserting U.S. Economic Leadership

The institutions that have defined the global economic order for the past century—organizations like the International Monetary Fund (IMF), the World Bank, and the World Trade Organization (WTO)—were built on the foundation of U.S. leadership. But in recent years, the influence of these institutions has been challenged. China has created its own financial institutions, such as the Asian Infrastructure Investment Bank (AIIB), as alternatives to the Western-led system. The BRICS nations—Brazil, Russia, India, China, and South Africa—are increasingly pushing for a global economic framework that operates outside U.S. control.

If the U.S. wants to maintain its position as the central force in global economic governance, it must reassert its leadership in these institutions. That means strengthening alliances with traditional partners while also engaging with emerging economies that are being courted by China. The U.S. cannot afford to take its influence for granted; it must actively shape the rules of global finance and trade to ensure that they continue to reflect American interests.

The use of economic sanctions as a geopolitical tool has also reached a critical juncture. While sanctions have historically been an effective mechanism for exerting pressure on adversarial regimes, overuse risks driving countries to develop financial systems that bypass U.S. controls. Russia's response to Western sanctions following the invasion of Ukraine has accelerated the shift toward non-dollar trade among its allies. While targeted sanctions remain a necessary tool, Washington must be mindful of the unintended consequences of broad economic restrictions that encourage the fragmentation of the global financial system.

The ability to influence global economic policy has long been one of America's greatest strategic advantages. Maintaining that influence in the face of rising competition will require a renewed commitment to shaping international economic institutions rather than assuming their continued dominance.

A Blueprint for U.S. Economic Power

The future of U.S. economic leadership will not be determined by tariffs, short-term trade deals, or reactive policy measures. It will be determined by the ability to anticipate and shape global economic trends before they take hold. That means investing in digital finance, securing leadership in critical technologies, and reinforcing America's role in global trade and financial institutions.

The U.S. has always thrived when it has embraced innovation and long-term vision. The postwar economic boom was not the result of protectionism or isolationism but of strategic engagement with the world, investment in infrastructure, and leadership in emerging industries. The same principles apply today. The path to continued dominance is not to close off the economy but to lead in the industries and financial systems that will define the 21st century.

Failure to act will not simply mean a slow erosion of influence — it will mean a fundamental shift in global economic power. The question is not whether the U.S. can maintain its leadership, but whether it has the foresight and political will to do so. The future of economic power is being written now, and history will judge whether America chose to shape it or be shaped by it.

The Decision Ahead – A Future of Strength or Decline?

The world is not waiting for the United States to decide its course. As policymakers in Washington debate the virtues of protectionism versus engagement, the rest of the world is already forging ahead. China is deepening its economic alliances across Asia, Africa, and Latin America, steadily reducing its dependence on the dollar and positioning itself as the economic counterweight to American dominance. The European Union is expanding its financial sovereignty, strengthening the euro's role in international transactions. The BRICS nations are working to establish alternative trade and financial mechanisms that bypass U.S. influence entirely.

For the first time in nearly a century, global economic leadership is up for grabs. The United States is no longer the unquestioned center of global finance and trade, and its ability to maintain that position depends entirely on the choices it makes today. The question is no longer whether America will face competition—it already does. The real question is whether it will respond with vision and strategy or with complacency and political short-termism.

This moment represents an inflection point. If the U.S. embraces a forward-looking strategy, reinvests in its economic foundations, and leads in shaping the next era of trade, finance, and technology, it will not only retain its dominance but reinforce it for another generation. If, instead, it turns inward, relying on tariffs and economic nationalism while allowing fiscal imbalances and infrastructure decay to continue unchecked, it will accelerate its own decline.

A nation's global economic standing is never a permanent fixture. Empires fall not because they are overtaken by superior competition overnight, but because they fail to recognize the shifting tides until it is too late. The British Empire, once the world's dominant economic force, ceded its role not through a singular moment of collapse but through decades of miscalculations, delayed reforms, and a refusal to adapt to new economic realities. The United States now faces a similar test.

The choices before the country are stark. It can choose to engage with the world on its own terms, leveraging its advantages in trade, finance, and technology to remain the dominant global force. Or it can allow its influence to erode, retreating from the world stage and watching as alternative financial and trade systems rise to replace it. There is no middle ground.

At the core of this decision is the role of the U.S. dollar. Its status as the world's primary reserve currency has provided economic stability and an unparalleled strategic advantage. But that status is not a given—it must be reinforced through prudent fiscal policy, trade leadership, and financial innovation. The more the U.S. weaponizes its economic influence through sanctions and trade barriers, the more it incentivizes other nations to find alternatives. The more it allows national debt to spiral unchecked, the more it risks undermining confidence in the dollar.

Leadership in the 21st century will not be secured through tariffs, isolation, or financial complacency. It will be secured through investment in the future—technology, infrastructure, and economic diplomacy that cements the U.S. as the indispensable global partner. The world is evolving, and the nations that shape this transformation will be the ones that define the coming century.

The United States can still lead, but time is not on its side. The decisions made today will determine whether it remains at the center of global trade and finance or whether, decades from now, it will be seen as the nation that let its economic supremacy slip away. The future is being written now. The question is: who will be the author?

PART V

THE NEXT GLOBAL ORDER
A Post-Dollar World?

"Fate leads the willing and drags along the unwilling."
— Seneca

The global monetary order is at a turning point. Part V examines the forces challenging the dollar's supremacy and the potential pathways the financial system could take in the years ahead. As economic power shifts, alternative financial systems expand, and geopolitical tensions mount, the question is no longer whether change is coming, but how rapidly it will unfold. Through three diverging scenarios, this section explores the resilience of the U.S. dollar, the emergence of a fragmented multipolar system, and the potential unraveling of dollar hegemony. While some nations seek to reinforce the status quo, others are actively working to reshape the financial landscape. The coming era will test the adaptability of the dollar-based system and determine whether global finance remains anchored in U.S. monetary dominance or transitions to a more decentralized order.

CHAPTER 11

THE FUTURE OF GLOBAL TRADE & FINANCE

— Three Diverging Paths —

The global economic order stands at a crossroads, with three possible futures for trade and finance. Will the U.S. dollar retain its dominance, upheld by institutional momentum? Will a multipolar system emerge, where regional blocs and alternative currencies—like the yuan and digital assets—challenge its supremacy? Or will a new financial paradigm take hold, driven by decentralization and technological disruption? This chapter examines the forces shaping these outcomes, from rising debt burdens and shifting trade alliances to the role of central bank digital currencies (CBDCs) and de-dollarization. Each path carries profound consequences for economic stability, geopolitical power, and the future of globalization. The choices made today will define the world's financial architecture for decades to come.

1

A WORLD AT A CROSSROADS

The global financial order stands at a pivotal moment. The forces that once cemented the U.S. dollar's status as the world's dominant reserve currency are now being tested by shifting geopolitical dynamics, technological innovations, and the growing determination of emerging economies to reduce their reliance on a financial system that they see as skewed in favor of the United States. The world has been here before.

Economic hegemonies rise and fall, and history is filled with examples of once-dominant currencies losing their grip. The pound sterling reigned supreme in the 19th and early 20th centuries, only to be overtaken by the U.S. dollar after World War II. The collapse of the gold standard and the emergence of fiat currency systems marked another major shift. Now, new forces are at play, challenging the system that has been in place for the past eight decades.

A closer look at history suggests that global reserve currencies rarely collapse overnight; instead, they tend to decline gradually before an external shock accelerates their demise. The British pound, for instance, remained the world's primary reserve currency well into the mid-20th century, even after the United States surpassed Britain economically. Its decline was accelerated by a combination of financial crises, shifting trade patterns, and geopolitical pressures — particularly Britain's debt burden after World War II.

Similarly, the Spanish real, which dominated global trade in the 16th and 17th centuries, saw a prolonged decline as economic power shifted away from Spain. If history is any guide, the U.S. dollar's fate will be shaped not just by current economic trends but also by policy decisions and unforeseen global disruptions in the years ahead.

Throughout this book, the discussion has traced the intricate web of trade, debt, and monetary policy that binds the global economy together. The fundamental question that emerges is whether this system, built on the primacy of the U.S. dollar, can withstand the pressures of de-dollarization, trade fragmentation, and rising protectionism. While no single event is likely to bring about an immediate transformation, the accumulation of economic and political shifts suggests that change is inevitable. The real question is not whether the global financial system will evolve, but how.

The Three Possible Futures

There are three distinct paths the world could take, each with profound implications. The first possibility is that the status quo endures, albeit with growing challenges. In this scenario, the U.S. dollar retains its dominance, supported by deep financial markets, the liquidity of U.S. Treasury bonds, and the absence of a credible alternative. This scenario assumes that, despite rising U.S. debt and economic competition, there is no single viable substitute that can fully replace the dollar's role as the world's preferred currency for trade and reserves.

The second possibility envisions a fractured world in which regional trade blocs begin to assert financial independence, creating a patchwork of competing reserve currencies that erode, but do not fully replace, the dollar's influence. The rise of the euro, yuan, and possibly digital assets backed by central banks could contribute to this shift. Trade and financial flows would become more localized, reducing the dollar's share in global transactions but not eliminating its role entirely. In this scenario, the U.S. would retain significant financial leverage, but it would face greater constraints as alternative currencies and payment systems gain traction, challenging its ability to unilaterally shape global economic policy.

The final and most dramatic scenario is one in which the U.S. dollar loses its status as the global reserve currency, leading to a wholesale restructuring of global trade and finance, with the potential for economic turmoil in its wake. This scenario could be triggered by a loss of confidence in U.S. fiscal policy, a major financial crisis, or the successful emergence of a competing global financial system. If demand for U.S. Treasuries collapses and capital flows shift elsewhere, the consequences for the American economy—and by extension, the global financial system—could be severe fueling inflation, weakening U.S. geopolitical influence, and accelerating the rise of alternative financial hubs.

The Key Forces Driving Change

The outcome will not be dictated by economic forces alone. The course of U.S. fiscal policy, the extent to which emerging economies embrace alternative financial frameworks, and the growing influence of digital currencies will all play a decisive role in shaping the global financial order. These factors have the potential to either accelerate or slow down the ongoing shifts in economic power, making the next decade a critical inflection point.

What unfolds in the coming years will not only redefine the financial landscape but also reshape the broader geopolitical order. The decisions made by policymakers, central banks, and major corporations will determine whether the United States retains its financial dominance, whether the world transitions into a multipolar economic system, or whether an entirely new global framework emerges

The Future of U.S. Fiscal and Monetary Policy

The strength of the U.S. dollar is inextricably linked to the credibility of American economic governance. For decades, the dollar has been seen as a safe haven, backed by a relatively stable political system, the rule of law, and a deep, liquid financial market. However, the sustainability of this advantage is increasingly in question. The U.S. national debt has soared past $34 trillion, with projections indicating further increases. At some point, foreign investors may begin to reassess the risk of holding U.S. assets, particularly if interest payments on government debt consume an ever-larger share of GDP.

The Federal Reserve's monetary policy will also play a defining role. During past economic crises, the Fed's ability to inject liquidity into the system reinforced the dollar's position as the global anchor. However, in an environment of *high inflation, rising interest rates, and growing fiscal deficits*, the Fed faces a dilemma. Tightening monetary policy too much could destabilize financial markets and debt-laden economies, while excessive loosening could fuel inflationary pressures and weaken confidence in the dollar's long-term stability. The dollar's dominance is built not only on its historical role but on the perception that U.S. policymakers can maintain economic stability. If that confidence is lost, the world will accelerate its search for alternatives.

The Acceleration of De-Dollarization Efforts

A growing number of countries are actively working to reduce their dependence on the U.S. dollar, a shift driven by geopolitical considerations as much as economic ones. The imposition of sanctions on Russia following its invasion of Ukraine demonstrated how the dollar's dominance can be weaponized, prompting other nations to explore alternative financial arrangements.

China, in particular, has taken a leading role in this effort, promoting the internationalization of the yuan through currency swap agreements, Belt and Road Initiative projects, and the development of CIPS as an alternative to SWIFT. Already, China and Russia have settled more than 70% of their bilateral trade in yuan and rubles, marking a sharp departure from dollar-denominated transactions of the past.

India and the broader BRICS bloc have also intensified their efforts to reduce reliance on the dollar. India has expanded rupee-based trade settlements with Russia, the UAE, and select African nations, while Brazil has increased yuan-denominated trade with China. The BRICS coalition is actively exploring the creation of a new reserve currency backed by a basket of member nations' currencies, aiming to provide an alternative to the dollar-dominated global financial system. These moves signal a broader realignment, where emerging economies are building parallel financial structures to insulate themselves from U.S. monetary policy and geopolitical pressures.

Geopolitical Tensions and Global Trade Fragmentation

The world is witnessing a shift from a unipolar order dominated by the U.S. to a more multipolar system in which China, Russia, and other emerging powers assert greater influence. If the U.S.-China rivalry escalates into a full economic decoupling, or if conflicts in the Middle East and Eastern Europe disrupt global trade, the financial system will be forced to adapt to new realities. Meanwhile, the European Union, long tethered to the U.S. financial system, has increased efforts to conduct energy trade in euros rather than dollars, particularly in deals with Russia and Iran.

History shows that major financial shifts are often triggered by crises rather than gradual, planned transitions. The collapse of the gold standard in 1971, the emergence of floating exchange rates, and the 2008 financial crisis all reshaped global finance in ways that were unplanned and often chaotic. A major shock—whether in the form of a U.S. debt crisis, a severe banking failure, or a global liquidity crunch—could force a faster transition toward an alternative system.

The world is at a crossroads. The decisions made in the coming years will determine whether the U.S. dollar retains its financial hegemony, whether trade and finance become increasingly fragmented, or whether an entirely new global financial order emerges. The next sections will explore these possibilities in detail, outlining how each scenario might unfold and what it would mean for the future of global trade and finance.

2

SCENARIO 1

The Resilient Dollar
U.S. Retains Financial Hegemony

The notion that the U.S. dollar could retain its dominance in the global financial system is not merely wishful thinking; it is supported by historical precedent, structural advantages, and the absence of a fully credible alternative. While the dollar's supremacy is frequently questioned, it continues to weather economic shocks, policy missteps, and geopolitical tensions. As of 2023, approximately 58% of global foreign exchange reserves are held in U.S. dollars, according to the International Monetary Fund, far surpassing the euro's 20% share and the yuan's modest 3%. This numerical reality underscores a fundamental truth: despite growing calls for de-dollarization, the dollar remains deeply entrenched in global finance—less by design and more by default.

The Foundations of Dollar Dominance

A key pillar of the dollar's resilience is the unparalleled depth and liquidity of U.S. financial markets. The U.S. Treasury market, valued at over $25 trillion, provides a level of security and liquidity that no other sovereign debt market can match. Investors, ranging from foreign central banks to multinational corporations, rely on Treasuries as a safe and accessible store of value. This demand is reinforced during times of global economic distress.

The 2008 financial crisis, often seen as a moment of reckoning for the U.S. financial system, paradoxically strengthened the dollar's dominance. As financial panic spread globally, capital flowed into U.S. assets, particularly Treasuries, reaffirming that even when the U.S. economy is the epicenter of a crisis, global trust in the dollar persists. A similar pattern emerged during the COVID-19 pandemic: between March and June 2020, foreign holdings of U.S. Treasuries surged by over $500 billion as investors sought stability amid market turmoil.

Moreover, the dollar benefits from a powerful network effect. The more the dollar is used in international transactions, the more indispensable it becomes. According to the Bank for International Settlements, nearly 90% of all foreign exchange transactions involve the U.S. dollar on one side—an unparalleled level of ubiquity that creates a self-reinforcing cycle. Businesses and governments prefer to transact in dollars not just out of convenience, but because its dominance ensures deep liquidity and predictable value. Even China, the most vocal proponent of de-dollarization, remains a major holder of U.S. Treasuries, with over $800 billion in reserves—an implicit acknowledgment that, for now, viable alternatives remain elusive.

Geopolitical alliances further bolster the dollar's position. U.S. military and economic influence spans the globe, providing an implicit guarantee that reinforces confidence in American financial instruments. From NATO allies in Europe to Pacific partners like Japan and South Korea, and trading blocs such as the USMCA, the dollar's reach extends far beyond financial markets into global strategic alignments. While economic ties alone may not guarantee the dollar's permanence, the geopolitical architecture built over decades ensures that many nations have vested interests in maintaining the current system.

Challenges to Dollar Hegemony

However, maintaining dollar hegemony is not without challenges. The U.S. national debt-to-GDP ratio, which stood at 123% in 2023, raises concerns about long-term sustainability. Repeated debt ceiling standoffs and persistent fiscal deficits are beginning to test investor patience, raising questions about Washington's ability to manage its growing financial obligations.

Yet, history offers a counterpoint: the British pound, despite Britain's declining empire, remained a significant global currency for decades due to trust in its institutions and financial markets. The U.S., with its technological innovation, economic dynamism, and robust legal framework, could follow a similar trajectory—even as its share of global GDP declines.

Perhaps the strongest argument for the dollar's resilience is the lack of a fully credible challenger. The euro, while a significant player, is hamstrung by political fragmentation within the European Union. The yuan, despite China's economic might, is constrained by Beijing's capital controls, lack of transparency, and concerns over political interference in financial markets. Gold, once the bedrock of the global monetary system, lacks the flexibility modern economies demand and cannot function as a primary reserve asset at scale. In essence, the dollar's dominance persists not because it is perfect, but because its alternatives are flawed in ways that markets cannot ignore.

If current trends continue, the dollar's share of global reserves may gradually decline, but its central role in trade, finance, and investment is unlikely to disappear in the foreseeable future. The resilience of the dollar is not merely a product of historical inertia; it rests on structural advantages that are difficult to replicate or dislodge. As the next section will explore, however, this resilience is not immune to the forces of fragmentation and regionalism that are increasingly shaping global economic alliances.

Why the Dollar Could Endure

The U.S. dollar's status as the world's dominant reserve currency has been challenged before, yet each time, it has demonstrated remarkable resilience. From the collapse of the Bretton Woods system in the 1970s to the oil shocks, inflationary crises, and global financial meltdowns, the dollar has repeatedly emerged as the anchor of global finance.

While de-dollarization efforts are gaining momentum and alternative financial systems are being explored, the reality remains that the global economy is deeply intertwined with the dollar in ways that cannot be unwound quickly or easily. The persistence of U.S. financial dominance is underpinned by three key factors: sustained investor confidence in U.S. Treasuries, the structural advantages of America's financial markets, and the geopolitical alliances that reinforce the dollar's role as the foundation of global commerce.

Investor Confidence in U.S. Treasuries

The demand for U.S. government debt remains one of the strongest pillars supporting the dollar's dominance. Treasuries are regarded as the safest and most liquid financial assets in the world, offering investors a refuge in times of uncertainty. This perception of safety has endured despite soaring U.S. debt levels, a feat few other nations have managed to achieve. No other country has been able to replicate the scale, transparency, and liquidity of America's bond market, where over $26 trillion in marketable securities circulate, providing unmatched depth and flexibility for global investors.

Historically, economic crises have reinforced—not weakened—demand for the dollar. In the aftermath of the 2008 financial crisis, global investors did not flee U.S. assets despite the crisis originating in American financial markets; instead, they flocked to Treasuries, driving yields to historic lows. A similar pattern emerged during the COVID-19 pandemic, when foreign holdings of U.S. Treasuries surged by over $500 billion between March and June 2020 as fears of economic collapse spread worldwide. These episodes highlight a critical dynamic: even when U.S. policies or institutions are at the center of turmoil, the global financial system continues to trust in the underlying stability of the American economic framework.

What reinforces this confidence? The sheer scale of the U.S. Treasury market provides liquidity unmatched by any other sovereign debt market. Even Japan, whose government debt exceeds 250% of GDP, cannot offer the same global acceptance due to its less liquid bond market and a narrower investor base. For central banks and sovereign wealth funds, holding Treasuries is not just a preference but a necessity—there are simply no other assets that offer the same combination of safety, liquidity, and ease of transaction. As long as this dynamic holds, the dollar will remain the anchor of the global financial system.

Structural Advantages of U.S. Financial Markets

Beyond the demand for Treasuries, the structural depth of U.S. financial markets gives the dollar an enduring advantage. The United States is home to the world's largest and most liquid capital markets, attracting investment from every corner of the globe. In 2023, U.S. stock markets accounted for approximately 42% of global equity market capitalization, far outpacing any other nation or region. The New York Stock Exchange and NASDAQ dominate global equity trading, while the depth of the U.S. banking system ensures that capital can move freely with minimal restrictions. The robust legal and regulatory framework, though occasionally criticized, provides investors with a level of transparency and protection that many emerging markets struggle to match.

These factors reinforce the dollar's supremacy by making it the default currency for global investors seeking stability, liquidity, and high returns. Even during periods of U.S. economic turmoil, such as the 2011 debt ceiling crisis, investors continued to view dollar-denominated assets as safer bets compared to alternatives.

The power of the U.S. financial system also extends beyond equities and bonds. The vast majority of international trade and cross-border transactions are still conducted in dollars. As of 2022, over 80% of global trade invoices were denominated in U.S. dollars, including in sectors where the U.S. is not the primary trading partner. This dominance creates a reinforcing cycle: businesses need dollars to settle trade, which increases demand for dollar-based banking systems, further deepening the dollar's entrenchment in global finance.

Even debt issued outside the United States often remains tied to the dollar. According to the Institute of International Finance, nearly 70% of emerging market corporate debt is denominated in dollars, reflecting investor preference for the U.S. currency over more volatile local alternatives. Attempts to break this cycle would require not only a viable alternative reserve currency but also the development of deep, trusted financial markets that can compete with the scale and sophistication of those in the United States. Currently, no such system exists.

Geopolitical Alliances and the Dollar's Security Premium

Economic dominance is rarely built on finance alone; military and geopolitical influences also play a decisive role in shaping the global monetary order. The dollar's hegemony is underpinned by U.S. military strength, which provides an implicit guarantee that bolsters confidence in American financial instruments. The American military presence across the globe, its network of alliances, and its ability to enforce economic and trade security contribute to the trust that underpins the dollar. For nations aligned with the U.S., such as NATO members, Japan, and South Korea, the dollar's dominance is not just a financial convenience but a strategic necessity.

Global trade agreements also work in the dollar's favor. The U.S. maintains a web of economic partnerships with key allies, from

NATO members in Europe to trade agreements with Japan, South Korea, and Canada. These alliances extend beyond commerce, encompassing coordinated banking regulations, shared financial infrastructure, and collective defense pacts that disincentivize any rapid shift away from dollar-based transactions.

Additionally, the geopolitical risks faced by America's primary economic rivals work to the dollar's advantage. While China has made strides in increasing the yuan's global use, the lack of full capital account convertibility and concerns over state intervention in financial markets remain significant obstacles. Investors and central banks remain wary of holding large yuan reserves when the Chinese government maintains strict capital controls and has demonstrated a willingness to intervene in financial markets. Even the euro, despite its strengths, suffers from political fragmentation within the EU, making long-term investor confidence more fragile.

The Dollar's Enduring Strength in a Changing World

Despite the growing momentum of de-dollarization and alternative financial systems, the U.S. dollar remains the foundation of global finance. Its resilience is reinforced not just by historical inertia, but by the unique blend of liquidity, transparency, and geopolitical assurance that the U.S. offers. For now, no viable contender has emerged that can match the full spectrum of advantages the dollar provides. While challenges to dollar dominance will continue to emerge, any replacement would need to offer comparable levels of security, liquidity, and global acceptance—an objective that remains elusive for even the most determined challengers.

The forces supporting the dollar are deeply embedded in the global economic framework. Even if de-dollarization efforts gain traction, the dollar's role in trade, finance, and investment will not vanish overnight. Understanding the durability of these foundations is crucial to grasping why the dollar remains so central to the world economy. The next section will explore how these structural advantages may be tested by shifting global trade patterns and emerging financial alternatives, raising the question of whether the world is moving toward a more fragmented, multi-currency system— or whether the dollar's dominance will continue to evolve but endure.

Challenges & Vulnerabilities

The resilience of the U.S. dollar is not without its weaknesses. While its deep financial markets and entrenched role in global trade have provided an enduring foundation, this dominance is increasingly being tested by internal fiscal pressures and shifting global economic strategies. The biggest risks lie not in external shocks, but in structural issues that threaten to weaken the dollar's standing from within. Debt accumulation, rising interest rates, and growing de-dollarization efforts are placing unprecedented pressures on U.S. financial hegemony. Even if the dollar retains its central position in global finance, these vulnerabilities could steadily erode the advantages that have defined American economic dominance for decades.

U.S. Finances under Strain

For years, the U.S. has benefited from a unique privilege: the ability to finance large deficits without triggering a loss of investor confidence. As the issuer of the world's primary reserve currency, Washington has been able to borrow extensively at relatively low interest rates, relying on steady demand for U.S. Treasuries from foreign governments, financial institutions, and private investors. But this privilege is showing signs of strain.

The national debt has surged past $34 trillion, fueled by persistent fiscal deficits, entitlement spending, and higher interest payments. In 2023 alone, interest payments on U.S. debt exceeded $659 billion—more than the budget for the Department of Defense—raising alarms about long-term fiscal sustainability. The issue is no longer simply one of scale but of sustainability. As borrowing costs increase, the U.S. government finds itself in a precarious position. The Federal Reserve's aggressive rate hikes in 2022–2023, aimed at taming inflation, have further amplified debt servicing costs, forcing policymakers into a fiscal corner.

At what point does the debt load become a crisis? Historically, markets have shown remarkable tolerance for U.S. debt, but this confidence is fragile. A sudden shift in sentiment, triggered by political gridlock over debt ceiling negotiations or rising inflation fears, could lead to a sharp sell-off in Treasuries, raising borrowing costs not just for the U.S., but globally. If investors begin questioning

Washington's ability—or willingness—to stabilize its finances, the consequences could be severe. Unlike past decades, where economic dynamism offset fiscal concerns, the current environment of slowing growth and mounting obligations presents new risks.

The political landscape further complicates matters. Fiscal responsibility has become a deeply partisan issue, with little consensus on how to address the growing debt burden. Repeated clashes over budget priorities, coupled with short-term political calculations, have eroded confidence in Washington's fiscal discipline. Economic hegemonies—from the British Empire to the Roman Empire—have faltered not solely due to external threats but because of internal mismanagement of their financial foundations. While the U.S. is far from the point of collapse, the cracks in its fiscal position are becoming more apparent, raising uncomfortable questions about the long-term viability of dollar dominance.

De-Dollarization: The Slow Erosion of Dominance

Even if the U.S. successfully manages its debt burden, it faces another long-term challenge: the gradual, but persistent, efforts by other nations to reduce their dependence on the dollar. This trend is not merely rhetorical but is increasingly reflected in global financial strategies and trade agreements.

China has been at the forefront of this effort, using a multi-pronged strategy to expand the yuan's role in global trade. Through bilateral trade agreements, such as those with Russia, Brazil, and Gulf nations, China has pushed for yuan-based settlements, reducing reliance on dollar transactions. The expansion of the Belt and Road Initiative has further accelerated this process, with over $400 billion in infrastructure financing increasingly denominated in yuan. Meanwhile, BRICS nations have made de-dollarization a key policy focus, culminating in recent discussions about creating a BRICS-backed settlement currency as an alternative to the dollar-dominated SWIFT system.

This shift is not limited to China. Countries in the Middle East, long aligned with the petrodollar system, are now considering diversifying their trade invoicing. Saudi Arabia's openness to pricing oil in yuan or euros, signaled during discussions with China in 2022, represents a seismic shift in energy markets long dominated by the dollar. While such moves remain incremental, they highlight a growing willingness to experiment with financial alternatives, even if no immediate replacement for the dollar exists.

One of the greatest strengths of the U.S. dollar has been its ubiquity—global businesses, investors, and governments rely on it because there has been no viable substitute. However, a world in which multiple competing financial ecosystems emerge presents new risks for the U.S. The more countries engage in non-dollar transactions, the easier it becomes for others to follow, creating a self-reinforcing trend that could gradually diminish the dollar's centrality. If this shift accelerates, the U.S. may find it increasingly difficult to wield financial influence through sanctions, control global liquidity, or sustain the dollar's privileged role in international markets.

This slow erosion of dominance carries significant implications. A reduced reliance on the dollar would mean higher transaction costs for U.S. firms, increased currency volatility, and a diminished ability for Washington to influence global economic affairs through monetary policy. While the dollar is unlikely to be overtaken in the near future, its influence could wane in subtle but significant ways.

The process of de-dollarization is slow-moving, but its momentum is growing. Over time, these shifts could lead to a more fragmented global financial system—one where the dollar remains a key player but must share the stage with alternative reserves such as the yuan, euro, and even digital assets like central bank digital currencies (CBDCs). While this does not mean the immediate collapse of dollar hegemony, it signals that the era of uncontested U.S. financial dominance is facing a slow but steady transformation.

A System under Pressure

The dollar's resilience has been tested before, and each time it has emerged intact. The oil crises of the 1970s, the inflationary shocks of the 1980s, the Asian financial crisis of the 1990s, and the global financial meltdown of 2008 all threatened U.S. economic hegemony, yet the dollar remained the world's safe-haven currency. In each case, the depth of American financial markets and the absence of a viable alternative allowed the dollar to maintain its dominance. Yet, history does not move in straight lines. The pressures facing the U.S. today—record debt levels, political gridlock, rising interest rates, and active de-dollarization efforts by major economies—are more complex than ever before.

Debt levels are unsustainable, and fiscal mismanagement could force difficult choices that test the limits of global confidence. At the same time, the persistent push for de-dollarization is no longer a distant possibility but a tangible policy direction for many economies. These challenges do not spell an immediate crisis, but they do raise the specter of a slow erosion of U.S. financial power—a process that, if left unaddressed, could reshape the global monetary order in profound ways.

The question remains: Will Washington recognize these warning signs in time to adapt, or will the world continue moving toward financial diversification with or without U.S. cooperation?

Outcome of Scenario 1: The Cost of Inaction

If the U.S. manages to retain its financial dominance in the years ahead, the dollar will remain the global reserve currency, but the landscape of international finance will not remain static. Even under this scenario, the forces challenging the dollar's supremacy—rising global debt, geopolitical rivalries, and alternative financial structures—will continue to shape the world economy. The resilience of the U.S. financial system will ensure that the dollar remains the anchor of global trade, but its position will be more precarious than in previous decades. Stability will come at a price, as maintaining the dollar's dominance will require periodic interventions from the Federal Reserve and the U.S. government to counter economic crises and prevent destabilizing capital flight.

The defining characteristic of this future will be heightened volatility. The dollar's dominance has long provided a stabilizing force for global markets, but as countries increasingly diversify their reserves, financial shocks could become more frequent and pronounced. The traditional cycle of dollar demand—where investors seek refuge in U.S. assets during global downturns—will remain intact, but each crisis will expose new vulnerabilities within the U.S. financial system.

In response, the Federal Reserve will likely resort to familiar tools: quantitative easing to inject liquidity, interest rate adjustments to manage inflationary pressures, and fiscal stimulus measures to stabilize domestic growth. While these interventions may provide short-term relief, they will also fuel long-term concerns about the sustainability of U.S. debt and the dollar's purchasing power. The delicate balance between stabilizing markets and maintaining fiscal discipline will become increasingly difficult to achieve, especially in an environment where investor scrutiny of U.S. debt levels is intensifying.

The U.S. economy itself will remain a dominant force, but its role as the world's undisputed financial hegemon will gradually erode. The global economy will still be dollar-centric, yet alternative financial structures will continue to emerge in parallel. The euro will retain its role as the second-most important reserve currency, while the Chinese yuan will make incremental gains, particularly in regional trade settlements across Asia, Africa, and parts of Latin America. Gold may experience a partial resurgence as a hedge against monetary instability, and digital assets—ranging from Bitcoin to central bank digital currencies—will gain traction in niche financial transactions, offering alternatives for cross-border payments and reserve holdings.

Rather than a dramatic shift, this scenario envisions a multipolar financial world, where the dollar remains dominant but must coexist with an increasingly complex system of competing assets. U.S. policymakers will face a constant balancing act: leveraging the dollar's reserve status to maintain economic influence while managing the risks that come with mounting debt and global diversification. The dollar's dominance will continue to provide immense benefits—lower borrowing costs, sustained demand for U.S. Treasuries, and the ability to finance trade deficits without immediate repercussions—but the growing reliance on these advantages will also heighten systemic risks.

As more countries diversify their reserves, the sensitivity of global markets to U.S. economic fluctuations will intensify. Debt ceiling debates, inflation cycles, and Federal Reserve policy decisions will trigger broader ripple effects, making financial markets more reactive and less predictable.

Ultimately, the endurance of the dollar in this scenario does not signal a return to the past. It represents a world where U.S. financial leadership persists, but with diminishing leverage. The global financial system will be more fragmented, with competing spheres of influence forming around alternative reserves. The dollar will remain the linchpin of international finance, but its grip will no longer be unchallenged.

This world will be marked by greater uncertainty, increased economic intervention, and a gradual shift toward a more decentralized monetary order. The U.S. will still hold the keys to the global financial system, but for the first time in nearly a century, it will not hold them alone.

3

SCENARIO 2

The Fragmented Future:
A Multipolar Financial System

The notion of a multipolar financial system—where the U.S. dollar no longer reigns supreme but coexists with other major currencies—is no longer a distant theoretical possibility; it is an emerging reality driven by shifting economic alliances, technological advancements, and geopolitical recalibrations. While the dollar's dominance has withstood numerous challenges over the past century, the accelerating pace of de-dollarization efforts, coupled with the rise of digital currencies and regional trade blocs, is steadily eroding the pillars of U.S. financial hegemony.

This shift is not born out of sudden economic upheaval, but from a gradual realignment of global power dynamics. As countries seek to reduce their reliance on the dollar, new financial ecosystems are beginning to take root—from the yuan's increasing role in Asian trade to the European Union's efforts to enhance the euro's global standing and the growing interest in digital assets as borderless financial instruments. The emergence of this fragmented financial landscape will not happen overnight, but the trend lines are clear: the world is inching toward a system where multiple currencies share influence, and no single nation wields uncontested monetary power.

This scenario envisions a future where the once-unquestioned centrality of the U.S. dollar gives way to a more diverse, albeit complex, financial order. While the dollar will remain a significant player, its dominance will be tempered by the rise of alternative currencies, regional trade agreements, and digital financial innovations that challenge traditional monetary frameworks. As the following sections will explore, this fragmented future promises both opportunities and uncertainties, forcing the U.S. and other economic powers to adapt to a rapidly evolving financial landscape.

Chapter 11: The Future of Global Trade & Finance

Catalysts for a Multipolar Financial System

The shift toward a multipolar financial system is being propelled by a combination of geopolitical, economic, and technological forces. While no single event has triggered this transition, the cumulative impact of trade realignments, technological disruptions, and political tensions has created fertile ground for financial diversification. As countries seek to hedge against the risks of an overreliance on the U.S. dollar, a new financial order is beginning to take shape—one that reflects the growing influence of emerging markets, regional alliances, and digital innovation.

Geopolitical Realignments and the Drive for Financial Independence

Geopolitical fractures are accelerating the push for a multipolar financial system. The growing rivalry between the U.S. and China has prompted many nations to seek financial independence from the dollar-dominated system, fearing that their economic stability could be compromised by geopolitical tensions or U.S.-imposed sanctions. The imposition of sanctions on Russia following its 2022 invasion of Ukraine, which froze hundreds of billions in Russian reserves held in Western financial institutions, served as a stark reminder to many countries of the potential vulnerabilities inherent in the current system.

In response, China has aggressively promoted the yuan as an alternative for trade settlements, particularly within Asia, Africa, and Latin America. The China-Russia bilateral trade relationship, for instance, has increasingly moved toward yuan-based transactions, with over 70% of bilateral trade settlements conducted in local currencies as of 2023. Similarly, the BRICS bloc has expanded its efforts to create financial mechanisms that bypass the dollar, including cross-border payment systems and regional reserve pools that reduce reliance on U.S.-led financial institutions such as SWIFT and the IMF.

These geopolitical shifts are not merely reactive measures; they reflect a broader ambition among emerging markets to assert greater financial autonomy. As countries diversify their trade partnerships and investment flows, the dollar's grip on global finance weakens, making room for a more balanced financial system where multiple currencies coexist.

The Rise of Regional Trade Blocs and Currency Agreements

The proliferation of regional trade blocs has also played a critical role in fostering a multipolar financial system. Agreements such as the Regional Comprehensive Economic Partnership (RCEP) in Asia, the African Continental Free Trade Area (AfCFTA), and the expansion of the European Union's single market have created ecosystems where local currencies are increasingly favored over the dollar.

RCEP, which encompasses 15 Asia-Pacific countries and accounts for nearly 30% of global GDP, has accelerated the use of local currencies in intraregional trade. By 2023, over 35% of trade within the RCEP bloc was settled in non-dollar currencies, with the yuan playing a particularly prominent role. Similarly, the AfCFTA has encouraged African nations to reduce dollar dependency by settling trade in regional currencies, with the Pan-African Payment and Settlement System (PAPSS) facilitating cross-border transactions without relying on U.S. financial intermediaries.

These regional agreements are more than just economic partnerships; they represent deliberate efforts to build financial resilience by reducing exposure to dollar volatility and U.S. monetary policy shifts. As more countries engage in currency swap agreements and local currency settlements, the dollar's dominance in global trade faces incremental, yet persistent, erosion.

Technological Innovation and the Emergence of Digital Currencies

Perhaps the most transformative catalyst for a multipolar financial system is the rapid advancement of digital financial technologies. The rise of central bank digital currencies (CBDCs), blockchain-based payment systems, and decentralized finance (DeFi) platforms has introduced new tools for cross-border transactions that bypass traditional banking systems—and, by extension, the dollar.

China's digital yuan, which has been piloted in major cities and used in cross-border payments with Hong Kong, Thailand, and the UAE, exemplifies how digital currencies can challenge the dollar's dominance. As of 2023, the digital yuan had facilitated over $100 billion in transactions, offering a glimpse into a future where digital currencies play a central role in global trade.

In addition, the growing acceptance of cryptocurrencies such as Bitcoin and Ethereum in international payments, remittances, and asset transfers underscores the potential for non-sovereign currencies to disrupt the existing financial order. While regulatory challenges remain, the increasing adoption of digital assets by both consumers and institutions suggests that a more decentralized financial landscape is on the horizon.

The combination of geopolitical shifts, regional alliances, and technological innovation is gradually reshaping the global financial system. As these forces continue to gain momentum, the dollar's singular dominance will give way to a more diverse array of currencies, each vying for influence in a rapidly evolving economic landscape.

The Role of China and the Yuan in a Multipolar World

China's ambition to reshape the global financial system is inseparable from its broader geopolitical and economic strategies. As the world's second-largest economy, China has positioned itself as the most formidable challenger to U.S. financial dominance, with the yuan playing a central role in this endeavor. While the dollar's entrenched status remains formidable, Beijing's concerted efforts to internationalize the yuan are gradually altering the global financial landscape.

China's push for yuan internationalization is not a recent development, but the scale and intensity of its efforts have accelerated in the past decade. Initiatives such as the Belt and Road Initiative (BRI), which spans over 140 countries and has mobilized more than $1 trillion in infrastructure investment, have served as a critical platform for expanding the yuan's global footprint. As of 2023, over 20% of BRI-related transactions were settled in yuan, reflecting China's deliberate strategy to reduce dollar dependency in its trade and investment partnerships.

In addition to infrastructure diplomacy, China has pursued bilateral currency swap agreements with more than 40 central banks worldwide, providing liquidity and facilitating yuan-based transactions. The People's Bank of China (PBOC) has also established offshore yuan clearing centers in major financial hubs, including London, Hong Kong, and Singapore, creating a network that enables seamless yuan transactions across continents.

These efforts are yielding tangible results. According to SWIFT, the yuan accounted for nearly 7% of global payments by value in 2023, up from just 1% a decade earlier. While this share remains modest compared to the dollar's dominance, the yuan's steady ascent signals a growing acceptance of China's currency in global finance.

Economic Influence and Trade Dynamics

China's economic influence, particularly as the world's largest trading nation, provides a strong foundation for yuan internationalization. In 2023, China's total trade surpassed $6 trillion, with major trading partners such as ASEAN, the European Union, and Africa increasingly conducting transactions in yuan. The Regional Comprehensive Economic Partnership (RCEP), which China spearheaded, has further boosted the yuan's prominence by promoting local currency settlements within the bloc.

The rise of the digital yuan has added another dimension to China's financial strategy. The digital currency, backed by the PBOC, offers a compelling alternative for cross-border payments, reducing transaction costs and bypassing U.S.-controlled financial intermediaries. In 2023, the digital yuan facilitated over $100 billion in cross-border transactions, particularly in pilot programs with Thailand, the UAE, and Hong Kong.

China's economic clout and technological advancements are creating a financial ecosystem where the yuan is increasingly viewed as a viable alternative, particularly among countries wary of U.S. sanctions or seeking to diversify their reserves. As China deepens trade ties and expands initiatives like the Belt and Road, more nations are integrating the yuan into their financial systems, accelerating the shift toward a multipolar currency landscape.

Challenges to Yuan Dominance

Despite these strides, China faces significant hurdles in establishing the yuan as a true rival to the dollar. The most formidable challenge is the lack of full capital account convertibility. Beijing's tight capital controls, aimed at preventing capital flight and maintaining economic stability, limit the yuan's liquidity and accessibility in global markets.

Moreover, concerns over China's financial transparency and the potential for political interference in its markets continue to deter many investors and central banks from holding large yuan reserves. The Chinese financial system, while vast, lacks the depth, liquidity, and regulatory transparency that characterize U.S. financial markets.

Additionally, the yuan's expansion is heavily dependent on China's geopolitical relationships. While Beijing has strengthened ties with many emerging markets, its strained relations with Western economies and ongoing trade tensions with the U.S. pose challenges to broader yuan adoption.

The Yuan's Role in a Fragmented Financial Future

In a multipolar financial system, the yuan is likely to play a significant, though not dominant, role. China's economic influence, extensive trade networks, and technological innovations provide a strong foundation for yuan adoption, particularly in Asia, Africa, and parts of Latin America. However, the structural limitations of China's financial system and the geopolitical complexities of U.S.-China relations will temper the yuan's rise.

Rather than replacing the dollar, the yuan will serve as a key pillar in a fragmented global financial system—one where multiple currencies share influence, and economic power is more distributed. As China continues to expand its financial reach, the yuan's role in global finance will grow, but its path to dominance remains fraught with challenges that Beijing will need to navigate carefully.

The Role of Digital Currencies in a Multipolar System

Digital currencies are rapidly emerging as a transformative force in global finance, challenging traditional monetary frameworks and accelerating the shift toward a multipolar financial system. While sovereign currencies like the U.S. dollar and the yuan continue to dominate, the rise of central bank digital currencies (CBDCs), cryptocurrencies, and blockchain-based payment systems is reshaping cross-border transactions and financial settlements.

Central bank digital currencies have moved from concept to reality at an unprecedented pace. Over 130 countries, representing more than 98% of global GDP, are actively exploring or piloting CBDCs, with several already in circulation. China's digital yuan leads this charge, serving not only as a domestic payment tool but also as a vehicle for cross-border trade. By 2023, the digital yuan had facilitated over \$100 billion in transactions, particularly within Asia and with Belt and Road partner nations, offering an efficient alternative to dollar-based systems.

Other major economies are following suit. The European Central Bank has committed to launching a digital euro by 2026, aiming to bolster the euro's international role and reduce dependence on U.S.-dominated financial channels. Similarly, the Bank of England and the Federal Reserve are accelerating their research into digital currencies, recognizing that the absence of a digital dollar could erode U.S. financial influence in an increasingly digitalized global economy.

CBDCs offer compelling advantages: reduced transaction costs, enhanced transparency, and greater efficiency in cross-border payments. More importantly, they provide countries with an opportunity to bypass traditional financial intermediaries, many of which are U.S.-controlled, thereby reducing their exposure to dollar-based sanctions and policies.

Cryptocurrencies and Decentralized Finance: A Borderless Alternative

Beyond state-backed digital currencies, cryptocurrencies like Bitcoin and Ethereum are carving out roles in global finance that were unimaginable a decade ago. While regulatory scrutiny remains intense, cryptocurrencies have found acceptance in remittances, cross-border payments, and as stores of value in economically unstable regions.

In 2023, Bitcoin transactions exceeded \$11 trillion globally, with significant adoption in countries like El Salvador, Nigeria, and Argentina, where inflation and currency volatility have driven demand for decentralized alternatives. Stablecoins, digital assets pegged to traditional currencies, have gained particular traction, providing the benefits of digital transactions without the volatility associated with traditional cryptocurrencies.

The decentralized finance (DeFi) ecosystem, built on blockchain technology, is further eroding the dominance of conventional banking systems. Platforms that allow peer-to-peer lending, borrowing, and trading are bypassing the need for traditional banks and, by extension, reducing reliance on dollar-based systems. As these platforms grow, they create a parallel financial network that is borderless, resilient, and increasingly influential.

The Digital Payment Infrastructure and Cross-Border Trade

The infrastructure supporting digital payments is expanding rapidly, providing the backbone for a multipolar financial system. Systems like China's Cross-Border Interbank Payment System (CIPS), which offers an alternative to the SWIFT network, are enabling seamless international transactions in yuan. Meanwhile, blockchain-based solutions such as Ripple's XRP Ledger are offering faster, cheaper cross-border settlements, challenging the dominance of the dollar in international trade.

This growing digital infrastructure reduces the friction traditionally associated with non-dollar transactions. As countries and businesses adopt digital payment solutions, the need to rely on dollar-denominated financial intermediaries diminishes, further weakening the dollar's central role in global finance.

A Digital Future: Challenges and Opportunities

While digital currencies offer a path toward financial diversification, challenges remain. Regulatory uncertainty, particularly in the U.S. and EU, poses risks to the widespread adoption of cryptocurrencies and decentralized finance. Moreover, the digital yuan's expansion is limited by geopolitical tensions and concerns over China's financial surveillance practices.

Nonetheless, the trajectory is clear: digital currencies are here to stay, and their influence will only grow. In a multipolar financial system, digital assets will serve as both complements and competitors to traditional currencies, offering flexibility, efficiency, and reduced dependency on any single monetary authority. As digital currencies continue to evolve, they will play a pivotal role in shaping the future of global finance, accelerating the shift away from a dollar-dominated system toward a more fragmented, dynamic financial landscape.

Implications of a Multipolar Financial System

The emergence of a multipolar financial system carries profound implications for global trade, investment, monetary policy, and geopolitical dynamics. While the dollar will remain a significant force, its gradual decline from unrivaled dominance will reshape the financial landscape, altering the balance of economic power and introducing new complexities for policymakers and businesses alike.

In a world where multiple currencies hold sway, global trade will become more fragmented. Businesses will need to navigate a more complex financial environment, managing currency risks across a broader spectrum of currencies rather than relying predominantly on the dollar. This shift will increase transaction costs and complicate pricing strategies, particularly for multinational corporations accustomed to dollar-based trade.

Investment flows will also be affected. As countries diversify their foreign exchange reserves, demand for U.S. Treasuries could soften, potentially raising borrowing costs for the U.S. government. Conversely, emerging markets that successfully promote their currencies could benefit from increased capital inflows, bolstering their financial markets and economic development. However, this redistribution of capital may also heighten volatility, as investors recalibrate their portfolios in response to shifting currency dynamics.

Monetary Policy Challenges for the U.S.

For the Federal Reserve, a multipolar system presents new challenges. The central bank's ability to influence global liquidity through monetary policy, a cornerstone of U.S. financial hegemony, may diminish as alternative currencies and digital assets reduce the world's dependence on dollar liquidity. This reduced influence could limit the effectiveness of U.S. monetary policy interventions, particularly during global crises.

Moreover, the U.S. could face higher inflationary pressures if reduced dollar demand weakens the currency's value, making imports more expensive and eroding purchasing power. Policymakers will need to balance domestic economic priorities with the demands of an increasingly fragmented global financial system, where the ripple effects of U.S. policy decisions may be less pronounced but more unpredictable.

Furthermore, the Federal Reserve may find itself navigating a more complex and less responsive global financial environment. In the past, the Fed's policy shifts—whether tightening or loosening monetary conditions—rippled through global markets almost immediately, reinforcing the dollar's centrality. However, in a world where multiple reserve currencies hold sway, international capital flows may no longer react as predictably to U.S. interest rate changes. This could weaken the Fed's ability to contain financial crises, as liquidity injections or rate cuts may not have the same stabilizing effect on global markets.

At the same time, a diminished role for the dollar could increase volatility in U.S. financial markets, as investors diversify away from Treasuries and seek alternative safe-haven assets. If demand for U.S. government debt declines, Washington may struggle to finance deficits at historically low costs, leading to higher borrowing expenses and greater fiscal pressure. In such a scenario, the U.S. would have to adapt to a new reality—one where its economic policies must compete for global capital rather than dictate its flow.

Geopolitical Shifts and Strategic Alignments

The geopolitical landscape will also be reshaped by financial fragmentation. Countries with strong regional currencies, such as China with the yuan and the EU with the euro, will wield greater economic influence, potentially challenging U.S. geopolitical supremacy. This shift could redefine alliances, with countries aligning more closely with financial powers that best serve their economic interests.

Sanctions, a key tool of U.S. foreign policy, may lose some of their potency. As countries develop alternative payment systems and hold reserves in non-dollar assets, the U.S.'s ability to enforce economic sanctions could be undermined. This erosion of financial leverage will force Washington to rely more heavily on diplomatic and military tools to achieve its foreign policy objectives. In turn, this shift could reshape global alliances, as nations previously vulnerable to U.S. financial pressure seek greater economic and strategic independence, reducing Washington's influence over international affairs.

Increased Currency Volatility and Financial Innovation

The transition to a multipolar system will likely be accompanied by increased currency volatility. With multiple reserve currencies competing for dominance, exchange rates may experience greater fluctuations, posing challenges for global trade and investment stability. However, this volatility could also spur financial innovation, as businesses and investors seek sophisticated hedging instruments and new financial technologies to manage currency risk.

Digital currencies and blockchain-based financial solutions will play a critical role in this environment, offering tools for efficient, low-cost cross-border transactions and reducing reliance on any single currency. This wave of innovation will not only reshape financial markets but also challenge traditional banking systems and monetary authorities. As central banks and private entities race to develop digital currencies, the competition to establish new standards for global transactions will intensify, potentially weakening the influence of traditional reserve currencies and shifting financial power toward decentralized networks and regional digital payment systems.

A More Equitable Financial Order or a Fragmented Future?

The rise of a multipolar financial system holds the potential for a more equitable global financial order, where economic power is more evenly distributed. Emerging markets and developing economies, long constrained by dollar dependence and U.S. monetary policy, could gain greater financial autonomy and resilience. Yet, this future also carries risks: financial fragmentation could lead to inefficiencies, higher transaction costs, and increased economic uncertainty.

Ultimately, the transition to a multipolar system is not merely a shift in financial instruments but a fundamental reordering of global economic power. The dollar's dominance may not vanish, but its singular hold on global finance is slipping, giving rise to a more complex, dynamic, and uncertain financial landscape that will demand adaptability from nations, businesses, and investors alike.

Outcome of Scenario 2: The Risks of Overreach

If the global financial system evolves into a truly multipolar framework, the consequences will be profound. The U.S. dollar, while still influential, will no longer enjoy its unchallenged status as the world's primary reserve currency. Instead, a constellation of currencies—including the yuan, euro, and digital assets—will share the stage, each playing a vital role in global trade, investment, and monetary policy. This shift will not happen overnight, but the momentum is undeniable.

In this scenario, the financial landscape will become more competitive and decentralized. Countries will diversify their reserves, reducing exposure to U.S. monetary policy but increasing the complexity of global financial management. For the U.S., this shift will mean higher borrowing costs, as demand for Treasuries declines and interest rates rise to attract investors. The era of financing fiscal deficits with minimal consequences, a privilege long enjoyed by Washington, will come under strain. Policymakers will need to adjust to a world where the dollar no longer carries the same weight in international finance.

Emerging markets, on the other hand, could see new opportunities. With reduced reliance on the dollar, they may benefit from increased investment and financial autonomy, fostering regional economic integration and innovation. However, the absence of a single, dominant reserve currency could introduce greater financial volatility, with more frequent shifts in exchange rates and capital flows. A fragmented system may empower some nations but leave others more exposed to financial shocks.

Geopolitically, a multipolar financial system will create a more fluid and dynamic environment. Economic alliances will become more transactional, with countries aligning based on financial convenience rather than historical ties. The U.S. will remain a key player, but its ability to wield financial influence through sanctions and monetary policy will diminish, forcing a recalibration of its global strategy. This transformation will not only reshape economic power but also redefine diplomatic relationships and global governance structures.

At the heart of this transition will be digital currencies and financial technology. As blockchain-based systems and central bank digital currencies (CBDCs) gain traction, they will facilitate faster, cheaper, and more transparent transactions, eroding the traditional dominance of the dollar-based banking system. This digital shift, while democratizing finance, will also challenge regulatory frameworks and necessitate global cooperation to prevent financial fragmentation. The rise of decentralized financial systems will pose new risks, particularly in terms of cybersecurity, regulation, and monetary policy coordination.

Ultimately, a multipolar financial system represents both opportunity and uncertainty. While it promises a more balanced distribution of economic power, it also raises the specter of increased volatility, regulatory challenges, and complex financial interactions. The U.S. will still play a critical role, but it will do so in a world where its financial influence is one among many rather than the singular force it once was.

The key question is whether global institutions and policymakers are prepared for this shift—or whether the transition to a multipolar financial system will be marked by turbulence. With no single currency poised to fully replace the dollar, the coming years could see a fragmented system where multiple reserve currencies compete for dominance. If the shift is poorly managed, it could trigger capital flight, liquidity shortages, and heightened financial instability—particularly in emerging markets that remain dependent on dollar-based trade and investment.

4

SCENARIO 3

The Decline Of The Dollar
A Post-Hegemonic Financial Order

The notion that the U.S. dollar could lose its status as the world's dominant reserve currency once seemed improbable. For decades, the dollar's supremacy has been underpinned by the size of the U.S. economy, the liquidity of its financial markets, and the geopolitical influence of Washington. Yet, history offers a sobering lesson: no global currency retains its dominance indefinitely. Just as the British pound ceded its role to the dollar in the mid-20th century, the possibility of a post-dollar financial order is no longer confined to academic speculation or political rhetoric—it is a scenario that global markets are increasingly considering.

What would a world without dollar hegemony look like? The decline of the dollar would usher in a fragmented financial order, where multiple currencies compete for influence, regional alliances dictate monetary flows, and the U.S. finds its economic leverage diminished. This scenario is not a distant fantasy but a plausible outcome driven by mounting U.S. debt, geopolitical shifts, and the rapid development of alternative financial ecosystems.

As of 2023, the U.S. national debt has surpassed $34 trillion, with interest payments alone exceeding $659 billion annually—a burden that threatens long-term fiscal stability. Rising debt, coupled with political gridlock and monetary policy missteps, could erode investor confidence in U.S. assets, triggering a flight from the dollar. At the same time, rival economic powers, particularly China and a coalition of emerging markets, are accelerating efforts to reduce their reliance on the dollar, building regional payment systems and expanding the use of local currencies in trade settlements.

A post-dollar world would not emerge overnight, but the gradual erosion of the dollar's dominance would reshape the global financial landscape. U.S. policymakers would lose the unparalleled flexibility they have long enjoyed—borrowing cheaply, imposing financial sanctions with ease, and influencing global monetary policy through the Federal Reserve. Instead, they would face a new reality where financial power is dispersed, and economic diplomacy becomes a more delicate balancing act.

The erosion of the dollar would carry profound implications not just for the United States, but for the entire global economy. Trade flows would become more complex, currency volatility would rise, and international debt markets would need to adapt to a world where the dollar is no longer the default benchmark. This section explores the key drivers behind a potential dollar decline, the structural changes that would accompany this shift, and the far-reaching consequences for global trade, investment, and economic stability.

The decline of the U.S. dollar as the world's dominant reserve currency would not occur due to a single event, but rather through a confluence of economic, political, and structural forces. While the dollar's resilience has been remarkable, the growing weight of U.S. debt, shifts in global trade patterns, and increasing efforts by other nations to bypass the dollar are creating conditions ripe for a gradual erosion of its supremacy.

Unsustainable U.S. Debt and Fiscal Imbalance

At the heart of the dollar's potential decline is the mounting fiscal burden of the United States. The national debt, which now exceeds $34 trillion, has surged from 55% of GDP in 2000 to 123% in 2023. This rapid accumulation has not only raised alarms among economists but also triggered concerns among global investors who have long viewed U.S. Treasuries as the safest financial assets. As interest payments on this debt surpassed $659 billion in 2023—more than the entire defense budget—the sustainability of U.S. fiscal policy is under increasing scrutiny.

The era of near-zero interest rates, which made servicing large deficits manageable, has come to an end. The Federal Reserve's aggressive rate hikes in response to post-pandemic inflation have sharply increased borrowing costs, pushing the U.S. government into a precarious position where debt servicing consumes an ever-larger share of its budget. If these trends continue, investor confidence in U.S. fiscal management could falter, leading to reduced demand for Treasuries and, consequently, a weaker dollar.

Historically, economic hegemonies have faltered when debt burdens became unsustainable. The British pound, once the backbone of global finance, saw its influence wane as Britain's post-war debt soared and its global economic dominance receded. The U.S. now faces a similar inflection point: failing to address its fiscal imbalance could accelerate the dollar's decline, as investors seek more stable and fiscally prudent alternatives.

The Rise of Alternative Financial Systems

The dollar's dominance has also come under threat from the rapid development of alternative financial systems, particularly in Asia and the Middle East. China's ambitious Belt and Road Initiative (BRI), which has financed over $1 trillion in infrastructure projects across more than 140 countries, has increasingly promoted the use of the yuan in trade and investment settlements. Additionally, the Cross-Border Interbank Payment System (CIPS), launched by Beijing in 2015, serves as a direct alternative to the U.S.-dominated SWIFT system, allowing for cross-border yuan transactions that bypass the dollar.

This shift is not confined to China. The BRICS coalition—comprising Brazil, Russia, India, China, and South Africa—has actively pursued de-dollarization, with recent discussions focusing on the creation of a BRICS-backed reserve currency. Meanwhile, Middle Eastern nations, traditionally reliant on the petrodollar system, have begun exploring alternative payment mechanisms. Saudi Arabia's openness to pricing oil in yuan, highlighted during high-level meetings with Chinese officials in 2022, signals a potential break from decades of dollar-denominated energy markets.

The cumulative effect of these developments is a slow but persistent chipping away at the dollar's centrality. As more countries adopt alternative financial systems, the global reliance on the dollar will diminish, reducing Washington's ability to influence international markets through its currency. While the transition will likely be gradual, the momentum toward a more multipolar financial order is becoming increasingly difficult to ignore. This shift could ultimately weaken the dollar's role as the default medium for global trade and investment.

Geopolitical Shifts and Eroding U.S. Influence

Geopolitical dynamics are also reshaping the global financial order. While the U.S. remains a formidable military and economic power, its unilateral influence is being challenged by rising regional blocs and shifting alliances. China's growing influence in Asia, Russia's deepening economic ties with non-Western economies despite sanctions, and the formation of new trade partnerships in the Global South are eroding the U.S.-led financial system.

Sanctions, long a powerful tool of U.S. foreign policy, have inadvertently accelerated de-dollarization. Nations targeted by these measures, such as Russia and Iran, have sought alternatives to mitigate their exposure to U.S. financial controls. The use of digital currencies, bilateral trade agreements in local currencies, and gold reserves have become part of a broader strategy to reduce dependence on the dollar and insulate economies from U.S. sanctions.

Additionally, the U.S.'s perceived political instability—marked by frequent debt ceiling standoffs, contentious fiscal debates, and growing polarization—has raised concerns about the long-term reliability of the dollar as a stable reserve currency. Investors and governments alike are beginning to hedge their bets, not because of an immediate crisis, but due to a recognition that the dollar's future may not be as secure as it once was.

Technological Disruption: Digital Currencies and Decentralized Finance

Technological advancements are further challenging the dollar's dominance. The rise of decentralized finance (DeFi), blockchain technology, and digital currencies is creating new avenues for cross-border transactions that bypass traditional banking systems. Central bank digital currencies (CBDCs), particularly China's digital yuan, are being positioned as alternatives for global trade settlements. As of 2023, over 100 central banks were exploring or developing CBDCs, signaling a significant shift in how global transactions might be conducted in the future.

The digital yuan's pilot programs, which have processed billions in transactions across China's major cities, illustrate how quickly technology can alter financial landscapes. If widely adopted in international trade, digital currencies could reduce the need for dollar intermediaries, further eroding its role as the default global currency.

A Gradual yet Inevitable Shift

The drivers of dollar erosion are numerous and interconnected. An unsustainable debt trajectory, the rise of alternative financial systems, geopolitical realignments, and technological disruptions are all converging to challenge the dollar's hegemony. While the dollar's fall will not be abrupt, the gradual erosion of its dominance is becoming increasingly plausible. The structural changes accompanying this shift would not merely reshape global finance—they would redefine economic power, trade dynamics, and the very architecture of the international monetary system.

This transition mirrors historical shifts, but with key differences. The British pound, once the backbone of global finance, saw its influence wane due to war-related debt and declining economic dominance. But today's shift is unfolding under different forces: rising multipolar trade alliances, decentralized financial technologies, and deliberate de-dollarization efforts by emerging economies. Unlike past transitions, where a single currency replaced another, the post-dollar world may not be led by just one successor—it could be a fragmented system where multiple financial hubs and competing reserve assets emerge.

Moreover, this transition is playing out against the backdrop of rapid monetary innovation. Digital currencies, blockchain settlements, and bilateral trade agreements in non-dollar currencies are already reshaping cross-border transactions. This shift is not just about currency dominance—it is about the very structure of global finance itself.

Structural Changes in a Post-Dollar World

A world where the U.S. dollar no longer holds unrivaled dominance would be marked by profound shifts in how financial power is distributed. The decline of the dollar's singular supremacy would not merely lead to a reallocation of reserve holdings—it would transform the way nations trade, invest, and manage financial risk.

One of the most immediate shifts would be the emergence of a multipolar currency system. While the dollar would still play a major role, it would no longer function as the default intermediary for global transactions. Instead, we would see the yuan, euro, and potentially a BRICS-backed reserve currency rise as viable alternatives in regional markets. This transition would increase currency diversification but also introduce new volatility, as no single currency would anchor global stability in the way the dollar has for decades.

Trade and investment strategies would also need to adapt. Businesses accustomed to dollar-based transactions would have to navigate multiple currency regimes, increasing exchange rate risks, hedging costs, and financial complexity. Central banks, in turn, would need to rethink their reserve strategies, holding a broader mix of assets beyond Treasuries and diversifying into gold, digital reserves, and regional currency swaps.

The very nature of financial infrastructure would evolve. As reliance on U.S.-controlled systems like SWIFT declines, alternative networks—such as China's CIPS or blockchain-based decentralized finance platforms—will gain traction. These systems, designed to bypass U.S. financial oversight, would reduce Washington's ability to impose sanctions, influence capital flows, or dictate liquidity conditions worldwide.

Ultimately, the post-dollar financial order would not be defined by a single event, but by a slow, strategic recalibration of global finance. While the world would still require a stable medium of exchange, it may no longer be anchored to just one dominant currency. Instead, financial power would become more regionally dispersed, introducing both opportunities and risks in the years ahead.

The Rise of a Multipolar Currency System

One of the most immediate structural changes would be the emergence of a multipolar currency system. In this new order, the dollar would coexist with other major currencies, such as the euro, the yuan, and potentially a BRICS-backed reserve currency, each holding significant but not dominant positions. The euro, despite its internal political challenges, would likely strengthen its role within Europe, North Africa, and parts of the Middle East, while the yuan would expand its influence across Asia, Africa, and Latin America, particularly through China's Belt and Road Initiative.

This fragmentation would alter the dynamics of global trade. Currently, over 80% of global trade invoices are denominated in dollars, ensuring seamless transactions across borders. In a post-dollar world, businesses would need to navigate multiple currency regimes, increasing transaction costs, exchange rate risks, and operational complexity. Financial institutions would need to adapt by offering more diverse hedging instruments, multi-currency accounts, and region-specific financial products.

Decentralized Financial Infrastructure

A decline in dollar dominance would also accelerate the development of decentralized financial infrastructure. As reliance on U.S.-based systems like SWIFT diminishes, alternative payment networks such as China's CIPS, Russia's SPFS, and blockchain-based solutions would gain prominence. These systems, designed to bypass U.S. financial controls, would enable faster, cheaper, and more secure cross-border transactions.

The adoption of central bank digital currencies (CBDCs) would further reshape global finance. China's digital yuan, which has already processed over $1.8 trillion in transactions since its pilot launch, could become the preferred medium for cross-border trade within Asia and beyond. In such a system, the need for dollar intermediaries would diminish, reducing transaction costs and enhancing financial autonomy for participating nations.

Decentralized finance (DeFi) platforms, which allow peer-to-peer financial services without traditional banks, would likely flourish in a post-dollar world. These platforms, powered by blockchain technology, would provide new avenues for borrowing, lending, and investing across borders, free from the constraints of centralized monetary systems.

Changes in Global Reserve Management

Central banks around the world would need to rethink their reserve management strategies. Currently, approximately 58% of global foreign exchange reserves are held in U.S. dollars, providing liquidity and stability. In a post-dollar era, reserves would become more diversified, with central banks holding larger shares of euros, yuan, gold, and digital currencies.

This diversification would have significant implications. The demand for U.S. Treasuries, which currently serve as the primary reserve asset, would decline, raising borrowing costs for the U.S. government. Simultaneously, countries with strong fiscal positions and stable political environments—such as Germany, Switzerland, and Singapore—could see increased demand for their sovereign debt, benefiting from lower borrowing costs and greater financial influence.

The shift would also impact global liquidity. The dollar's dominance has ensured that U.S. monetary policy decisions—such as interest rate changes by the Federal Reserve—have immediate and far-reaching effects on global financial conditions. In a multipolar system, monetary policies from multiple central banks would shape global liquidity, creating a more complex and less predictable financial environment.

Trade and Investment Realignments

Global trade patterns would also undergo significant changes. The U.S. has long enjoyed the privilege of financing its trade deficits by issuing dollar-denominated debt, but in a post-dollar world, this advantage would erode. U.S. exports would face higher costs, as foreign buyers would no longer rely exclusively on dollars, while American imports would become more expensive due to currency exchange fluctuations.

Emerging markets, which have historically faced higher borrowing costs due to their reliance on dollar-denominated debt, could benefit from a more diversified financial system. Countries like Brazil, Indonesia, and South Africa could issue debt in regional currencies, reducing their exposure to U.S. monetary policy and currency volatility. However, this shift would also introduce new risks, as fragmented markets often face higher transaction costs and reduced liquidity.

Foreign direct investment (FDI) flows would become more regionally concentrated. Investors, seeking to hedge currency risks, would likely favor projects within their own economic spheres, leading to greater regionalization of investment. This trend could benefit regional economic blocs, such as the European Union, ASEAN, and the African Continental Free Trade Area, but might limit cross-regional investment opportunities.

Diminished U.S. Economic Leverage

Perhaps the most significant structural change would be the diminished economic leverage of the United States. For decades, the U.S. has wielded its currency as a tool of foreign policy, imposing sanctions, controlling capital flows, and influencing global trade through the dollar's dominance. In a post-dollar world, this leverage would weaken, as countries adopt alternative payment systems and diversify their reserves.

Sanctions, which have been a cornerstone of U.S. foreign policy, would lose much of their efficacy. Nations targeted by U.S. sanctions, such as Russia, Iran, and Venezuela, have already begun establishing financial channels that bypass the dollar, a trend that would accelerate if the dollar's dominance erodes further.

The U.S. would also face higher borrowing costs and reduced fiscal flexibility. Without the automatic global demand for its debt, Washington would need to adopt more disciplined fiscal policies to maintain investor confidence. This constraint could limit the scope of U.S. economic interventions, both domestically and internationally.

A New Era of Financial Multipolarity

The structural changes in a post-dollar world would usher in an era of financial multipolarity, where no single currency dictates global economic flows. While this system would offer greater financial autonomy to individual nations, it would also introduce new complexities, from fluctuating exchange rates to increased transaction costs.

For the U.S., the challenge would lie in adapting to a reduced role without losing influence entirely. For emerging markets, the opportunity would be in leveraging new financial instruments and regional alliances to drive growth. And for global investors, a decentralized financial landscape would present both new risks and untapped opportunities, requiring a shift in strategies as capital flows become more fragmented.

As this transition unfolds, the global economy will experience a fundamental reshaping of trade, investment, and economic power dynamics. The institutions and mechanisms that have long relied on dollar stability will need to adjust to a world of competing currencies and shifting financial alliances. While some nations will benefit from reduced dependence on the U.S. financial system, others may struggle with heightened volatility, new transaction costs, and a lack of a singular, stabilizing force in global finance.

Global Trade Disruptions and Rising Costs

One of the most immediate consequences would be disruptions to global trade. The dollar currently serves as the universal medium for international transactions, reducing currency conversion costs and ensuring price stability across borders. Without a single dominant currency, businesses would face higher transaction costs, increased currency volatility, and more complex financial planning.

For instance, a multinational corporation exporting goods from Southeast Asia to Europe might need to navigate multiple currency exchanges—from the local currency to yuan, then euros—rather than a single dollar-based transaction. These added layers would increase operational costs, which would likely be passed on to consumers through higher prices.

Smaller economies, particularly those heavily reliant on exports, could face greater financial strain, as currency fluctuations erode profit margins and complicate trade financing. The predictability provided by dollar-based contracts would be replaced by the need for constant hedging and risk management, adding another layer of cost and complexity.

Higher Borrowing Costs for the U.S.

For the United States, the decline of the dollar would have profound fiscal implications. The U.S. has long benefited from the "exorbitant privilege" of issuing debt in its own currency, enabling it to finance large deficits without facing the full wrath of currency depreciation. A diminished dollar would erode this privilege, forcing the U.S. to offer higher yields to attract investors, thereby increasing borrowing costs.

The national debt, already at $34 trillion, would become even more burdensome as interest payments surged. Fiscal policy would need to become more disciplined, potentially leading to cuts in social programs, infrastructure spending, and defense budgets. The U.S. government's ability to implement large-scale stimulus packages during economic downturns would be constrained, making recessions deeper and recoveries slower.

Weaker U.S. Economic Influence

The dollar's decline would also weaken U.S. economic influence globally. For decades, the U.S. has used its financial system as a tool of diplomacy, from imposing sanctions to providing aid. A fragmented currency system would reduce this influence, as countries turn to alternative financial channels that bypass U.S. controls.

Sanctions on nations like Russia and Iran have been effective largely due to the dollar's centrality in global finance. In a post-dollar world, these measures would lose much of their bite, as targeted nations shift to alternative payment systems. U.S. diplomatic leverage, long bolstered by its financial clout, would be significantly diminished.

Shifts in Global Investment Flows

Investment patterns would also shift dramatically. Currently, U.S. assets—ranging from Treasuries to equities—are considered the safest and most liquid investment options. A weaker dollar would prompt investors to diversify their portfolios, increasing allocations to European, Asian, and emerging market assets. This shift could accelerate the development of alternative financial hubs, challenging the U.S.'s historical dominance in global capital markets.

This diversification could benefit emerging markets, providing them with greater access to capital, but it could also introduce more volatility, as global capital flows become more fragmented and sensitive to regional economic conditions. U.S. markets, which have long enjoyed a steady influx of foreign investment, could face reduced liquidity and higher volatility. As investor confidence in the dollar fluctuates, central banks and sovereign wealth funds may also rethink their reserve allocations, further reshaping global financial dynamics.

Impact on Consumers and Businesses

For American consumers, a weaker dollar would mean higher prices for imported goods, from electronics to energy. Inflationary pressures would mount, reducing purchasing power and altering consumption patterns. U.S. businesses, particularly those reliant on imported materials, would see costs rise, potentially leading to reduced profit margins or higher prices for consumers.

Conversely, American exporters could benefit from a weaker dollar, as U.S. goods become cheaper for foreign buyers. However, the benefits could be offset by higher input costs and reduced global demand due to broader economic uncertainty.

Opportunities for Emerging Markets

While the decline of the dollar would pose challenges, it would also present opportunities—particularly for emerging markets. Countries that have long struggled with currency volatility due to dollar-denominated debt could find relief by issuing debt in regional currencies.

For example, African nations participating in the African Continental Free Trade Area could settle trade in a common regional currency, reducing reliance on external financing and mitigating exchange rate risks. Similarly, Latin American countries could strengthen intra-regional trade, fostering economic resilience and growth.

However, these opportunities would come with risks. Emerging markets would need to develop robust financial infrastructure, enhance regulatory frameworks, and build investor confidence in local currencies. Without these measures, the transition away from the dollar could lead to financial instability rather than empowerment.

Technological Innovation and Digital Finance

The decline of the dollar would likely accelerate innovation in digital finance. Central bank digital currencies, decentralized finance platforms, and blockchain-based payment systems would gain traction, offering alternatives to traditional banking systems.

China's digital yuan, already used in cross-border trade pilots, could become a model for other countries, enabling seamless transactions without dollar intermediaries. Private digital currencies, such as stablecoins pegged to various assets, could also play a significant role, particularly in regions with underdeveloped financial systems.

This technological shift would democratize access to global finance but would also raise regulatory challenges, as countries grapple with ensuring financial stability while fostering innovation.

A New Financial Order Emerges

Ultimately, the decline of the dollar would mark the beginning of a new financial order—one characterized by multiple competing currencies, decentralized financial systems, and regional economic blocs. While the transition would be fraught with challenges, it would also pave the way for a more diversified and resilient global economy. This shift could reduce the systemic risks associated with over-reliance on a single reserve currency, fostering a more balanced distribution of economic power.

For the U.S., the challenge would be to adapt to this new reality, balancing fiscal discipline with economic growth. Maintaining credibility in global markets will require a careful recalibration of monetary policy, trade strategy, and diplomatic engagement to sustain confidence in U.S. financial institutions.

For emerging markets, the opportunity lies in building financial systems that can thrive in a multipolar world. Developing strong regional trade networks, robust monetary frameworks, and alternative payment systems will be crucial in mitigating external vulnerabilities and ensuring long-term stability.

And for global businesses and investors, navigating the complexities of a post-dollar era will require agility, innovation, and a keen understanding of evolving financial landscapes. Success in this environment will depend on the ability to anticipate geopolitical shifts, manage currency risks, and adapt to a financial system no longer dominated by a single anchor currency.

Outcome of Scenario 3: The World After Dollar Hegemony

The global financial system is entering a period of profound transformation. While the U.S. dollar remains dominant today, the forces challenging its supremacy are becoming too significant to ignore. Mounting debt, shifting geopolitical alliances, and the rise of alternative financial systems are reshaping the economic landscape.

The question is no longer whether the dollar will face challenges, but how quickly the world will adapt to a future where its role is diminished.

History has shown that no reserve currency holds its position indefinitely. The British pound, once the backbone of global commerce, saw its influence fade as Britain's economy weakened. Now, the dollar faces a similar trajectory. Unlike past transitions, this shift will not be driven by a single successor but by a fragmented, multipolar system. The euro, yuan, gold, digital currencies, and regional financial blocs will all play expanding roles, reducing dependence on any single currency.

For the U.S., the stakes are high. The loss of dollar dominance would complicate monetary policy, increase borrowing costs, and limit Washington's ability to project financial power globally. The U.S. must adapt by strengthening its economic fundamentals, reinforcing trade partnerships, and innovating within financial technology. Failing to do so could lead to a faster erosion of influence, forcing a painful adjustment to a world where America's financial leverage is significantly weaker.

For emerging markets and global investors, a post-dollar world presents both risks and opportunities. Greater financial autonomy, reduced exposure to U.S. interest rate cycles, and more diversified trade relationships could enhance economic resilience. However, a fragmented currency system will bring greater complexity, higher transaction costs, and increased volatility in global markets. Nations that fail to prepare for this transition will find themselves vulnerable rather than freed from dollar dependence.

This transformation will not happen overnight, but the trends are clear. The global monetary order is shifting, and those who anticipate and adapt will be best positioned for the decades ahead. The age of absolute dollar hegemony may be ending, but what comes next remains an open question—one that will define the future of global finance.

A world after dollar dominance will also reshape global governance and economic diplomacy. The U.S. has long used its currency as a tool of influence, enforcing sanctions, shaping global liquidity conditions, and maintaining a central role in international financial institutions. As alternative systems gain traction, institutions like the International Monetary Fund (IMF) and the World Bank may need to recalibrate their frameworks to reflect a more multipolar financial reality. The emergence of regional development banks and alternative payment networks will likely shift economic power toward blocs that previously operated on the periphery of global finance.

At the same time, the erosion of dollar dominance will test the resilience of the global economy. While diversification of reserve currencies may reduce over-reliance on a single monetary anchor, it could also introduce greater instability, particularly during financial crises. Without a universally trusted safe-haven asset, future economic shocks may trigger more fragmented and unpredictable responses from central banks and policymakers. The challenge ahead is not just adjusting to a world with reduced dollar dominance, but ensuring that the transition does not bring heightened economic fragmentation and volatility.

CHAPTER 12

THE TIPPING POINT

— Forces Shaping the Next Global Order —

The global financial order is at a tipping point. Decades of U.S. dominance are being challenged by soaring debt, shifting trade alliances, and the rise of alternative financial systems. Chapter 12: explores how these forces—digital currencies, regional economic blocs, and de-dollarization—are reshaping power dynamics. Will the world shift toward a multipolar system, or will a new hegemon emerge? As economic fractures deepen, the next decade will determine whether this transition unfolds gradually or leads to a seismic break from the system that has defined the modern era.

1

THE GLOBAL ORDER IN FLUX

For over seven decades, the global financial system has been anchored by a singular reality: the dominance of the U.S. dollar. The dollar has not only functioned as the world's primary reserve currency but also as the bedrock of international trade, investment, and financial stability. Governments hold their reserves in U.S. Treasuries, commodities are priced in dollars, and multinational corporations rely on the liquidity of American financial markets. This system has persisted through wars, recessions, sovereign debt crises, and even the near-collapse of the global banking system in 2008— each time emerging intact, if not stronger.

But the foundation upon which this dominance rests is shifting beneath our feet. The post-war economic order is fracturing, challenged by rising debt burdens, shifting trade alliances, technological disruptions, and geopolitical realignments. The future of global finance is no longer guaranteed to follow the path of the past. The world is at a tipping point.

A Financial Order on the Brink of Change

The previous chapter explored three diverging paths for the future of global finance. But whether the world remains anchored to the dollar, shifts toward a multipolar system, or experiences a complete transition into a new financial order depends on a complex interplay of forces. Each scenario carries its own implications, but no single trajectory is inevitable. Instead, financial hegemony—historically— has been shaped by a series of incremental shifts, market reactions, and policy choices that ultimately determine the direction of global finance.

Unlike the seamless transitions envisioned in economic models, real-world financial shifts are rarely smooth, predictable, or preordained. The rise of the U.S. dollar to global dominance after World War II did not occur in a single moment, nor was the British pound's decline a sudden collapse. These transformations unfolded over decades, shaped by war, political choices, and economic mismanagement. Today's uncertainty follows a similar trajectory — but with one critical difference: the forces driving change are no longer linear, nor are they unfolding in isolation.

A Convergence of Disruptive Forces

This time, multiple forces are colliding simultaneously, forming a complex web of competing financial realities. An era of unsustainable U.S. debt is raising doubts about Washington's ability to maintain fiscal discipline, while emerging economies are actively working to reduce their dependence on the dollar. Alternative economic alliances, particularly among BRICS nations, are accelerating efforts to settle trade in local currencies, gradually chipping away at the dollar's near-monopoly in global transactions.

At the same time, the increasing use of economic sanctions as a geopolitical weapon is prompting targeted nations to develop independent financial infrastructures, reducing their exposure to the Western-led banking system. Perhaps most disruptive of all, breakthroughs in financial technology — ranging from central bank digital currencies (CBDCs) to decentralized blockchain payment networks — threaten to upend the traditional structures that have underpinned the global financial system for decades.

Each of these shifts alone would be manageable. Together, they create a moment of profound uncertainty.

The Tipping Point: When Gradual Change Becomes Sudden

Historically, global financial shifts unfold gradually — until they don't. The world rarely moves in straight lines; instead, tipping points — moments of crisis or policy shifts — accelerate change far faster than expected. The collapse of the gold standard, the rise of petrodollar agreements, and the structural realignments following financial crises all illustrate that the most significant financial transformations are often triggered by events that force abrupt adjustments. The question today is whether we are nearing such a moment.

The global financial order may not collapse overnight, nor will a single event suddenly dethrone the dollar. Instead, the coming years will be defined by a series of incremental decisions, crises, and policy responses that will dictate the shape of the next financial era. How governments, central banks, and financial institutions respond will determine whether the world drifts into a multipolar monetary system, retains U.S. financial hegemony, or enters a radically transformed order.

The United States still has a choice—it can adapt and reshape its role in the evolving system or cling to outdated assumptions of uncontested dominance, risking its position in global finance. Meanwhile, other players—China, Europe, BRICS, and new financial networks—are making their own moves, accelerating the pace of change.

The tipping point is fast approaching. The forces shaping the future of finance are already in motion. The question is no longer whether change is coming—but how quickly, under what conditions, and to whose benefit.

2

THE FOUR KEY FORCES DRIVING CHANGE

The future of global finance will not be dictated by a singular event or a predetermined trajectory. Instead, it will be forged at the intersection of four defining forces—U.S. fiscal discipline, the rise of alternative financial systems, the weaponization of finance, and disruptive financial technologies—each exerting pressure on the current financial order in different ways. Some of these forces, such as U.S. fiscal discipline, have the power to reinforce the dollar's global role, while others, such as the rise of alternative financial networks, may accelerate its erosion. What remains uncertain is which force will prove dominant in shaping the next era of finance.

The four fundamental variables that will determine whether the world continues to operate under a U.S.-led financial order, transitions into a fragmented multi-currency system, or moves toward a fundamentally new global paradigm are now coming into sharper focus.

The U.S. Fiscal Dilemma – Can it Rein in its Debt in Time?

For decades, global confidence in the U.S. dollar has been anchored in three pillars: the world's deepest financial markets, a relatively stable political system, and the perceived safety of U.S. Treasuries as the world's primary reserve asset. However, all three of these foundations are now under stress, as the United States grapples with unprecedented debt accumulation, political dysfunction, and questions about its long-term fiscal sustainability.

With national debt surpassing $34 trillion and projections indicating it could exceed $50 trillion by the early 2030s if current spending patterns persist, the strain is becoming increasingly difficult to ignore. More concerning is the cost of servicing this debt—interest payments on U.S. government bonds now rival defense spending and are set to become the single largest line item in the federal budget within the next decade. Rising interest rates are compounding the burden, creating a dangerous feedback loop where more debt is required just to cover existing obligations.

The consequences of fiscal mismanagement are not confined to abstract policy debates; they directly impact global confidence in the U.S. financial system. If debt continues to grow unchecked, foreign investors and central banks may begin to reassess the safety of Treasuries. A shift away from U.S. debt as the global reserve asset would weaken dollar demand, pushing borrowing costs higher. The Federal Reserve, already navigating a precarious balancing act, could be forced into drastic interventions, raising concerns about debt monetization and inflationary spillovers.

A historical parallel looms large. In the aftermath of World War II, Britain, once the epicenter of global finance, was burdened with high debt and declining economic competitiveness. The pound gradually lost its role as the world's primary reserve currency, not through a single event, but through decades of fiscal mismanagement, economic stagnation, and the gradual erosion of investor confidence. While the U.S. today retains unparalleled financial depth and geopolitical influence, the lesson remains: financial dominance is not permanent if fiscal mismanagement erodes credibility.

In the bond market, foreign central banks have already begun reducing their holdings of U.S. Treasuries. China, once the largest foreign holder, has been steadily offloading U.S. debt. Japan, another major investor in U.S. bonds, has also been trimming its exposure, reflecting growing concerns over fiscal sustainability. If confidence in U.S. financial stability erodes further, it could trigger a liquidity crunch or force the Federal Reserve to intervene, raising concerns about debt monetization. Such a scenario would weaken the dollar's role as the world's primary reserve currency, accelerating the transition toward a multipolar financial system.

The question now is whether the U.S. government and Federal Reserve can restore fiscal credibility before global investors begin actively seeking alternatives. Failure to do so could accelerate capital outflows, weaken demand for U.S. debt, and hasten the rise of competing financial centers poised to reshape global markets. Time is no longer a luxury; each year of delay compounds the risks. A slow erosion of confidence can be just as devastating as a sudden crisis, gradually undermining America's position at the core of the global financial system.

China's Challenge – The Yuan's Potential vs. Its Structural Limits

China has spent nearly two decades working to reduce its dependence on the U.S.-led financial system. Through currency swap agreements, trade settlement in yuan, and the creation of alternative financial institutions such as the Asian Infrastructure Investment Bank and the Cross-Border Interbank Payment System, Beijing has steadily chipped away at the dollar's monopoly in global trade.

Momentum has accelerated in recent years. Yuan-denominated trade settlements have surged, particularly among BRICS nations, while Saudi Arabia, Russia, and other energy-exporting economies have begun accepting non-dollar payments for oil and gas sales. China has also made significant strides in expanding the use of its digital yuan, positioning it as an alternative to SWIFT-based transactions.

Despite these efforts, the yuan remains far from replacing the dollar as a global reserve currency. The most significant obstacles lie within China's own financial system. Strict capital controls continue to limit yuan convertibility, deterring foreign investors who prefer transparency and liquidity. While Beijing has encouraged international use of the yuan in trade, the lack of a fully open financial market prevents the currency from achieving the scale and trust necessary for reserve status.

Structural economic risks also weigh on China's ambitions. A deteriorating real estate sector, slowing GDP growth, and mounting demographic pressures undermine investor confidence. The yuan's limited liquidity in global markets further complicates matters. The U.S. dollar is still used in 88 percent of global foreign exchange transactions, while the yuan accounts for less than 5 percent. Without meaningful financial liberalization, China's ability to position the yuan as a credible alternative to the dollar remains constrained.

While China is the most frequently discussed challenger to the dollar, India is also emerging as a financial player. With an economy projected to surpass Japan and Germany in size by the early 2030s, India is positioning itself as a key force in global trade. The Indian government has been pushing for rupee-based trade settlements, particularly with Middle Eastern energy suppliers and neighboring economies. If successful, these efforts could further reduce dependence on the dollar in regional trade, adding another dimension to the evolving multipolar financial system.

Sanctions, Trade Wars, and the New Economic Blocs

The U.S. dollar's dominance has long been reinforced by its use as a geopolitical tool. The power of sanctions, SWIFT access, and U.S. financial regulations has allowed Washington to control global financial flows, freezing assets and restricting access for nations that fall out of favor.

This very strategy, however, is accelerating the push for alternatives. The freezing of Russian central bank assets following the Ukraine conflict spurred Moscow to deepen economic ties with China, India, and the Middle East, shifting trade away from dollar-based transactions. Saudi Arabia's growing openness to pricing oil in yuan and the expansion of BRICS are further signs that countries are seeking ways to insulate themselves from Washington's financial reach.

Even in Europe, long considered a financial ally of the U.S., policymakers are pushing for greater "strategic autonomy" in finance. The European Union has explored alternative payment systems to bypass U.S. sanctions, signaling a broader dissatisfaction with Washington's financial leverage. While the euro remains secondary to the dollar, the EU is increasingly vocal about reducing its reliance on U.S.-led financial mechanisms.

Could Digital Currencies Reshape Finance?

Beyond geopolitics, technological innovation is reshaping global finance. Central bank digital currencies, decentralized payment systems, and blockchain-based financial networks have the potential to bypass traditional banking and currency systems altogether.

China's digital yuan is already in large-scale use for domestic transactions and cross-border pilot programs. The BRICS bloc is exploring a digital payments framework that could reduce reliance on Western banking networks. Meanwhile, decentralized finance and stablecoins continue to offer an alternative for emerging markets grappling with currency volatility.

While CBDCs could reduce dependence on the dollar, they also raise concerns about government surveillance of transactions and financial fragmentation. If major economies push for national digital currencies rather than a unified global system, financial markets may become more fractured rather than seamlessly multipolar. The risk of financial surveillance and state-controlled monetary systems could also deter investors, limiting widespread adoption of CBDCs outside of state-backed economies.

These four forces—fiscal stability, China's financial ambitions, the weaponization of finance, and the rise of digital currencies—will shape the future of global finance. Whether they reinforce the existing system or lead to an entirely new order remains uncertain. What is clear, however, is that the world has already begun its transition toward a new financial reality.

3

TIPPING POINTS

The global financial system may appear stable on the surface, but history has shown that financial transitions do not always unfold gradually. While long-term structural trends, such as rising U.S. debt and the increasing use of alternative currencies, suggest an evolving monetary order, the actual shift could be triggered by a tipping point—an event or policy decision that accelerates change far faster than most expect.

Financial hegemons rarely collapse under the weight of a single crisis. Instead, they erode through a series of shocks and policy missteps that weaken confidence in their stability. The dollar's dominance has persisted through multiple global recessions, banking crises, and geopolitical conflicts, yet it has remained resilient due to its deep liquidity and institutional trust. The question now is whether a catalyst event—economic, technological, or geopolitical—could disrupt this equilibrium and push the world toward a new financial order.

Several factors could serve as potential tipping points, accelerating the transition away from dollar dominance. A U.S. debt crisis that erodes confidence in Treasuries, a coordinated de-dollarization effort by BRICS nations, breakthroughs in financial technology such as central bank digital currencies (CBDCs), shifts in commodity pricing mechanisms, and geopolitical conflicts all have the potential to trigger a rapid financial realignment. While some of these risks are slow-burning trends, others could emerge suddenly, reshaping global finance in unpredictable ways.

U.S. Debt and the Risk of a Confidence Crisis

The most immediate and structurally significant risk is a U.S. debt crisis that shatters confidence in Treasuries. As debt levels soar beyond $34 trillion, the cost of servicing U.S. obligations is reaching historic highs. Investors have long viewed Treasuries as the world's safest asset, but if Washington fails to demonstrate long-term fiscal responsibility, the very foundation of dollar dominance could weaken. A scenario in which bond markets demand higher yields, forcing the Federal Reserve to intervene by purchasing even more debt, would risk triggering a crisis of confidence.

Foreign central banks, already reducing their U.S. bond holdings, could begin offloading Treasuries at an accelerated pace. If markets perceive that the U.S. is veering toward debt monetization rather than genuine fiscal reform, the credibility of the dollar could deteriorate rapidly. In such a scenario, capital flight would intensify, and investors would seek alternative stores of value, putting enormous pressure on the global financial system. Beyond concerns over U.S. debt sustainability, broader structural shifts in global finance are also challenging the dollar's dominance.

The Forces Reshaping Global Finance

Another potential tipping point could come from China and BRICS nations formalizing a large-scale non-dollar trade mechanism. While efforts to de-dollarize have been incremental, a coordinated move — such as a formal announcement of a BRICS-backed financial settlement system that bypasses SWIFT — could have an immediate impact. Already, China and Russia are settling energy transactions in yuan, while Brazil, India, and the Gulf states are exploring bilateral agreements that limit dollar exposure. If a critical mass of major economies agrees to price commodities in alternative currencies, the global reliance on the dollar could shift rapidly.

However, while such a transition is possible over time, it remains less likely to happen in an overnight transformation. The dollar's liquidity and deep financial infrastructure still make it indispensable for global trade, meaning this scenario would require sustained geopolitical coordination and years of trust-building. Even with growing momentum, shifting away from a currency system as entrenched as the dollar will likely be a gradual process rather than a sudden break.

Beyond state-driven initiatives, technological innovation could produce a financial breakthrough that fundamentally alters the way money moves across borders. The emergence of central bank digital currencies (CBDCs), blockchain-based financial systems, or decentralized payment networks has already begun challenging traditional banking. If a major economy—China, the European Union, or a coalition of emerging markets—successfully deploys a CBDC that operates outside U.S. financial control, it could create a parallel financial system independent of dollar-based transactions. The implications of such a development would be profound. If businesses and consumers worldwide can conduct transactions seamlessly in digital currencies that bypass Western banking intermediaries, the role of the dollar as the default medium of exchange could erode far more quickly than anticipated.

Another factor that could accelerate the financial realignment is the role of commodities and gold in a potential currency crisis. Historically, during periods of currency instability, gold has reasserted itself as a financial anchor. The 1970s oil crisis, the collapse of the Bretton Woods system, and hyperinflationary episodes across emerging markets have all demonstrated gold's ability to serve as a hedge against monetary uncertainty. Recognizing this, central banks have been steadily increasing their gold reserves as a hedge against dollar uncertainty.

Additionally, major commodity exporters like Saudi Arabia and Russia have hinted at pricing oil in gold or alternative currencies—potentially reshaping commodity markets. If a major geopolitical shift or financial panic leads to a sudden loss of faith in fiat currencies, gold and other tangible assets could play an even greater role in global trade. Such a move could accelerate the de-dollarization trend, prompting central banks and investors to increase their holdings of gold as a hedge against currency volatility and geopolitical uncertainty.

Finally, a geopolitical crisis—whether in Taiwan, the Middle East, or another flashpoint—could accelerate financial fragmentation. The weaponization of the dollar through sanctions has already forced some nations to explore financial alternatives, but a full-scale geopolitical conflict could speed up this transition dramatically. A crisis that disrupts global trade routes or leads to further fragmentation between economic blocs could force rapid adaptation to non-dollar financial mechanisms, particularly in regions that are already looking to reduce their exposure to Western financial dominance.

How Likely Are These Tipping Points?

Not all tipping points carry the same probability or timeline. Some are immediate risks that could unfold in the next few years, while others remain long-term possibilities. The likelihood of a U.S. debt crisis accelerating financial realignment is significantly higher than the probability of BRICS replacing the dollar overnight. Markets are already signaling unease over U.S. fiscal policy, and bond investors are increasingly wary of unchecked government borrowing. If there is a sudden loss of confidence in Treasuries, the financial shift would not be gradual—it would be swift and destabilizing.

By contrast, a formalized BRICS-led non-dollar system remains a longer-term possibility rather than an imminent threat. While individual nations are conducting trade outside the dollar system, the trust and scale required for a new reserve structure remain formidable barriers. The most likely outcome is a gradual diversification rather than a wholesale rejection of the dollar.

Technological disruption through CBDCs or decentralized finance is difficult to predict. If a global-scale digital currency system emerges outside U.S. control, it could accelerate de-dollarization far faster than policymakers anticipate. However, such a shift requires not only technological capability but also broad-based adoption. At present, central banks remain hesitant to relinquish control over traditional monetary frameworks, making this a mid-term rather than immediate tipping point.

Geopolitical crises, on the other hand, remain wildcard events with unpredictable consequences. While financial trends often develop over decades, war and conflict can force nations into abrupt financial realignments. The impact of U.S.-China tensions, European economic shifts, and energy market disruptions will continue to act as catalysts that could either reinforce or weaken the dollar's role in the global system.

Ultimately, tipping points are impossible to predict with absolute certainty, but the conditions for a major financial realignment are already forming. Whether through a debt crisis, a coordinated shift in global trade mechanisms, a breakthrough in financial technology, or an external geopolitical shock, the stability of the current system is more fragile than it appears.

4

ADAPTING TO THE NEW FINANCIAL ORDER

The forces shaping the next global financial order are already in motion. The question is no longer whether change will come, but how nations, institutions, and investors will adapt to the evolving landscape. Unlike previous financial transitions, where power shifted gradually over decades, today's environment is defined by unprecedented speed, technological disruption, and geopolitical fragmentation. The ability to anticipate, respond, and position strategically will determine whether economic actors thrive in the new era or struggle to keep pace with forces beyond their control.

The United States, as the incumbent financial hegemon, faces the most critical decisions. Its ability to maintain global financial leadership depends on navigating mounting fiscal challenges, managing geopolitical alliances, and adapting to innovations in digital finance. While past financial powers—such as Britain in the early 20th century—clung to outdated economic assumptions and suffered slow decline, the U.S. still has the opportunity to shape rather than resist the transition. The key question is whether policymakers in Washington will recognize the urgency of the moment. If they fail to act decisively, the dollar's dominance could erode not through a direct challenge, but through a slow, self-inflicted unraveling.

Britain's experience serves as a cautionary tale. In the aftermath of World War II, the British pound—once the cornerstone of the global financial system—faced declining trade influence, an unsustainable debt burden, and reduced confidence in its economic strength. As investors gradually lost trust in sterling, capital flowed toward the rising power of the U.S. dollar. The transition did not happen overnight, but Britain's failure to adjust to new financial realities ensured that the pound never recovered its former dominance. The United States now stands at a similar crossroads. Will it acknowledge the shifting landscape and adapt, or will it cling to outdated assumptions of unchallenged financial hegemony?

Global Capital Shift: Are Investors Betting Against the Dollar?

While governments and policymakers debate the future of global finance, capital markets are already making moves. Institutional investors—sovereign wealth funds, pension funds, asset managers, and hedge funds—control trillions of dollars in capital flows, and their decisions shape the direction of the financial system long before official policy shifts.

There are already signs that global investors are hedging against the dollar's long-term supremacy. Sovereign wealth funds in Asia and the Middle East have steadily increased allocations to gold and alternative currencies, diversifying away from U.S. Treasuries. Central banks in China, Russia, and Brazil have been reducing their exposure to dollar-denominated assets, signaling a broader shift in reserve management. If these trends continue—or accelerate—they could undermine the very foundation of the global financial order faster than policymakers anticipate.

This does not mean a sudden collapse of the dollar, but it does indicate a growing recognition that the global reserve system may not remain static. If capital continues to reallocate toward alternative stores of value, the financial order could shift not through political decisions, but through sheer market momentum. The actions of these financial giants will not only reflect changing economic realities but also reinforce them, accelerating trends that, once set in motion, are difficult to reverse.

The Investor's Dilemma: Navigating a Shifting Financial Order

For ordinary investors, the shifting financial order presents both new risks and new opportunities. For decades, the stability of the U.S.-led financial order has provided a sense of security to multinational corporations, pension funds, and retail investors alike. The dollar's dominance helped keep global inflation in check, ensured deep capital markets, and allowed for long-term stability in savings and investments. But as nations hedge against a future where the dollar is no longer unchallenged, these guarantees are becoming less certain.

If global capital flows begin to shift away from dollar-denominated assets, the ripple effects will be felt not only in government bond markets but also in investment stability, the cost of imports, and the purchasing power of households. Investors who have long relied on predictable financial conditions may find themselves navigating a more volatile environment where multi-currency exposure and diversification become essential. Those who fail to adapt their investment strategies may face unexpected shocks as the financial order realigns.

While some see risk in this transition, others see opportunity. Emerging markets may benefit from a more balanced financial system, with new pathways for investment and alternative trading arrangements outside the traditional Western financial centers. Countries and corporations that align themselves with the shifting flow of capital may find themselves better positioned for the future than those that continue to operate under outdated assumptions of dollar permanency.

The Digital Currency Race: Will the U.S. Lead or Lag Behind?

Beyond geopolitics and institutional investment shifts, financial technology is emerging as one of the most transformative forces in global finance. The rapid rise of central bank digital currencies (CBDCs), decentralized payment systems, and blockchain-based financial networks has the potential to fundamentally alter the mechanics of trade, investment, and monetary control.

China has already recognized this reality and moved aggressively to shape the future of digital finance. The digital yuan (e-CNY) has been integrated into cross-border trade pilot programs, allowing China to bypass Western financial systems and reduce dependence on dollar-based transactions. The BRICS bloc has also begun exploring a digital payments system, aiming to create an alternative to SWIFT and other Western-dominated financial networks.

The United States, by contrast, has been slow to embrace digital financial innovation. While the Federal Reserve has discussed the possibility of a digital dollar, no decisive action has been taken. If Washington continues to view financial technology as a secondary concern rather than a defining feature of global economic power, it risks falling behind as the architecture of global finance shifts beneath it. The future will not be determined solely by traditional economic policies—it will be shaped by who controls the infrastructure of digital finance.

A New Financial Era Is Coming: Who Will Shape It?

The global financial order is entering a period of profound transformation. The forces at play—fiscal policy, capital flows, technological disruption, and geopolitical realignment—are already shaping the next era of global finance. The question now is who will adapt and seize the moment, and who will be left behind.

For the United States, the opportunity still exists to lead rather than lag behind in shaping the evolving financial landscape. But that will require bold policy decisions, a rethinking of its debt trajectory, and an embrace of financial technology rather than resistance to it. Failure to act will not result in an immediate collapse, but in a gradual erosion of financial influence—just as it did for past economic hegemons that failed to recognize the changing tides.

The coming transition will test the adaptability of nations, the foresight of policymakers, and the resilience of investors. The dollar's future will not be determined by its historical legacy alone, but by the choices made today. The question is no longer whether change is coming—it is whether the key players in global finance are prepared to meet it head-on.

5

FINAL REFLECTION

The future of global finance will not be dictated by inevitability but by choices—choices that will determine whether the United States remains at the center of the world's financial system or is gradually displaced by an emerging order. For over seven decades, the dollar has been the foundation of global trade, investment, and monetary policy, a status reinforced by deep capital markets, institutional trust, and the strength of the U.S. economy. Yet history has shown that financial hegemony is never permanent. *The rise and fall of dominant currencies follow a familiar pattern: stability, expansion, excess, and decline.* The question now is whether the United States will recognize the shifting landscape and adapt accordingly, or whether it will cling to outdated assumptions until it is too late.

Financial transitions rarely unfold in a single moment. The British pound did not lose its global dominance overnight, nor did the U.S. dollar ascend in an instant. These shifts are shaped by decades of policy decisions, geopolitical events, and market forces. The same forces that elevated the dollar—economic strength, strategic alliances, and financial innovation—can just as easily become forces of decline if mismanaged. Today, the warning signs are clear. The rise of alternative economic networks, the growing reliance on non-dollar trade settlements, the increasing appeal of digital financial technologies, and the widening fractures in U.S. fiscal policy all point toward a world that is no longer unquestioningly anchored to the dollar.

The tipping point has not yet arrived, but the trajectory is unmistakable. The cracks in the system are no longer theoretical; they are evident in the shifting alliances, policy maneuvers, and financial experiments unfolding across the globe. Washington still holds immense structural advantages, yet they are eroding under the weight of rising debt, political dysfunction, and the increasing weaponization of financial dominance. The ability of the U.S. to maintain its leadership will depend on its willingness to engage with reality—acknowledging that financial power cannot be maintained through force alone. It requires credibility, adaptability, and a recognition that the global economy is evolving in ways that cannot simply be ignored.

The moment of reckoning will come not in a single dramatic event but in a series of incremental shifts, each reinforcing the next. The choices made now will shape global finance for decades to come. History offers a clear lesson: dominant financial powers rarely adjust willingly. Most are forced into adaptation by crisis, responding only when the cost of inaction becomes unbearable. Whether the U.S. will break that pattern remains an open question.

The world is watching. The tipping point is at hand. The choices made today will determine whether the dollar remains the foundation of global finance or fades into history like the pound before it. This is not just about currency—it is about power, influence, and the structure of the global order itself. What happens next will not simply define the future of finance. It will define the balance of power for decades to come.

APPENDIX

THE PILLARS OF GLOBAL FINANCE

Systems That Shaped and Challenged
Dollar Dominance

"Paper money eventually returns to its intrinsic value—zero."
—Voltaire

This appendix offers a concise exploration of five key financial systems that have shaped the global economy and the U.S. dollar's hegemony. From the disciplined era of the Gold Standard to the postwar Bretton Woods framework, and from the rise of the Petrodollar System to the digital frontiers of Central Bank Digital Currencies, each system reveals how global finance has evolved. Understanding these systems provides critical insights into the forces driving today's de-dollarization trends and the challenges facing the dollar's future as the world's dominant reserve currency.

1

THE GOLD STANDARD

The Gold Standard was a global monetary system where currencies were directly tied to a specific amount of gold. Every dollar, pound, or franc represented a claim to a piece of gold held in reserve, creating a sense of stability and trust in financial transactions. This system dominated global finance from the 19th century until the early 20th century, providing a predictable framework for international trade. However, its rigid structure often amplified economic downturns, making financial crises more painful and prolonged.

How It Works

Under the Gold Standard, countries established a fixed price for gold and issued currency based on the amount of gold they held. For instance, when the United States set the price of gold at $20.67 per ounce, it meant that for every ounce of gold in its reserves, the U.S. could issue exactly $20.67. This created a natural limit on how much money a country could print, as every unit of currency had to be backed by physical gold. International trade under this system involved the physical movement of gold between countries to settle trade balances. A nation that imported more than it exported would see its gold reserves diminish, forcing it to reduce its money supply. This often led to higher interest rates and economic contraction, while countries with trade surpluses gained gold reserves, allowing them to expand their money supply and stimulate growth.

Historical Context

The Gold Standard's rise began in 1821 when Britain became the first major economy to formally adopt it. During the 19th century, its influence spread as France, Germany, and the United States joined the system. The Gold Standard's stability facilitated international trade during the Industrial Revolution, providing a reliable foundation for economic expansion. However, its inherent rigidity became evident during times of crisis. World War I marked a turning point as countries abandoned gold backing to finance their war efforts, shattering confidence in the system. Although some nations attempted to return to the Gold Standard in the 1920s, the Great Depression highlighted its limitations, forcing many countries to abandon it once again. The final chapter came in 1971 when U.S. President Richard Nixon ended the dollar's convertibility to gold, signaling the end of the Gold Standard era and ushering in the modern age of fiat currencies.

Benefits and Drawbacks

The Gold Standard brought both significant benefits and considerable challenges. Its fixed exchange rates provided stability, reducing currency fluctuations and promoting international trade. It also imposed monetary discipline on governments, preventing them from printing excessive amounts of money and thereby controlling inflation. However, this very rigidity often turned economic shocks into prolonged downturns. Countries could not adjust their money supply to respond to economic crises, leading to deflation, unemployment, and recessions. Additionally, the dependence on gold reserves limited economic growth, not by a country's potential, but by the finite supply of gold available.

Legacy and Modern Relevance

Though long abandoned, the legacy of the Gold Standard endures in modern debates over monetary policy. Advocates argue that returning to a gold-backed system would prevent reckless government spending and inflation, while critics point to the economic constraints it imposes. Even today, central banks around the world hold thousands of tonnes of gold as a reserve asset, underscoring its lasting importance. In the context of de-dollarization, several countries are increasing their gold reserves as a hedge against reliance on the U.S. dollar, reflecting a desire for the kind of stability once provided by the Gold Standard.

2

THE BRETTON WOODS SYSTEM

The Bretton Woods System, established in 1944, created a new global financial order that cemented the U.S. dollar's dominance in the post-war world. Unlike the rigid Gold Standard, this system introduced a more flexible framework where major currencies were pegged to the dollar, which in turn was tied to gold. This shift not only stabilized war-torn economies but also positioned the United States at the heart of global finance, a position that would define international economic relations for decades.

How It Works

At the core of the Bretton Woods System was a simple yet transformative idea: instead of directly tying every currency to gold, most currencies would be pegged to the U.S. dollar, and the dollar alone would be convertible to gold at a fixed rate of $35 per ounce. This arrangement made the dollar the world's primary reserve currency, much like a global financial anchor. Countries maintained their currency's value within a narrow margin against the dollar, and when deviations occurred, central banks intervened by buying or selling their currency. The International Monetary Fund (IMF) was created to provide short-term financial assistance to countries struggling to maintain their exchange rates, while the World Bank focused on long-term economic development and reconstruction.

Historical Context

The Bretton Woods System emerged from the economic devastation of World War II, when global leaders recognized the need for a stable international monetary framework to prevent the financial chaos that had followed World War I. Led by the United States and Britain, the conference held in Bretton Woods, New Hampshire, brought together 44 nations to design a system that would promote economic growth, prevent competitive devaluations, and foster international trade. The U.S., emerging from the war as the world's largest economy and holding the majority of global gold reserves, was in a prime position to shape the system. For over two decades, the Bretton Woods System facilitated economic recovery and unprecedented growth, particularly in Western Europe and Japan. However, by the late 1960s, mounting U.S. deficits and dwindling gold reserves created pressures that the system could no longer withstand. The final blow came in 1971, when President Richard Nixon announced the suspension of the dollar's convertibility to gold, effectively ending the Bretton Woods era and leading to the system of floating exchange rates we see today.

Benefits and Drawbacks

The Bretton Woods System provided much-needed stability in the post-war period, promoting international trade and economic cooperation. By anchoring currencies to the dollar, it reduced exchange rate volatility and fostered investor confidence. However, its reliance on the U.S. dollar also meant that global economic stability hinged on America's financial discipline. As U.S. spending soared in the 1960s—driven by the Vietnam War and expansive social programs—the system's foundation began to crack. The requirement to maintain gold reserves limited U.S. monetary flexibility, while other countries, especially France, criticized the "exorbitant privilege" that allowed the U.S. to print dollars without the same constraints they faced. When trust in the U.S. ability to honor its gold commitments eroded, the system's collapse became inevitable.

Legacy and Modern Relevance

The Bretton Woods System's legacy endures in the U.S. dollar's dominance and institutions like the IMF and World Bank, which remain central to global finance. Though dissolved, it shaped today's financial architecture. As de-dollarization gains momentum, the era serves as a reminder that economic power defines financial systems— and shifts in power reshape them. Today's debates on reducing dollar reliance echo past concerns, as nations seek alternatives for greater financial independence and stability.

3

THE DOLLAR SYSTEM
AFTER BRETTON WOODS

The collapse of the Bretton Woods System in 1971 marked the beginning of a new era in global finance—the Dollar System, where the U.S. dollar reigned supreme without the constraints of gold backing. This shift allowed the United States unprecedented monetary flexibility, enabling it to print dollars at will while maintaining its status as the world's primary reserve currency. Over the following decades, the Dollar System underpinned global trade, investment, and finance, giving the U.S. unmatched influence over international economic affairs. However, this newfound dominance also introduced vulnerabilities, as the global economy became increasingly dependent on U.S. monetary policy and dollar liquidity. This reliance meant that economic disruptions in the U.S.—from inflationary spikes to financial crises—had far-reaching consequences, amplifying instability across global markets.

How It Works

In the post-Bretton Woods era, currencies began to float freely, with their values determined by market forces rather than fixed exchange rates. The dollar, no longer tied to gold, became a fiat currency, backed solely by the U.S. government's credibility and economic strength. Despite this, the dollar remained the preferred currency for international trade, especially in commodities like oil, and as the primary reserve currency held by central banks worldwide. The SWIFT network, dominated by the U.S., facilitated global financial transactions in dollars, further entrenching its dominance. This system allowed the U.S. to finance deficits by issuing debt in its own currency, a privilege few other nations enjoyed. As countries accumulated dollars through trade surpluses, particularly China and Japan, they recycled these dollars back into U.S. Treasury bonds, effectively funding U.S. government spending and keeping interest rates low.

Historical Context

The Dollar System's ascent coincided with the U.S. economic boom of the 1980s and 1990s, driven by financial deregulation, technological innovation, and globalization. The petrodollar agreement between the U.S. and Saudi Arabia in the 1970s, which ensured that oil would be priced in dollars, solidified the dollar's role in global trade. However, cracks began to emerge in the early 2000s as U.S. debt levels soared and financial crises, particularly the 2008 global financial crisis, exposed vulnerabilities in the system. Despite these challenges, the dollar's dominance persisted, buoyed by the absence of a viable alternative and the depth of U.S. financial markets.

Benefits and Drawbacks

The Dollar System provided the U.S. with significant economic advantages, including the ability to borrow cheaply and finance its deficits through global demand for dollars. For the rest of the world, the system offered liquidity, stability, and a common medium for international trade. However, it also exposed economies to U.S. monetary policy decisions, often leading to currency crises in emerging markets when the Federal Reserve tightened interest rates. The U.S. itself faced criticism for exploiting its exorbitant privilege, using the dollar's dominance to impose economic sanctions and influence global finance.

Legacy and Modern Relevance

The Dollar System remains the backbone of the global economy, but its future is increasingly questioned. Rising U.S. debt, geopolitical tensions, and the emergence of alternative financial systems, including China's yuan-based trade agreements and Central Bank Digital Currencies (CBDCs), challenge the dollar's supremacy. As countries seek to reduce their reliance on the dollar, the post-Bretton Woods era stands as both a testament to U.S. financial power and a cautionary tale of the risks that come with overreliance on a single currency in an evolving global landscape.

4

THE PETRODOLLAR SYSTEM

The Petrodollar System emerged in the 1970s as a critical pillar of U.S. financial dominance, linking the global oil trade to the U.S. dollar. By ensuring that oil, the world's most essential commodity, was priced and traded exclusively in dollars, the system created consistent demand for the American currency, reinforcing its status as the global reserve currency. This arrangement not only stabilized the dollar after the collapse of the Bretton Woods System but also gave the U.S. extraordinary influence over global economic and geopolitical affairs.

How It Works

The mechanics of the Petrodollar System are straightforward yet profound in their implications. Following agreements between the United States and Saudi Arabia in the mid-1970s, oil-exporting countries in the Organization of the Petroleum Exporting Countries (OPEC) agreed to price and sell oil exclusively in U.S. dollars. In return, the U.S. provided military protection and economic incentives to key oil producers. This meant that any country wishing to buy oil had to first acquire dollars, often through trade or by holding reserves, thus maintaining a constant global demand for the U.S. currency. Oil-exporting nations, flush with dollar revenues, reinvested these earnings into U.S. assets, particularly Treasury bonds, further financing U.S. deficits and keeping interest rates low.

Historical Context

The birth of the Petrodollar System can be traced back to the 1973 oil crisis, when OPEC nations, led by Saudi Arabia, imposed an oil embargo against the U.S. and its allies, causing oil prices to skyrocket. In response, the U.S. sought to secure its economic interests by forging an agreement with Saudi Arabia in 1974, ensuring that oil would be sold in dollars, thereby stabilizing the currency and protecting the U.S. economy from future shocks. Over the decades, the Petrodollar System became deeply entrenched, with oil pricing in dollars becoming a global norm. However, recent geopolitical shifts and the push for de-dollarization, especially by major economies like China and Russia, have begun to challenge this long-standing system.

Benefits and Drawbacks

The Petrodollar System has provided significant benefits to the United States, ensuring a steady global demand for its currency and enabling it to run persistent trade deficits without facing severe economic consequences. It has also allowed the U.S. to finance its military and economic policies with ease, leveraging its currency dominance to impose economic sanctions and influence global markets. However, for oil-importing countries, the system has meant vulnerability to U.S. monetary policy and the constant need to maintain dollar reserves, sometimes at the expense of their own economic stability. Moreover, oil-exporting nations tied to the dollar have occasionally faced challenges when U.S. policy shifts impacted the value of their reserves.

Legacy and Modern Relevance

The Petrodollar System remains a cornerstone of the global financial system, but its future is increasingly uncertain. As countries like China seek to establish yuan-based oil trading platforms and others explore alternatives like gold-backed trade agreements or CBDCs, the dominance of the petrodollar faces growing pressure. The system's legacy is one of strategic economic diplomacy that solidified U.S. financial hegemony, but the rise of new economic powers and the increasing complexity of global energy markets signal that the era of uncontested petrodollar dominance may be approaching its end.

5

CENTRAL BANK DIGITAL CURRENCIES

Central Bank Digital Currencies (CBDCs) represent the next frontier in global finance, offering a digital form of a country's official currency issued and regulated by its central bank. Unlike cryptocurrencies, which are decentralized and often volatile, CBDCs are state-backed and designed to function as a stable digital alternative to cash. As nations explore ways to modernize their financial systems, CBDCs have emerged as a potential disruptor to the U.S. dollar's dominance, offering countries new tools to conduct trade, manage monetary policy, and reduce reliance on existing global financial infrastructure.

How It Works

CBDCs function as a digital version of fiat currency, accessible through digital wallets provided by central banks or authorized institutions. Each CBDC unit equals its physical counterpart, ensuring 1 digital dollar, yuan, or euro holds the same value. Transactions occur on a centralized digital ledger managed by the issuing central bank, allowing for instant transfers, real-time settlement, and enhanced security. Unlike traditional banking systems, where transfers take days, CBDC transactions are completed in seconds. Central banks can issue or retract supply as needed, offering unprecedented control over monetary policy. For individuals and businesses, using a CBDC feels similar to an online banking app but without intermediaries, as transactions occur directly through the central bank's system..

Historical Context

The concept of CBDCs gained momentum in the early 2010s, but significant interest surged when China launched its digital yuan pilot program in 2020, becoming the first major economy to introduce a functioning CBDC. This move spurred other countries, including the European Union, India, and the United States, to accelerate their own research and development of digital currencies. Proponents see

CBDCs as a response to the growing influence of cryptocurrencies and a means to modernize financial infrastructure, while critics warn of potential risks to privacy and financial stability. Today, more than 130 countries, representing over 98% of global GDP, are exploring or developing CBDCs, highlighting the growing consensus that digital currencies are not a passing trend but a fundamental shift in the financial landscape.

Benefits and Drawbacks

CBDCs offer several benefits, including faster, cheaper transactions, improved financial inclusion, and enhanced control over monetary policy, including direct stimulus payments. They also reduce reliance on cash, improving efficiency and lowering costs for governments. However, CBDCs raise privacy concerns, as centralized ledgers allow governments to track transactions. Additionally, CBDCs could disrupt banking systems, as individuals and businesses might bypass banks, reducing deposits and raising lending costs. For the global financial system, widespread CBDC adoption challenges the dollar's dominance, as countries could trade directly using digital currencies without converting to the U.S. dollar.

Legacy and Modern Relevance

While still in its early stages, the legacy of CBDCs is already taking shape as a potential game-changer in international finance. For nations seeking to reduce dependence on the U.S. dollar, CBDCs offer a new mechanism for cross-border transactions, bypassing traditional dollar-based systems like SWIFT. As more countries adopt CBDCs, the global financial system may become increasingly multipolar, with digital currencies challenging the dollar's long-standing supremacy. In the broader context of de-dollarization, CBDCs represent both an opportunity and a threat, signaling a future where digital financial systems redefine economic power and global monetary dynamics.

GLOSSARY

THE LANGUAGE OF GLOBAL FINANCE

Key Terms in Global Finance
& De-Dollarization

Understanding global finance requires clarity on key terms shaping currency markets, monetary systems, and geopolitical shifts. This glossary provides concise definitions of essential concepts, categorized for thematic coherence while maintaining logical sequencing where historical progression is relevant. From the Gold Standard to the Bretton Woods System and the Nixon Shock, these terms trace the evolution of financial power. Meanwhile, entries on reserve currencies, capital controls, and foreign exchange reserves explain the mechanics of today's monetary order. Together, these definitions offer a quick-reference guide to the forces driving de-dollarization and the challenges facing the U.S. dollar's dominance.

1

MONETARY AND RESERVE CURRENCY SYSTEMS

Reserve Currency

A reserve currency is a foreign currency held in large quantities by central banks to facilitate global trade, stabilize exchange rates, and back financial obligations. The U.S. dollar is the world's dominant reserve currency, making up over half of global reserves. Countries use reserves to intervene in currency markets, settle international transactions, and manage economic crises.

Fiat Currency

Fiat currency is money that has no intrinsic value and is not backed by a physical commodity like gold. Instead, its value comes from government decree and public confidence. Most modern currencies, including the U.S. dollar, euro, and yuan, are fiat currencies. Unlike gold-backed money, fiat currencies allow central banks to expand the money supply, but excessive issuance can lead to inflation.

Hard Currency vs. Soft Currency

A *hard currency* is a stable and widely accepted currency used in global trade and held in reserves, such as the U.S. dollar, euro, and Swiss franc. A *soft currency*, by contrast, is more volatile and often subject to capital controls or inflation, making it less desirable for international transactions. Hard currencies are trusted due to strong economic fundamentals, while soft currencies may struggle with devaluation.

Foreign Exchange Reserves

Foreign exchange reserves are the foreign currencies, gold, and other liquid assets held by central banks to manage exchange rates, settle trade balances, and stabilize financial markets. The U.S. dollar and euro make up the largest share of global reserves. Countries with large reserves can defend their currency during financial crises or de-dollarise by shifting reserves into gold or non-dollar assets.

Gold Standard

The gold standard was a monetary system where currencies were directly tied to a fixed amount of gold. Governments guaranteed convertibility, ensuring stability but limiting monetary flexibility. The system dominated global finance until the early 20th century but was gradually abandoned due to its rigidity, particularly during economic crises. The last remnants disappeared in 1971 when the U.S. ended the dollar's convertibility to gold.

Bretton Woods System

Established in 1944, the Bretton Woods System pegged major global currencies to the U.S. dollar, which was convertible to gold at $35 per ounce. This system created post-war economic stability but collapsed in 1971 due to U.S. deficits and declining gold reserves. Bretton Woods cemented the dollar's role as the world's primary reserve currency, a dominance that continues today.

Nixon Shock

The Nixon Shock refers to U.S. President Richard Nixon's 1971 decision to end the dollar's convertibility to gold, effectively dismantling the Bretton Woods System. This move shifted the global economy to a fiat currency system, where exchange rates float freely. While this gave governments more monetary flexibility, it also enabled unlimited money printing, fueling inflation and financial instability over time.

Special Drawing Rights (SDRs)

SDRs are an international reserve asset created by the IMF to supplement global liquidity. Their value is based on a basket of major currencies, including the U.S. dollar, euro, yuan, yen, and pound. SDRs are not a currency but can be exchanged for reserve currencies. Some nations advocate expanding SDRs to reduce dependence on the dollar in global finance.

Eurodollar System

The Eurodollar system refers to U.S. dollars held in foreign banks, particularly outside U.S. regulatory oversight. These offshore dollars play a critical role in global finance, allowing international trade, lending, and investment beyond U.S. jurisdiction. The Eurodollar market grew after World War II and remains a key pillar of dollar dominance, though alternative financial systems are emerging.

Dollar Liquidity

Dollar liquidity refers to the availability of U.S. dollars in global markets, crucial for trade, debt repayment, and financial stability. Since the dollar is the dominant reserve currency, shortages can trigger crises, especially in emerging markets reliant on dollar funding. The Federal Reserve provides liquidity through swap lines with other central banks, reinforcing the dollar's global influence.

Currency Peg

A currency peg occurs when a country fixes its exchange rate to another currency, typically the U.S. dollar, to maintain stability in trade and investment. Pegs can prevent currency volatility but limit monetary independence. Nations like Saudi Arabia and Hong Kong maintain dollar pegs, while others, such as China, manage their currency within a controlled range against the dollar.

Capital Controls

Capital controls are government-imposed restrictions on the flow of money in and out of a country to stabilize the economy, prevent currency crises, or manage inflation. These controls can include limits on foreign exchange transactions, taxes on capital movements, or restrictions on repatriating profits. Countries facing financial instability, such as Argentina or China, often use capital controls to protect their currency from excessive depreciation.

2

THE DOLLAR SYSTEM AND ITS GLOBAL ROLE

Dollar Hegemony

Dollar hegemony refers to the U.S. dollar's dominant role in global trade, finance, and reserves, giving the U.S. unique economic advantages. Since the 1940s, most international transactions have been conducted in dollars, reinforcing its status as the world's primary currency. This dominance allows the U.S. to finance deficits cheaply and impose financial sanctions with global reach. However, growing efforts by other nations to bypass the dollar are challenging this system.

Petrodollar System

The petrodollar system links global oil sales to the U.S. dollar, ensuring worldwide demand for the currency. Since the 1970s, OPEC nations have priced oil in dollars, forcing countries to hold dollar reserves. In return, the U.S. provided military and economic incentives to key oil producers. Recently, nations like China and Russia have begun settling oil trade in non-dollar currencies, threatening the petrodollar's dominance.

Dollar-Denominated Debt

Debt issued in U.S. dollars by governments, corporations, or institutions outside the U.S. This type of debt is common in emerging markets, where borrowing in dollars often provides lower interest rates. However, countries with high dollar-denominated debt can face crises when the dollar strengthens, making repayments more expensive. De-dollarisation efforts aim to reduce reliance on such debt.

U.S. Treasury Market

The U.S. Treasury market is the global marketplace for U.S. government debt securities (Treasury bonds, notes, and bills). As the deepest and most liquid bond market, it attracts central banks and investors worldwide. Foreign governments, particularly China and Japan, hold large amounts of Treasuries as reserves. A shift away from Treasuries—especially by major economies—could weaken dollar dominance.

Federal Reserve Swap Lines

A mechanism where the U.S. Federal Reserve provides dollar liquidity to foreign central banks during financial crises. These swap lines help stabilize global markets by ensuring access to dollars when liquidity is tight. While this reinforces the dollar's role as the world's reserve currency, it also highlights global dependence on U.S. monetary policy.

Exorbitant Privilege

A term describing the U.S. advantage of issuing the world's reserve currency. Because global trade and finance rely on the dollar, the U.S. can borrow at lower costs and run persistent trade deficits without major currency devaluation. However, this privilege has fueled resentment, prompting efforts to reduce reliance on the dollar in international transactions.

Triffin Dilemma

An economic paradox where a reserve currency issuer (like the U.S.) must run trade deficits to supply the world with liquidity, but excessive deficits erode confidence in the currency over time. This dilemma creates tension between global financial stability and the sustainability of the dollar's dominance. Calls for de-dollarisation partly stem from concerns about the risks this imbalance poses to the global economy.

Quantitative Easing (QE)

A monetary policy tool where central banks inject liquidity into financial markets by purchasing government bonds and other assets. The U.S. Federal Reserve's large-scale QE programs after the 2008 financial crisis and during COVID-19 expanded the dollar supply. While QE supports economic growth, it can also weaken confidence in the dollar, prompting countries to seek alternative reserve assets like gold and non-dollar currencies.

3

DE-DOLLARISATION – KEY CONCEPTS AND TRENDS

De-Dollarisation
The process of reducing reliance on the U.S. dollar in trade, finance, and central bank reserves. Countries engage in de-dollarisation to protect themselves from U.S. sanctions, reduce currency risk, and increase financial independence. Key examples include Russia and China shifting trade to local currencies and the rise of non-dollar payment systems like CIPS (Cross-Border Interbank Payment System).

Non-Dollar Trade Settlements
International trade transactions conducted in currencies other than the U.S. dollar. This trend is growing as countries like China, India, and Russia settle oil and commodity trades in yuan, rupees, and rubles to bypass dollar dependence.

Bilateral vs. Multilateral Trade in Local Currencies
- *Bilateral trade settlements* involve two countries agreeing to trade in their own currencies, bypassing the dollar (e.g., India and Russia trading in rupees and rubles).
- *Multilateral settlements* involve multiple countries using a common framework to settle trade in non-dollar currencies, such as BRICS initiatives to promote yuan-based transactions.

Yuanisation
The increasing use of China's yuan (renminbi) in global trade and finance, often as an alternative to the U.S. dollar. This trend is driven by China's economic rise, trade agreements with partners like Russia and Saudi Arabia, and the yuan's inclusion in the IMF's Special Drawing Rights (SDRs).

Petroyuan
A Chinese-led effort to price and settle oil transactions in yuan instead of U.S. dollars. China has signed deals with major oil

exporters like Russia and Saudi Arabia to accept yuan for crude oil sales, challenging the traditional petrodollar system.

De-SWIFTing

The removal of a country or financial institution from SWIFT (the global messaging system for international payments), effectively cutting off access to dollar-based transactions. The U.S. has used this as a financial weapon against nations like Iran and Russia, prompting them to develop alternative systems like China's CIPS (Cross-Border Interbank Payment System) and Russia's SPFS (System for Transfer of Financial Messages). As de-dollarisation accelerates, more countries are exploring backup payment networks to reduce vulnerability to Western financial sanctions.

BRICS Currency Initiatives

Efforts by BRICS nations (Brazil, Russia, India, China, and South Africa) to reduce dependence on the dollar, including proposals for a common BRICS currency or expanded use of local currencies in trade. These initiatives aim to create a multipolar financial system. While no single BRICS currency exists yet, member states are increasing bilateral trade in non-dollar currencies, signaling a shift toward regional financial autonomy.

Asian Clearing Union (ACU)

A regional payment arrangement among Asian central banks that facilitates trade settlements in local currencies, reducing the need for U.S. dollars. Countries like India and Iran have used ACU mechanisms to bypass Western financial restrictions. As interest in de-dollarisation grows, ACU is being strengthened with new settlement options, including direct rupee and yuan transactions.

Monetary Unipolarity vs. Multipolarity

- *Monetary unipolarity* refers to a system where a single currency (the U.S. dollar) dominates global trade and finance.
- *Monetary multipolarity* envisions a world where multiple reserve currencies—such as the yuan, euro, and gold-backed assets— share influence, reducing dependence on any one currency. The shift toward a multipolar system is being driven by increasing use of regional trade currencies and alternative payment mechanisms.

4

FINANCIAL SYSTEMS AND ALTERNATIVE CURRENCIES

Central Bank Digital Currencies (CBDCs)
CBDCs are digital versions of a country's official currency, issued and regulated by its central bank. Unlike cryptocurrencies, they are state-backed and designed for secure, fast transactions. Many countries are developing CBDCs to modernize payments and reduce reliance on the dollar for trade. China's digital yuan is a major step toward de-dollarisation.

Cryptocurrency-Based Systems
Cryptocurrencies like Bitcoin operate on decentralized networks without central bank control. Unlike traditional currencies, they rely on blockchain technology to enable peer-to-peer transactions. Some countries view them as alternatives to dollar-based systems, but their volatility limits mainstream adoption. El Salvador made Bitcoin legal tender, while others explore stablecoins for trade settlement.

Stablecoins
Stablecoins are digital currencies pegged to assets like the U.S. dollar or gold to reduce volatility. They offer the benefits of cryptocurrencies—fast, low-cost transactions—without wild price swings. Some nations explore using stablecoins for cross-border payments, bypassing dollar-based financial systems. However, regulatory concerns remain about their impact on monetary stability.

Monetary Regionalism
Monetary regionalism refers to economic blocs or groups of countries creating their own financial systems to reduce dependence on global reserve currencies like the U.S. dollar. Examples include the euro in the European Union and ongoing discussions within BRICS to create a shared settlement currency. These initiatives aim to strengthen economic sovereignty and reduce exposure to dollar volatility.

Gold-Backed Currencies

Gold-backed currencies are tied to a fixed amount of gold, limiting excessive money printing and inflation. While most modern economies use fiat money, some countries, like Russia and China, are increasing gold reserves as a hedge against the dollar. Calls for a return to gold-backed trade settlements have grown amid de-dollarisation efforts.

BRICS Alternative Financial Infrastructure

BRICS nations (Brazil, Russia, India, China, South Africa) are developing financial systems outside U.S. influence, including non-dollar payment networks and a potential new currency. The BRICS Contingent Reserve Arrangement (CRA) offers an alternative to the IMF, and Russia's SPFS system rivals SWIFT. These efforts aim to challenge dollar dominance in global trade.

IMF SDRs as a Dollar Alternative

Special Drawing Rights (SDRs) are reserve assets issued by the International Monetary Fund (IMF) to supplement global liquidity. SDRs are valued based on a basket of major currencies, including the dollar, euro, yuan, yen, and pound. Some advocate for expanded SDR use to reduce global reliance on the U.S. dollar, but adoption remains limited.

5

TRADE, SANCTIONS, AND GEOPOLITICAL FINANCE

Balance of Payments

The balance of payments (BOP) is a record of a country's economic transactions with the rest of the world, including trade, investment, and financial transfers. It consists of the *current account* (exports, imports, and services) and the *capital account* (investment flows). Persistent deficits can weaken a currency, while surpluses strengthen it. Countries seeking de-dollarisation aim to settle trade in local currencies to avoid dollar-driven imbalances.

Geoeconomics

Geoeconomics refers to the use of economic policies, trade, and finance as tools of geopolitical influence. Countries leverage trade agreements, investment, and financial sanctions to shape global power dynamics. For example, the U.S. uses the dollar's dominance to enforce sanctions, while China promotes the yuan through infrastructure projects like the Belt and Road Initiative. De-dollarisation is partly driven by the desire to reduce vulnerability to geoeconomic pressure.

Financial Sanctions

Financial sanctions restrict a country's access to global markets by freezing assets, blocking transactions, or limiting access to the dollar-based financial system. The U.S. frequently imposes such sanctions through SWIFT or asset freezes, targeting countries like Russia, Iran, and Venezuela. As a result, affected nations are seeking alternatives, including trade in local currencies and digital payment networks, to bypass U.S. financial controls.

Weaponisation of Finance

The weaponisation of finance occurs when economic tools—such as sanctions, asset seizures, and trade restrictions—are used to achieve political or strategic objectives. The dominance of the U.S. dollar allows Washington to control global financial flows, cutting off adversaries from key markets. However, this has accelerated de-dollarisation efforts, with countries developing alternative payment systems like China's CIPS (Cross-Border Interbank Payment System) and Russia's SPFS (System for Transfer of Financial Messages) to reduce reliance on the dollar-based system.

Trade Imbalances

Trade imbalances occur when a country's imports exceed its exports (trade deficit) or vice versa (trade surplus). Persistent deficits weaken a currency and increase reliance on foreign borrowing, while surpluses strengthen reserves. The U.S. runs chronic trade deficits, sustained by global demand for dollars. Countries seeking de-dollarisation aim to settle trade in local currencies to correct imbalances and reduce exposure to U.S. monetary policy shifts.

Petrodollar System

The petrodollar system refers to the global practice of pricing and settling oil transactions in U.S. dollars. Established in the 1970s through agreements between the U.S. and oil-producing nations, particularly Saudi Arabia, this system has reinforced demand for the dollar as the world's primary reserve currency. As more countries explore pricing oil in alternative currencies like the yuan or gold, the petrodollar's dominance is being challenged, accelerating de-dollarization trends.

Currency Wars

A currency war occurs when countries deliberately devalue their currencies to gain a trade advantage by making exports cheaper. Competitive devaluations can lead to inflation, capital flight, and economic instability. The U.S. has accused China of manipulating the yuan to maintain trade surpluses, while some emerging markets de-dollarise to reduce reliance on the dollar and shield their economies from currency fluctuations tied to Federal Reserve policy.

Belt and Road Initiative (BRI)

The Belt and Road Initiative (BRI) is China's massive infrastructure project aimed at expanding trade routes across Asia, Africa, and Europe. By financing projects in yuan, China increases the global use of its currency and reduces dependence on the U.S. dollar. Some BRI participants now settle trade in yuan, reinforcing China's role in global finance and challenging dollar dominance in emerging markets.

Geopolitical Risk Premium in Currencies

The geopolitical risk premium refers to the extra cost embedded in a currency's value due to political and economic instability. Countries facing sanctions, conflict, or policy uncertainty often see their currencies depreciate as investors demand higher returns for risk exposure. The U.S. dollar benefits from a safe-haven status, but de-dollarisation trends could shift geopolitical risk to other currencies like the yuan or euro over time.

Reserve Currency Diversification

Reserve currency diversification occurs when central banks and sovereign wealth funds shift away from holding U.S. dollars as their primary reserve asset. Traditionally, the dollar has dominated global reserves, but recent trends show increased holdings of euros, yuan, and gold. This shift reflects growing concerns over U.S. fiscal policy, sanctions risk, and the desire for a more multipolar monetary system.

SWIFT (Society for Worldwide Interbank Financial Telecommunication)

SWIFT is the global messaging system that enables banks to communicate securely for cross-border transactions. It does not move money but facilitates payment instructions between financial institutions. SWIFT dominates international finance, processing trillions of dollars daily, primarily in U.S. dollars. The U.S. leverages SWIFT for financial sanctions, cutting off targeted nations from the global banking system. This has accelerated de-dollarisation efforts, with some countries exploring SWIFT alternatives.

CIPS (Cross-Border Interbank Payment System)

CIPS is China's alternative to SWIFT, designed to facilitate international trade in yuan (RMB) without relying on the U.S. dollar. Unlike SWIFT, which only provides messaging, CIPS also settles payments, offering a more direct transaction system. China launched CIPS in 2015 to promote de-dollarisation and reduce reliance on Western financial networks. While still smaller than SWIFT, CIPS is expanding as more countries use yuan-based trade settlements to bypass dollar dependence.

SPFS (System for Transfer of Financial Messages)

SPFS is Russia's alternative to SWIFT, designed to keep domestic and international financial transactions running despite Western sanctions. Launched by the Central Bank of Russia in 2014, SPFS allows Russian banks to send secure payment messages without relying on U.S.-controlled networks. Though primarily domestic, Russia is expanding SPFS for cross-border trade, with some BRICS and Eurasian Economic Union countries connecting to the system as part of broader de-dollarisation efforts.

SWIFT vs. CIPS vs. SPFS

SWIFT is the dominant global financial messaging system, handling most cross-border transactions in U.S. dollars. CIPS is China's alternative, facilitating yuan-based trade settlements, while SPFS is Russia's response to financial sanctions, allowing domestic and limited international transactions. Countries targeted by U.S. sanctions, including Russia and Iran, are expanding links to CIPS and SPFS to bypass the SWIFT system, accelerating global de-dollarisation efforts.

BIBLIOGRAPHY

1. BOOKS

- Baldwin, Richard. *The Great Convergence: Information Technology and the New Globalization*. Harvard University Press, 2016.
- Bordo, Michael D. *A Monetary and Fiscal History of the United States, 1961–2021*. University of Chicago Press, 2023.
- Eichengreen, Barry. *Exorbitant Privilege: The Rise and Fall of the Dollar and the Future of the International Monetary System*. Oxford University Press, 2011.
- Frieden, Jeffry A. *Currency Politics: The Political Economy of Exchange Rate Policy*. Princeton University Press, 2015.
- Friedman, Milton. *Money Mischief: Episodes in Monetary History*. Houghton Mifflin Harcourt, 1992.
- Irwin, Douglas A. *Clashing Over Commerce: A History of U.S. Trade Policy*. University of Chicago Press, 2017.
- Kindleberger, Charles P. *The World in Depression: 1929–1939*. University of California Press, 1986.
- Krugman, Paul. *The Return of Depression Economics and the Crisis of 2008*. W.W. Norton & Company, 2009.
- Pettis, Michael. *The Great Rebalancing: Trade, Conflict, and the Perilous Road Ahead for the World Economy*. Princeton University Press, 2013.
- Prasad, Eswar. *The Dollar Trap: How the U.S. Dollar Tightened Its Grip on Global Finance*. Princeton University Press, 2014.
- Reinhart, Carmen M., and Kenneth Rogoff. *This Time Is Different: Eight Centuries of Financial Folly*. Princeton University Press, 2009.
- Rodrik, Dani. *The Globalization Paradox: Democracy and the Future of the World Economy*. W.W. Norton & Company, 2011.

- Stiglitz, Joseph E. *Globalization and Its Discontents Revisited: Anti-Globalization in the Era of Trump*. W.W. Norton & Company, 2018.

- Subramanian, Arvind. *Eclipse: Living in the Shadow of China's Economic Dominance*. Peterson Institute for International Economics, 2011.

- Tooze, Adam. *Crashed: How a Decade of Financial Crises Changed the World*. Viking, 2018.

- Tooze, Adam. *Shutdown: How COVID Shook the World's Economy*. Viking, 2021.

- Triffin, Robert. *Gold and the Dollar Crisis: The Future of Convertibility*. Yale University Press, 1960.

- Wolf, Martin. *The Shifts and the Shocks: What We've Learned — and Have Still to Learn — from the Financial Crisis*. Penguin Books, 2015.

2. JOURNAL ARTICLES & RESEARCH PAPERS

- Autor, David H., David Dorn, and Gordon H. Hanson. *The China Shock: Learning from Labor Market Adjustment to Large Changes in Trade*. National Bureau of Economic Research, 2016.

- Bordo, Michael D., and Anna J. Schwartz. *Monetary Policy Regimes and Economic Performance: The Historical Record*. NBER Working Paper No. 6201, 1997.

- Gopinath, Gita, and Kenneth Rogoff. *Dominant Currency Paradigm: Implications for Global Trade and Policy*. IMF Working Papers, 2019.

- Obstfeld, Maurice, and Kenneth Rogoff. *Global Imbalances and the Financial Crisis: Products of Common Causes*. Federal Reserve Bank of San Francisco, 2009.

- Reinhart, Carmen M., and Vincent Reinhart. *After the Fall*. NBER Working Paper No. 16334, 2010.

- Williamson, John. *The Evolution of the International Monetary System*. Princeton Essays in International Finance, 1977.

3. GOVERNMENT & INSTITUTIONAL REPORTS

- Bank for International Settlements (BIS)
  - *Global Liquidity Indicators*. Various Reports.
  - *Quarterly Review*. Various Issues.
  - *Triennial Central Bank Survey: Global Foreign Exchange Market Turnover*. Various Years.
- Federal Reserve
  - *FRED Economic Data*. St. Louis Federal Reserve Bank.
  - *Monetary Policy Report*. Various Years.
  - *U.S. Treasury Holdings by Foreign Governments*.
- International Monetary Fund (IMF)
  - *Annual Report on Exchange Arrangements and Exchange Restrictions*. Various Years.
  - *Currency Composition of Official Foreign Exchange Reserves (COFER)*.
  - *Financial Stability Reports*. Various Years.
  - *World Economic Outlook*. Various Issues.
- Organisation for Economic Co-operation and Development (OECD)
  - *Economic Outlook*. Various Issues.
  - *Trade and Investment Statistics*.
- U.S. Bureau of Economic Analysis (BEA)
  - *National Income and Product Accounts (NIPA)*.
- U.S. Bureau of Labor Statistics (BLS)
  - *Consumer Price Index Reports*. Various Years.
  - *Unemployment Reports*. Various Years.
- U.S. Department of the Treasury
  - *Annual Report on the U.S. International Economic Position*. Various Years.
  - *International Capital Flows Reports*.
- World Bank
  - *Global Economic Prospects*. Various Years.
  - *Global Financial Development Report*. Various Years.

- World Trade Organization (WTO)
  - *World Trade Statistical Review.* Various Years.

4. ECONOMIC DATA & STATISTICAL SOURCES

- Bank for International Settlements (BIS) Global Liquidity Data.
- Federal Reserve Economic Data (FRED) – St. Louis Federal Reserve Bank.
- International Monetary Fund (IMF) Balance of Payments Data.
- OECD Trade and Investment Statistics.
- United Nations Conference on Trade and Development (UNCTAD) – World Investment Report.
- U.S. Census Bureau – Trade and Economic Indicators.
- World Bank Development Indicators.

5. ONLINE & DIGITAL SOURCES

- Bloomberg News. *Reports on Currency Markets and Global Trade.*
- Financial Times. *Analysis of Global Trade and Monetary Policy.*
- Reuters. *Coverage of U.S. Dollar Trends and Economic Policies.*
- The Economist. *Reports on Protectionism and Economic Shifts.*

ABOUT THE AUTHOR

 RANGA CHAND is an international economist and financial author whose work has shaped discussions on global finance, monetary policy, and investment strategy. Born in Uganda in 1946, he was educated in England, attending The King's School Worcester, before earning an MA in Economics from the University of Toronto in 1970. He spent his entire professional career in Canada, holding senior positions with Canada's Department of Finance and serving as a director of the Conference Board of Canada before joining a major stock brokerage firm. He represented Canada at prominent international economic forums, including the OECD in Paris, the United Nations, and the Kiel Institute for the World Economy in Germany.

At the invitation of Nobel Laureate Robert Mundell, he taught economics at the University of Waterloo from 1973 to 1974. From 2000 to 2003, he hosted the popular television show *Talking Mutual Funds with Ranga Chand*, which aired weekly on Canada's Report on Business Television (ROBTV) and reached over four million viewers nationwide. A prolific writer, he has authored several bestselling investment books and was a regular contributor to *The Globe and Mail*, Canada's leading national newspaper.

Today, Ranga Chand brings his global perspective and decades of experience to bear on the critical financial transformations reshaping the world economy.

.

Printed in Great Britain
by Amazon

62106096R00201